Designer's Guide to OSHA

Architectural Record Series

Architectural Record Books:

Hospitals, Clinics and Health Centers

Motels, Hotels, Restaurants and Bars, 2/e

Campus Planning and Design

Interior Spaces Designed by Architects

Houses Architects Design for Themselves

Techniques of Successful Practice, 2/e

Office Building Design, 2/e

Apartments, Townhouses and Condominiums, 2/e

Great Houses for View Sites, Beach Sites, Sites in the Woods,
Meadow Sites, Small Sites, Sloping Sites,
Steep Sites, and Flat Sites

Other Architectural Record Series Books:

Ayers: Specifications: for Architecture, Engineering,
and Construction

Feldman: Building Design for Maintainability

Heery: Time, Cost, and Architecture

Hopf: Designer's Guide to OSHA

Designer's Guide to OSHA

**A Design Manual for Architects, Engineers, and Builders
to the Occupational Safety and Health Act**

Peter S. Hopf, AIA

Robert D. Ascione   Chief Illustrator

McGRAW-HILL BOOK COMPANY

New York   St. Louis   San Francisco   Auckland   Düsseldorf
Johannesburg   Kuala Lumpur   London   Mexico   Montreal
New Delhi   Panama   Paris   São Paulo
Singapore   Sydney   Tokyo   Toronto

Library of Congress Cataloging in Publication Data

Hopf, Peter S, date.
  Designer's guide to OSHA.

  "The Occupational safety and health act": p.
  1. Building laws—United States. 2. Industrial
safety—Law and legislation—United States. I. United
States. Laws, statutes, etc. Occupational safety and
health act of 1970. 1974. II. Title.
KF5701.H67   344'.73'0465   74-16441
ISBN 0-07-030314-2

  234567890   BPBP   78321098765

The editors for this book were Jeremy Robinson
and Robert Braine, the designer was Naomi Auerbach,
and its production was supervised by Stephen J. Boldish.
It was set in Optima by University Graphics, Inc.,
and John C. Meyer & Son, Inc.

It was printed and bound by The Book Press.

Contents

Preface

Not long after the enactment of the Occupational Safety and Health Act of 1970, my local newspaper reported a tragic accident in a nearby town. A nineteen-year-old laborer had been checking some sewer pumps in the basement of a building when his longish hair got caught in the shackle on a shaft spinning at 1,100 revolutions per minute. A fellow worker, who heard a loud scream, scrambled down a ladder to the basement and recalled, "I saw Paul with a big hole in his head." He called the police, who took the youth to a nearby hospital.

After three hours of surgery, doctors reported that a large piece of the scalp was torn off, the skull was cracked, there were many bone cracks, and the patient was put on the critical list. The hospital stated he was "in pretty bad shape." The youth's father said, "All we can do now is hope."

My first reactions, after having read the article, were feelings of horror and sympathy. I wondered, Where were such elemental safety provisions as head covering for long hair and wire guards for moving parts of machinery? The newspaper reported that the young man usually worked in a different department and had been asked to work in the pumping station because the normal employee was sick.

Had he received any training in the maintenance of machinery? Did anyone brief him in even the barest of safety precautions? These were some of the elements, it seemed to me, which Congress had in mind when it enacted OSHA. Then my thoughts turned in a different direction. What about the engineer who had designed the plant? Had he specified everything to provide reasonable safeguards against this type of accident? Would he now possibly be dragged through the courts as a defendant in a third-party suit involving the designing engineer? Our current court calendars are loaded with litigation of this sort. Would this claim become another one of the statistics that were constantly increasing professional liability insurance premiums of architects and engineers?

Because I am an architect in private practice, this case was of particular significance to me. We had just completed plans for a large bus maintenance facility which would have all sorts of pits, as well as lifts, cranes, and other moving machinery. I recalled having briefly mentioned OSHA to my client and stating, "This whole OSHA thing is brand new and very few people are familiar with it. They're still developing standards and it will probably be a few years before we know very much about it."

What I had said was true. I had read an occasional article on the subject in various professional magazines. Once in a while, a small paragraph had appeared in architectural newsletters or in advertising noting that OSHA had just implemented one or another new regulation. I particularly recall seeing a photo taken during a congressional hearing showing a United States senator sitting next to a table with a five-foot-high stack of books on OSHA standards. These regulations were still in formulation and were only two-thirds completed at the time the picture was taken. This material, together with newsletters from the American Institute of Architects, as well as special circulars on OSHA from my insurance company, had convinced me that I, as the designer of plants where people work, had suddenly received some very heavy new responsibilities, actual and implied.

We who are constantly involved in building design barely have enough time to keep up with necessary reading. We are constantly looking things up in zoning codes, building codes, catalogs, specifications, manuals, and brochures. It seemed to me that we would now also have to get familiar with the contents of a new set of regulations that were to be contained in a stack of books that could be eight or ten feet high.

My practice in a metropolitan area such as New York City should have been able to provide me with access to virtually every available resource in this matter. I bought a copy of the actual statute. It provided no details except to state, essentially, that everyone had to work in a safe place. A seminar on OSHA by our local A.I.A. chapter was useful to me but left many questions unanswered and provided me with none of the "nitty-gritty" to be applied in my everyday work. Discussions with other concerned architects raised many more questions. First of all, where could we obtain the applicable detailed OSHA requirements so we could begin to apply them to our projects? We recognized that, as employers ourselves, we had to provide safe working conditions for our own employees. But, as building designers, were we really concerned about whether or not a machine operator had to wear safety goggles while operating his lathe? The OSHA regulations contain thousands of items of little practical application to designers of buildings. How could we sort the wheat from the chaff in order to have easy access to those provisions that applied specifically to our needs as architects and engineers? Clearly, the need existed for the publication of a concise, practical handbook on OSHA which an architect or engineer could use as an everyday guide in the design of his buildings.

In the preparation of this book I have kept the language brief, relying, where possible, on graphics. I recognize that the illustrations and/or abbreviated text may not be exactly applicable to all situations. An easy-to-follow numerical reference to the actual text of the OSHA regulations has therefore been included, enabling the designer to read and evaluate for himself the full intent of the applicable regulation. Users of the book are urged to read through the first two chapters to gain a better comprehension of the intent of OSHA and a basic understanding of the application of the Act.

When I undertook the preparation of this book I was cautioned that I might be treading on thin ice in trying to "interpret" the written text as it appears in the Federal Register. It should be made very clear that *only the Department of Labor can make such interpretations* and that the material in this book is solely my own professional judgment concerning the application of the standards. I have therefore deliberately tried to illustrate the book from a "narrow" view of the standards, even though there may be inconsistencies between the book and, say, local codes or practical experience. The cautionary note in the chapter "How to Use This Book" may be worth repeating here: the user is advised that the material in the book has neither official nor implied governmental approval, and he should not use the graphic material verbatim, but rather as a guide toward solving his own particular design problem. If, in this manner, we have at least made the architect/engineer aware of the need for including some particular OSHA requirement in design, our main purpose will have been accomplished.

A final word concerns the currency of the material herein. Although the basic content of the OSHA regulations is not likely to change over the years, some of the standards will undergo a process of modification; others may be added or deleted. The contents of this book are as up to date as possible at time of publication, but users are encouraged to contact area or regional OSHA offices to keep abreast with any late changes or additions.

I am grateful to Robert D. Ascione, architect, for his help in developing and following through with the graphic design and the illustrative material and to M. J. Poll, professional engineer, for the development of the engineering portions of the book. Particularly, I am grateful for the encouragement of Jeremy Robinson, my sponsoring editor at McGraw-Hill and for the help of the many staff members at McGraw-Hill. Jeremy's enthusiasm, encouragement, and help were invaluable to me in making this book possible. Finally, my thanks to my wife Edith for her support in this undertaking.

Peter S. Hopf

Designer's Guide to OSHA

ONE

The Design Professional and OSHA

A SAFE PLACE FOR ALL AMERICANS TO WORK IN! Few would argue with this elemental concept which Congress had in mind when it passed the Occupational Safety and Health Act of 1970. The law applies equally to the rich and the poor, the radicals, the liberals, and the conservatives; it is for people of all races, and it knows no religious boundaries.

And yet, in the early years after the enactment of a law which makes it illegal to work in an unsafe place, a general feeling of fear pervaded industry. What caused this fear? There were three major areas of concern.

Those large corporations which, for years, had staff members concerned with safety and health problems were now faced with a situation where their compliance to previously voluntary health and safety standards would now be a matter of law. These firms were best equipped to deal with this new situation because, in many cases, it simply meant the investment of money (often hundreds of thousands of dollars) in order to achieve compliance. Not only were these firms reasonably well equipped to deal with this situation, but they also recognized that the cost of any necessary upgrading could be quite simply passed on to the consumer.

The second group beset by fear consisted of the small businessmen who had been getting by all these many years with either marginal or unsafe working conditions. They recognized this situation to be so, and were truly concerned that the cost of upgrading their facilities would be so immense that they might no longer be able to compete and might have to go out of business. This fear made them more determined than ever that ignorance is bliss, and that the less they knew about these new-fangled requirements, the happier they would be and the longer they could remain in business. In the end, however, they may turn out to be the real losers. Not only may they be cited for safety violations, but by not being familiar with the law they may not even recognize that a pro-

Roof under construction showing absence of railings or barricades and loose debris which could easily be blown or pushed over edge.

1

vision exists in the Act whereby the Small Business Administration can make loans (with maximum repayment term of 30 years) to help them upgrade their facilities.

By far, however, the largest group that was beset by fear were the so-called "average businessmen" in every part of the country. Through reading their newspaper, or perhaps the journal of their trade association, they recognized that they were required to provide safe and healthy working conditions for their employees. They may even have heard that for every violation cited against them they might have to pay a penalty ranging up to $1,000 per day for each violation while it remained unabated. These businessmen were, in the main, enlightened employers favoring safe working conditions, but what troubled them mostly was the big unknown of it all.

To this latter group belonged those architects and engineers charged by law to design those buildings which would become places of employment. Building designers had an everyday exposure to zoning laws and building codes and thus had a general awareness and concern with safety and health. Nevertheless, this last consideration had never before had the force of a federal law behind it. Historically, building codes had concerned themselves with the safety of buildings (they should not collapse) and the protection of property (fire cutoffs and sprinklers to limit flame spread). Architects were trained to prevent or minimize *unusual* things from happening to their buildings.

With the passage of OSHA, building designers were now faced with a new responsibility and a significant potential new liability. They now had to concern themselves with the *usual* things that occur in the buildings they design—the fact that people work there. It now became possible that responsibility for a work accident could be placed at the architect's doorstep if his design failed to comply with OSHA standards. Even without an accident, the building owner might hold his architect responsible for the cost of changes to a building that failed to comply with OSHA requirements because the owner had been reasonably assured that his architect would design the building to comply with appropriate laws, including OSHA.

The initial fear of architects and engineers of this potential new liability can, therefore, be easily understood. The larger design firms were able to come to grips with the problem most easily. They designated a member of their staff to investigate and collect data on OSHA requirements and to keep others in the firm advised of them. In the main, however, most architects and engineers had neither the resources to devote to this new field nor any knowledge as to how to obtain the appropriate new information. Those who did explore the matter further found that there was considerable material, printed both by government and by private sources, but that it was scattered in terms of its availability and, when they did manage to obtain the data, they were not sufficiently concise for use by building designers. No single, concise reference existed which the architect or engineer could use in the day-to-day application to work.

It should be clearly understood that the Occupational Safety and Health Act of 1970 applies to all places where people work. It affects more than 57 million workers in some 4.1 million workplaces across the United States. Commonplace thinking has led us to believe that occupational hazards occur mainly in factories or other similar industrial buildings. Whereas there may be some truth in this conception, OSHA applies to *all* places where people work. Office buildings, shopping centers, schools, shipyards, and undertaking establishments, among others, are all places where people work. The Act covers only workers. Therefore, in a shopping center, OSHA does not concern itself with the majority of the people who use these buildings, that is, the shoppers, but only with those people, such as salesclerks and janitors, who may be employed there. An example of this situation concerns several apartment houses which were built in the air rights of a major highway in New York City not long ago. Readings of the quality of air at the building face over the roadway revealed that these buildings were subject to a much higher carbon monoxide intake from the street below than were other buildings which were more conventionally located at or near the side of a road. Paradoxically, OSHA would not concern itself with the thousands of tenants living in this apartment house, but *would* be concerned with the elevator operators and custodial employees in this building.

The Williams-Steiger Act, known as the Occupational Safety and Health Act of 1970, was signed by the President on December 29, 1970, and became effective 120 days thereafter on April 28, 1971. The Act covers every employer in a business affecting commerce who has one or more employees (subject to a limited list of exceptions). The full text of the Act appears in Appendix C of this book. In addition to its administrative sections, it provided four principal elements:

1. The Secretary of Labor was charged with establishing detailed standards and appropriate enforcement.
2. The National Institute of Occupational Safety and Health, under the Secretary of Health, Education, and Welfare, was established. Its principal function is to provide research in the field of occupational health.
3. The Occupational Safety and Health Review Commission was established as an independent quasi-judicial body to pass upon the appropriateness of citations and proposed penalties.
4. Provisions were included whereby states were encouraged to assume full responsibility for their own occupational safety and health laws, thus removing it from federal enforcement.

Hoisting open bucket of sand; note lack of protective helmet and inadequate footgear.

Of the foregoing, architects and engineers, as well as building operators, will be most concerned with the safety and health standards issued by the Secretary of Labor.

When Congress enacted the OSHA law, it provided for the rapid promulgation of such safety and health standards. Set forth in the Act is the basis for these standards:

1. Those already on the books, such as the older Walsh-Healey Act
2. The immediate inclusion of consensus standards generally recognized by the industry
3. Emergency standards under Section 6 (c) (rarely used, and, as the subtitle implies, only for emergencies)
4. The rule making process under Section 6 (b) requiring the publishing of proposed new standards

During the first 120 days after the new law was enacted, such existing consensus standards as had existed at that time were adopted and published. In the process a number of inconsistencies (many minor and a few major ones) were incorporated. For example, the Uniform Building Code (used by over 900 municipalities) requires a minimum ceiling height of 7 feet, whereas OSHA required 7 feet 6 inches. Many local codes call for 5-inch-high lettering on exit signs, whereas OSHA required 6-inch, etc. Significantly, most local codes do not have retroactive compliance provisions, but OSHA standards apply to all new as well as existing places of employment.

Then, too, professionals became concerned that the provisions for state enforcement could mean that architects and engineers might have to become familiar with up to fifty sets of separate state laws. As of March 1974, twenty-four states (plus the Virgin Islands) had received approval of state plans, and many others had applications pending for approval of their respective state plans. As of this writing, it appears that perhaps nine or ten states will not follow federal standards, with the balance of the states following existing federal standards. In any event, the law requires that state legislation be "at least as effective as the standards" promulgated by OSHA. Time and experience, it seems, will be needed to resolve the many potential difficulties with which the design professions are faced.

Architects and engineers are well advised to familiarize themselves with this new law. Just as they retain consultants in such specialized fields as acoustics and landscaping, they may now find they need to retain consultants who specialize in the subject of OSHA. The Economics Department of McGraw-Hill Publications Company had reported that American business intended to spend $3.03 billion in 1974 to improve health and safety conditions for its workers, much of it to comply with OSHA. This was a walloping 18 percent increase over such spending in 1973.

Even with limited experience and a relatively small staff, the enforcement people at OSHA have established an impressive record. In the first half of fiscal 1974, *only 25 percent of all facilities inspected were found to be in compliance*. From its inception up to January 1974, OSHA had made inspections alleging over 386,000 violations and had proposed over $10 million in penalties. Employee complaints were running at a rate of about 5,000 per year.

OSHA has set up a priority system of inspections to provide attention to the worst situations first, as follows:

1. Catastrophes and other fatal accidents
2. Valid employee complaints
3. Special Emphasis Programs (see below)
4. Random selection from all types and sizes of work places in all sections of the country

The Special Emphasis Programs include the Target Industry Program (TIP) and the Target Health Hazards Program.

Under the TIP a major effort is being undertaken to reduce working hazards in those industries with the highest injury frequency rate. In the year ending May 1, 1973 these industries were longshoring, meat and meat products, roofing and sheet metal, lumber and wood products, and miscellaneous transportation equipment (primarily manufacturers of mobile homes, campers, and snowmobiles). Whereas the national average was 15.2 disabling injuries per million employee hours worked, the injury frequency rate of these target industries was up to almost 70 injuries per million·employee hours worked.

The Target Health Hazards Program is focused on five of the most commonly used and hazardous of the more than 15,000 toxic substances that have been identified by the National Institute of Occupational Safety and Health: asbestos, carbon monoxide, cotton dust, lead, and silica.

Architects and engineers must realize that in addition to their professional responsibilities toward their clients, they too are employers and are thus covered under the Act. Their own offices must comply with the same OSHA regulations that apply to any other place where people work.

A two-day conference was held in Washington, D.C., in mid-1973, sponsored by the American Institute of Architects and co-sponsored by the American Society of Civil Engineers, Consulting Engineers Council of the U.S., and National Society of Professional Engineers, entitled "The Architect, the Engineer and OSHA." The transcript of this conference totals 180 pages and is filled with the very real concerns of the design professions in their roles as employers and as building designers vis-à-vis OSHA. Questions asked included these: "What is the architect's responsibility now that OSHA has been enacted, and what should he do in his contract documents to recognize this fact?" "To what degree does the architect have responsibility to see that a building contractor complies with OSHA during the construction period?" "How does the architect make provisions for OSHA in plans and specs beyond inclusion of AIA General Conditions?" "What is the obligation of the architect or engineer on a construction job when a violation is noted?"

Very few such questions could be answered definitively because of the newness of the law and the lack of experience in dealing with it. It was evident, however, that with the passage of time, the design professional will be caught up, on an increasing basis, with the implications and the applications of OSHA. What goes on his drawings and into his specs today may require two to three years to reveal itself as a violation or as a claim against him. The engineers and architects gathered at this conference were concerned with the steps they should take today to guard against problems developing tomorrow.

Although few hard rules came out of the conference, it was clear that the design professional must, in an enlightened self-interest, familiarize himself with the provisions of the Act so that he can conduct himself accordingly not only as a designer, but as an employer as well. The author, upon returning from the conference, issued the following memorandum to his staff:

TO: ALL STAFF MEMBERS
FROM: PETER S. HOPF

As most of you know, the Occupational Safety and Health Act of 1970 provides, essentially, that every employee has the right to work under safe conditions. To us, the Act has two principal applications:

(1) As a place in which we work, and
(2) Potential liability for compliance when we design buildings in which others will work.

In order to assure maximum adherence with the provisions of this law, we ask that all staff members comply with this directive:

(1) (a) Be on the alert and advise me of any unsafe conditions in the office so that appropriate remedies can be instituted.
    (b) For on-site visits of construction, if there is an unsafe condition which you believe is a violation of OSHA requirements, LEAVE THE PREMISES and return to the office. Prior to leaving the job site, advise the contractor's superintendent of this condition. Under the AIA General Conditions (Docu-

Stairway under construction, showing lack of railings at stair and unprotected well opening.

ment A-201) it is the contractor's responsibility, under his contract, to provide safety measures and to comply with appropriate federal laws. His noncompliance could be a breach of this contract. Upon your return to the office, prepare a letter to the Owner advising him of the situation. (You are specifically instructed *not* to instruct the contractor in what remedies to undertake. Such an action could mitigate the contractor's responsibility for job safety.)

(2) With regard to including OSHA requirements into our projects, the following points will be helpful to you: .

(a) Each of our offices has a copy of Section 1910, which is the applicable part as it affects our design. You should acquaint yourself with its provisions, and specifically refer to it when preparing contract documents. Specific questions can be referred to me inasmuch as I now have fairly good in-depth knowledge on the subject and quite a bit of resource material.

(b) Project Managers should get a clear definition from the client on the intended use of the building where a specific tenant is anticipated so that appropriate OSHA provisions can be included. Where a speculative project is being designed and specific tenancies are not known, the project will also be designed accordingly. In both cases, the intended use should be documented in writing.

(c) The owner must be made aware that OSHA requirements may impose additional costs on a project (current estimates range from 5 to 10 percent).

(d) In case of a conflict between local codes and OSHA, the more stringent will prevail. (Example: the Uniform Building Code requires a minimum of 7 feet headroom while OSHA requires 7 feet 6 inches).

(e) Under OSHA, the states are encouraged to implement their own safety laws in lieu of OSHA. The law provides that such plans meet the minimum requirements of OSHA (but may be more severe). To date, ten states have such approved plans. This is an additional burden on us because we now must check whether each state has such a plan, which is the Project Manager's responsibility. Nevertheless, as a *minimum,* use OSHA requirements.

The subject is complex and fraught with problems, compounded by the fact that architects and engineers have only limited experience with the subject. Furthermore, constant revisions are forthcoming. Nevertheless, it is here and here to stay. (In fiscal 1972–1973 alone 111,000 violations were reported and $3,100,000 in fines were assessed.) We have a professional obligation to our clients (and a protective obligation to ourselves) in this matter.

The law is very specific as to the procedures to be used in case of an employee complaint and furthermore specifies heavy penalties for illegal "tip-offs" warning an employer that an inspector has been called. Thus, any one of our millions of employees has the legal right to ask for an OSHA inspector to examine the premises of his employer. Except in cases of imminent danger, the request must be submitted in writing, but there are no lengthy formalities involved and the employee can be reasonably assured that if his complaint has validity such inspection will be promptly undertaken.

Notwithstanding the rights of employees to file complaints against their employers, the employer is not without certain rights. The following speech was given by Robert D. Moran as Chairman of the Occupational Safety and Health Review Commission on March 9, 1973 at the National Home Improvement Council in St. Louis, Missouri, and makes for worthwhile reading because it gives a simple and concise picture of what happens when a complaint has been filed:

The Occupational Safety and Health Act of 1970 led to the creation of three new federal agencies—each with separate duties and responsibilities—and each with a distinct role to play in achieving the purpose for which this law was enacted: reducing the number of job-related deaths, injuries, and illnesses. Two of the three were additions to existing cabinet-level departments: the Occupational Safety and Health Administration in the U.S. Department of Labor; and the National Institute of Occupational Safety and Health in the Department of Health, Education, and Welfare. The third, the Occupational Safety and Health Review Commission, is a newly created, independent agency. I'm not sure if there is a complete definition of an independent agency that fits all forty to fifty of them except that none of them are part of the eleven federal agencies which are headed by members of the President's cabinet.

The Labor Department's Occupational Safety and Health Administration is already familiarly known by its four-letter acronym: OSHA (and, I understand, among some employers by other four-letter combinations as well). It has been delegated the Secretary of Labor's authority to establish occupational safety and health standards, to conduct inspections to see if those standards are being observed, and to initiate enforcement actions whenever they believe an employer is not in compliance.

The National Institute of Occupational Safety and Health (NIOSH) was established to perform research and to conduct educational and training programs on occupational safety and health. It is also responsible for identifying unknown workplace hazards and developing ways to eliminate them. The information they develop is submitted to the Secretary of Labor and forms the basis for promulgation of new standards.

No railings have been provided for these masons.

The Occupational Safety and Health Review Commission, the agency with which I am associated, is a court, nothing more—and certainly nothing less—established to adjudicate disputed enforcement actions. For almost two years I've been trying to get this point across, and last month I thought we'd finally made a breakthrough: the Wall Street Journal, in an excellent article, identified us as "a relatively new federal 'court.'" However, I must admit I was somewhat underwhelmed by this when I noticed that the Journal had surrounded "court" with quotation marks. I think you can appreciate how I felt if you imagine a newspaper article describing you as so-called home improvement contractors. Well, regardless of quotation marks, parentheses, brackets, braces, or whatever, we are a court and function solely as a court of occupational safety and health.

Doubtless, many of you have heard horror stories of OSHA inspectors coming onto job sites, spotting what they think are violations, and "fining" employers princely sums. Fortunately it doesn't work that way. At least, not unless the employer is satisfied that he has been treated justly by OSHA.

All enforcement actions under this Act begin when the man from OSHA visits the factory or job site and conducts his inspection. About 25 percent of the time he will find no violations of job safety or health standards. If the compliance officer does find what he thinks is a violation, the employer will, shortly thereafter, receive two documents from the Labor Department: (1) a citation listing the specific standards or sections of the law which the employer is alleged to have violated and (2) a notification of proposed penalty. The employer must take affirmative action within 15 working days of receiving the notification of proposed penalty if he wants to contest this action. If he fails to do so, he is, in effect, conceding that OSHA's allegations are correct and agreeing to do exactly as the citation says and to pay the amount of the penalty proposed.

It's like the system some states use to enforce traffic tickets. A motorist is given a ticket by a police officer. The ticket specifies a certain fine which can be sent in if the motorist decides not to show up in court to contest.

So far employers have voluntarily accepted citations and proposed penalties in 95 percent of the more than 45,000 enforcement actions which have been brought since the law went into effect. The fact that 95 percent of OSHA's alleged victims have not disputed citations served upon them is, in my opinion, a fairly good refutation of some of the criticism they have received.

Of course, any employer who thinks the action initiated against him is wrong can and should exercise his right under the Act to contest the Department's action against him. To do so, he must simply send a letter to the Area Director of the Labor Department's Occupational Safety and Health Administration, whose name and address will appear on both the citation and the notification of proposed penalty. There are no particular formalities involved in this. The letter can simply say, "I disagree with the citation you have served on me." This is notice to OSHA that you are disputing their allegations and it automatically suspends the action until a decision is made after a full-scale hearing unless the parties agree on a settlement.

When the OSHA director receives this notice of contest, the Commission's rules require that he must forward it to us within 7 days of receipt. Once we receive the case it is assigned for hearing to one of the 41 Administrative Law Judges employed by the Review Commission. At this point, I'd like to reemphasize that when the case has reached us, it has reached a court in fact, if not in name. The Commission is not a part of the Labor Department; it is a wholly separate, wholly independent agency which had nothing to do with the development of the standard under which an employer is charged, nothing to do with the inspection that uncovered the alleged violation, and nothing to do with the decision to cite the employer. When the employer contests, that's the first we hear of the case.

The Administrative Law Judge to whom the case is assigned is a highly qualified jurist with many years' experience in trying and adjudicating legal proceedings. All Review Commission judges are. Each judge has career tenure and no duties other than hearing and deciding cases under the Job Safety Act. I might add that each judge is his own man; no one, including the Chairman of the Review Commission who appoints him, can discipline or reward a judge as a result of his actions in a case.

Now, of the cases filed with the Commission, most are settled to the satisfaction of the employer before actually reaching the formal hearing stage. This can happen in various ways: by the withdrawal of contest by an employer who, upon further consideration, decides he will comply with OSHA's wishes, by a motion from the Labor Department to vacate a citation it decides was issued in error, or by a compromise settlement reached by the parties before the opening of the formal hearing.

All cases, both those that reach a final hearing and those that do not, are conducted with scrupulous regard for due process of law. When Congress placed the powers of investigation and prosecution in the Labor Department and wholly separated the power of adjudication by creating the Review Commission as an autonomous agency to rule on disputed enforcement actions, it divided these powers along traditional lines of federal law enforcement. It was aware of the impact the Act would have on business and was concerned about assuring that it would be enforced with fairness, due process, and impartiality. The Commission record to date is evidence that this congressional purpose is being fully observed.

When a case does go to hearing, the employer does not have to travel to Washington, D.C., or to any one of the other eight cities where our judges are based. We recognized at the outset that travel costs alone could deter small businessmen from contesting citations that they sincerely thought were wrong, so we established a system in which the judge goes to the community in which the alleged violation is purported to have occurred unless a suitable hearing room is not available there. If one is not, the hearing is held at the nearest town having such facilities. We have the rather unique distinction of being one of the few federal agencies which conduct nearly all of their program activity outside of Washington, D.C.

Nor are lawyers required at Review Commission hearings. We've worked hard to eliminate legalistic gobbledygook from our Rules of Procedure. We have even taken this one step further by publication of a Guide to our procedures so that a non-attorney can carry his own case through all of the procedural steps before, during, and after hearing. This Guide is sent automatically to anyone who contests a Labor Department enforcement action.

Although I don't keep a score card on this, I do know that a rather significant number of employers have handled their own cases.

At the hearing the Labor Department has the burden of proving its allegations with substantial evidence. The employer is presumed to be *not* in violation when he has filed a timely objection to the charge. If the Secretary of Labor fails to present convincing evidence which will substantiate the charges, he will lose his case. This is not an unusual occurrence. It has happened many times.

When the Department is able to sustain its case, it is the Review Commission Judge who makes the penalty determination. The judge gives no more weight to the OSHA penalty proposal than he does to its charges. If he decides that a civil penalty should be assessed, he decides what amount, if any, is appropriate.

The judge then writes his decision and mails it to the parties. It will become final 30 days thereafter unless one of the three members of the Commission elects to exercise his right of discretionary review. This has happened in about 10 percent of the cases to date. When it does happen the decision in the case is made by the Commission members rather than the judge. It doesn't really make much difference, for once a decision has become final in either of these ways, any party aggrieved by it can appeal the ruling to the U.S. Court of Appeals, if he does so within 60 days.

I'd like to turn now to some of the decisions that have been issued by the Commission in the areas of penalty assessments, the responsibility of employers for unsafe acts or omissions of their employees, and the principles for deciding whether the prime contractor or a subcontractor is the violator when a job safety standard is not being observed at a construction site.

PENALTIES

The Act requires the Commission to take four things into consideration in deciding the amount of any penalty to be assessed: the size of the business, the gravity of the violation, the good faith of the employer, and the employer's history of previous violations.

In one of the earliest Commission decisions, we ruled that any one of the four criteria may be so important as to make the other three secondary in deciding on a penalty. In the particular case, the gravity of the violation, brief use of a forklift lacking overhead protection, was deemed low and the penalty reduced. Growing out of this decision, the Commission subsequently ruled that where violations of job safety and health standards were of extremely low gravity, minor penalties did nothing to help gain the objectives of the Act to achieve a safe and healthful workplace for all employees. The Commission saw that in many cases where these small penalties were proposed employers understandably viewed them as harassment. As a result, the Commission has in quite a few instances thrown out small penalties for low-gravity violations, such as uncovered trash cans, inadequate lunch facilities, unclean rest rooms, ungrounded coffee pots, and the like. It is my opinion that there is nothing at all wrong with a penalty of zero dollars and zero cents where the purposes of the Act are achieved by full abatement.

You shouldn't get the impression from the foregoing that the Commission throws out all small penalties as a matter of course. The Commission has also ruled that where nonserious violations are of a higher gravity, where the potential of possible harm to employees is greater, penalties do serve a purpose—even small ones. We've allowed penalties of this kind for failure to provide railings around open-sided floors and stairs, failure to ground power tools, and the improper storage of flammable liquids, among other things.

In another case where the gravity of the nonserious violations was also relatively high, however, the Commission ruled that the small size of the firm and its poor financial condition were grounds for eliminating any penalty. The Commission sought in this case to avoid destructive penalties, particularly in view of the subject firm's successful and prompt abatement of the hazards. This is an instance where one of the four criteria—the size of the firm—outweighed the others.

This laborer is not wearing a protective helmet, neither have any barricades been provided for him in case he loses his balance.

NONCOMPLIANCE BY EMPLOYEES

The law exhorts employees to comply with job safety health standards, but penalties for failure to comply can only be assessed against employers. There is logic to this, since an employer can discipline his employees. In most cases I think employers would prefer to retain this authority, rather than give it over to the government. The Commission has already decided a number of cases in which the central issue was the responsibility of the employer for acts and omissions of his employees.

In several cases in which the violations resulted from a failure of employees to use required protective equipment, such as earmuffs to protect them from excessive noise levels or safety belts to prevent fall injuries, the Commission in a series of similar dispositions ruled that the employer was at fault because he failed to live up to his responsibilities. The Commission decided that these employers should have done more than merely make protective equipment available; they must also establish an effective policy to ensure that the equipment is used and must continually monitor the program to see that their employees are complying with it.

However, where an employer does have a good program, it is not reasonable to hold him in violation for a brief, isolated failure of his employees to use their protective equipment. The Commission made just such a ruling in a case in which two employees of a company with a good program failed to wear their hard hats. The Commission does not believe that an employer can absolutely guarantee that his employees will always observe good safety practices. If an employer does his best to see that his employees comply with job safety standards designed for their own protection he needn't fear being in violation when the employees go wrong.

The Commission has also ruled that an employer has not violated the Act when noncompliance results from the sudden and unpredictable act of an employee in ignoring a standing work rule and exposing himself to an obvious hazard. Another Commission decision vacated a citation against an employer because the hazard involved had been created by an experienced, well-qualified technician who had always scrupulously observed excellent safety practices in the past. The only way the accident in the case could have been prevented would have been for the employer to provide constant one-on-one supervision for the technician, and this, the Commission ruled, was an impractical solution and an unreasonable burden for *any* employer in all but the most unusual circumstances.

PRIME CONTRACTOR-SUBCONTRACTOR RELATIONSHIP

I know that as home improvement contractors you are particularly concerned about the contractor-subcontractor relationship and its effect on your responsibilities under the Act.

The Act does not, of course, speak of contractors and subcontractors; it refers only to "each employer." And it requires of each employer that he comply with those of the Secretary of Labor's job safety and health standards that are applicable to his operations and that he "furnish to each of *his* (emphasis added) employees employment and a place of employment which are free from recognized hazards. . . ." Starkly put, that means that each employer, be he general contractor or sub, is responsible for the exposure of his employees to any hazards, unless, naturally, that employer couldn't reasonably be expected to know of the hazards. And each employer is responsible for the hazards to which his employees may be exposed wherever his employees happen to be working and regardless of who created the hazards or who may be formally or informally responsible for their elimination or prevention.

Let's say, hypothetically, that a general contractor has formally agreed to supply the employees of all the subcontractors with hard hats for use wherever they are required at a job site. If he should fail to provide the hats, then it would be up to each sub to see to it that his employees got hats from another source or to prohibit them from going into hard hat areas until the general contractor met his obligation and supplied the protective gear. If a sub were to allow his employees to work in the hard hat areas without the protective headgear, then he could be found in violation of the Job Safety Act, even though the prime has signed a contract promising to provide the equipment.

On the other hand, even if a hazard exists at a job site, but the subcontractor's employees working there aren't exposed to this hazard, the subcontractor would not be in violation. In one of the early cases involving the prime-sub relationship, for example, a citation was issued to a subcontractor whose employees were working near some stairs that lacked handrails in violation of a job safety standard. The stairs had been installed by the prime contractor. At the hearing for the case, it was not shown that the sub's employees ever used the stairs and were, thus, exposed to the hazard created by the lack of handrails. The Review Commission Judge who heard the case, therefore, threw out the charge against the subcontractor.

In other words, the employer's obligation under this Act is to provide for the job safety of his own employees. If a contractor fails to comply with a safety standard, he is not in violation of the Act unless some of his own employees are thereby exposed to a hazard. On the other hand, if Contractor A has scrupulously complied with all safety standards and his employees are working in an area which is hazardous because Contractor B has failed to erect perimeter protection, for example, Contractor A is in violation (Contractor B is also—if he has employees working there).

You violate the Act when you expose your employees to hazards—regardless of who created the hazardous conditions.

In conclusion, I'd like to thank you for extending to me the privilege of addressing your Council. I have always felt that the more people know about this law, the better they'll be able to meet its many requirements and that this will help reduce workplace illnesses and injuries as effectively as a personal visit from the OSHA inspector.

Scaffolding (from bottom looking up) for ceiling tile installers. Note lack of adequate ties between vertical poles and horizontals, as well as gaps in planking.

TWO

Designer's Quick-Reference Guide to OSHA

This Guide presents the technical subparts of Part 1910 in six major categories. A seventh category covers regulations applicable to all employers. These categories are:

1. Workplace Standards
2. Machines and Equipment Standards
3. Materials Standards
4. Employee Standards
5. Power Source Standards
6. Process Standards
7. Administrative Regulations

Page references are made to material included in this book.

Note: Only those standards most frequently used and of most common application by architects and engineers have been detailed in this book. For complete list of all standards refer to page 45.

Occupational Safety and Health Standards

Workplace Standards

A ELECTRICAL WIRING, FIXTURES AND CONTROLS

B EXITS AND ACCESS

C FIRE PROTECTION

D HOUSEKEEPING AND GENERAL WORK ENVIRONMENT

E ILLUMINATION (LIGHTING)

F SANITATION AND HEALTH

G SIGNS, LABELS, MARKINGS AND TAGS

H VENTILATION

I WALKING AND WORKING SURFACES

Occupational Safety and Health WORKPLACE STANDARDS	**1**		29 CFR 1910	
		Sub-part	Section	Page
A. ELECTRICAL WIRING, FIXTURES AND CONTROLS				235
1. General (National Electrical Code)		S	309	235
2. Grounding			309	235
3. Hazardous Locations (Classes I-III)			309(a)	235
4. Lighting Fixtures			309	235
5. Overcurrent Protection (NFPA Article 240)			309	
B. EXITS AND ACCESS				93-94
1. Access to Exits, Exterior		E	37(g)	90-92
2. Access to Exits, Interior			37(f)	
3. Application and General Requirements			36(a)	89
4. Arrangement			37(e)	88
5. Capacity, Occupancy Loads			37(d)	
6. Fundamental Requirements			36(b)	97
7. Maintenance, Path of Travel			37(k)	93-94
8. Markings, Locations and Illumination			37(g)	98
9. Obstructions and Decorations			37(l)	
10. Permissible Exit Components			37(a)	
11. Protection During Construction and Repair			36(c)	85-87
12. Special Buildings, Rooms and Operations				
Acetylene generator houses		G	252(a)(6)	
Bulk plant storage, flammable and combustible liquids		H	106(f)(2)	179
Gaseous hydrogen systems		H	103(b)(3)	149
Liquefied hydrogen systems		H	103(c)(2)&(3)	
Sawmills, emergency exits, doors and fire escapes		R	265(c)(6)	
Sawmills, fuel hoses and bins		R	265(c)(23)	
13. See also G. Signs, Labels, Markings, and Tags on next page				
C. FIRE PROTECTION				
1. Automatic Sprinklers, Fixed Systems		L	159	232
Fire department connections			159(b)	
General requirements			159(a)	232
Maintenance			159(d)	
Sprinkler alarm systems			159(c)	232
Sprinkler head clearances			159(e)	232

			Sub-part	Section	Page
		Spray booths	H	107(b)(10)	
		Storage areas, indoor	N	177(f)(1)	
F.		SANITATION AND HEALTH			
	1.	Application and General Requirements	J	141(a)	
		Laundry operations	R	264(f)(2)	
		Pulp, paper and paperboard mills	R	261(g)(15)	
		Sawmills	R	265(k)	
	2.	Change Rooms	J	141(e)(1)	
		Asbestos Workers	G	93a(d)(4)	
		— Clothes lockers		93a(d)(4)	
		— Contaminated clothes, laundering		93a(d)(4)	
	3.	Laundries	R	264(f)(2)	
	4.	Lunchrooms	J	141(g)	
	5.	Retiring Rooms		141(f)	
	6.	Temporary Labor Camps		142	
	7.	Toilet Facilities		141(c)	
	8.	Washing Facilities		141(d)	
	9.	Waste Disposal Systems		141(a)(3)	
		— Non-water carriage		143	
	10.	Water Supply			
		— Non-potable		141(b)(2)	
		— Potable		141(b)(1)	
		— Standpipe and hose systems		141(g)	
G.		SIGNS, LABELS, MARKINGS AND TAGS			
	1.	Application and Design	J	145	
	2.	Labels			
		Acceptable certifications, electrical equipment	S	308(d)	
		Asbestos	G	93a(g)	
		Electrical equipment (NFPA/NEC)	S	309	
		Respiratory protection equipment	I	134	
		— Breathing gas containers, air quality		134(d)(4)	
		— Canisters, gas mask identification		134(g)	
		Welding rods, fillers and coatings	Q	252(f)	
	3.	Markings			
		Compressed gas cylinders	Q	252(a)(2)	
		Explosive beads, power actuated hand tools	P	243(d)(3)	
		Load ratings, markings and charts			
		— Crawler, locomotive and truck cranes	N	180(c)(2)	
		— Derricks	N	181(c)	
		— Powered industrial trucks	N	178(a)(3)	
		— Powered platforms	F	66(c)(7),(21)	
		Standpipes, hose connections	L	158(b)(7),(c)(4)	
	4.	Physical Hazards, Color Coding	J	144(a)	
		Sawmills	R	265(c)(11)	
	5.	Signs			
		Asbestos caution signs and labels	G	93a(g)	
		Exit signs and markings	E	37(q)	
		Exits, emergency — sawmills	R	265(c)(6)	
		Extinguishers, locations	L	175(a)(3)	
		Extinguisher systems, carbon dioxide	L	161(a)(2)	
		Fuel gas systems, cylinder storage	Q	252(a)(2)	
		Lawn mowers, caution signs	P	243(2)(1)(v)	
		Manlifts, warning signs	F	68(c)(7)	

WORKPLACE STANDARDS (Cont'd.)	**1**	29 CFR 1910		
		Sub-part	Section	Page
Manifold systems, oxygen		Q	252(a)(3)	
Radiation signs, signals and labels				
– Ionizing		G	96(e)	
– Non-ionizing			97(a)(3)	
Storage areas, sawmills		R	262(l)(2)	
Sprinkler systems, automatic		L	159(b)(4)	
Standpipes, hose connections			158(b)(7)&(c)	
			(4)	
Traffic, in-plant		J	145(d)(8)	
Vehicles, slow moving			145(d)(10)	
Water, non-potable			141(b)(2)	
6. Tags				
Bio-hazard		J	145(f)(8)	
Caution			145(f)(5)	
Danger			145(f)(4)	
Defective equipment			145(f)(1)	
Defective ladders, metal		D	26(c)(2)	
Defective ladders, wood			25(d)(1)	
Do not start		J	145(f)(3)	
Out of order			145(f)(6)	
Radiation			145(f)(7)	
Scope and purpose			145(f)(1)	
H. VENTILATION				
1. Air Requirements–Sawmills		R	265(c)(7)	
2. Maintaining Comfortable Working Conditions–Laundries		R	264(d)	
I. WALKING AND WORKING SURFACES				
1. Application and General Requirements		D	22	
Aisles and passageways			22(b)	
Covers and guardrails, pits, tanks and ditches			22(c)	
Floors				
– general requirements			22(a) & 23(a)	
– loading protection			22(d)	
Housekeeping		D	22(a)&(b)	
– general		J	141(a)	
– storage		N	176(c)	
Safety factors–sawmills		R	265(c)(1)	
2. Floors				
Crane access, footwalks and catwalks		N	179(c)&(d)	
Guarding openings and holes		D	23(a)	46-48
– Chutes, hatchways, ladderways		R	261(k)	
– Manholes, pits, trap doors and skylights		R	265(i)	
Loading protection		D	22(d)	
Open-sided floors, ramps, runway walkways				
– bakery operations		R	263(d)(1)	
– general requirements		D	23(c)	51-52
– pulp, paper and paperboard mills		R	261(b),(i),(j),&	
			(k)	
– sawmills		R	265(c)(3),(4)	
Sanitation, maintenance and construction				
– general requirements		D	22(a)&(b)	
		J	141(a)(1),(2)&	
			(c)(2)	

Occupational Safety and Health Standards

Machines and Equipment Standards

A   APPLIANCES, ELECTRICAL UTILIZATION

B   COMPRESSED GAS AND COMPRESSED AIR EQUIPMENT

C   CONVEYORS

D   CRANES—CRAWLER, LOCOMOTIVE AND TRUCK

E   CRANES—OVERHEAD AND GANTRY

F   DERRICKS

G   HAND AND PORTABLE POWERED TOOLS

H   MACHINERY AND MACHINE GUARDING

I   MISCELLANEOUS EQUIPMENT USED IN GENERAL INDUSTRY

J   MISCELLANEOUS EQUIPMENT USED IN SPECIAL INDUSTRIES

K   TRUCKS

Occupational Safety and Health MACHINES AND EQUIPMENT STANDARDS	**2**		29 CFR 1910	
		Sub-part	Section	Page
A. APPLIANCES, ELECTRICAL UTILIZATION		S	309	235
B. COMPRESSED GAS AND COMPRESSED AIR EQUIPMENT				
1. Air Receivers		M	169	
2. Compressed Gas Cylinders, Inspection		M	166	
3. Safety Relief Devices				
Cargo and portable tanks		M	168	
Cylinders			167	
C. CONVEYORS				
1. Bakeries		R	263(d)(7)&(i)(7)	
2. Pulp, Paper and Paperboard Mills		R	261(f)(4)	
			261(c)(15)	
3. Sawmills		R	265(c)(18)	
4. Spray Booths, Spray Finishing			107(h)(7)	
D. CRANES—CRAWLER, LOCOMOTIVE AND TRUCK				
1. Application and General Requirements		N	180(b)	
Crane mounting, load tipping, and posting load rating charts			180(c)	
Design, construction and modification specifications; effective dates			180(b)(2)	
Load rating, stability and lifting performance			180(c)	
2. Crane Testing		N	180(e)	
Operational tests			180(e)(1)	
Rated load tests			180(e)(2)	
3. Inspection		N	180(d)	
Records			180(d)(6)	
Types			180(d)	
4. Load Handling		N	180(h)	
Attaching loads			180(h)(2)	
Holding and controlling loads			180(h)(4)	
Moving loads			180(h)(3)	
Restrictions on load size			180(h)(1)	
5. Maintenance, Repair Procedures and Operational Restrictions		N	180(f)	
6. Operating Near Electric Power Lines and Overhead Wires		N	180(i)	

		Sub-part	Section	Page
7.	Other Requirements	N	181(j)	
	Cabs or operating enclosures, maintenance		181(j)(6)	
	Fire extinguishers		181(j)(3)	
	Guarding exposed machinery		181(j)(1)	
	Hook specifications		181(j)(2)	
	Refueling		181(j)(4)	
8.	Testing			
	Anchorage	N	181(e)(2)	
	Operational tests		181(e)(1)	
G.	HAND AND PORTABLE POWERED TOOLS			
1.	Abrasive Wheels, Portable	P	243(c)	
2.	Explosive Actuated Fastening Tools		243(d)	
3.	General Requirements		242(a)	
	Signs, markings and color codes			
	— explosive actuated fastening tools		243(d)	
	— lawn mowers		243(e)	
4.	Lawnmowers, Powered		243(e)	
5.	Other Portable Equipment		244	
	Abrasive blast cleaning nozzles		244(b)	
	Electrode holders, welding	Q	252(b)(4)	
	Gas torches and valves		252(d)(4)	
	Hand tools—logging	R	266(c)(2)	
	Jacks	P	244(a)	
	Miscellaneous electrical equipment	S	309(a)	235
6.	Pneumatic Powered Hand Tools and Hoses	P	243(b)	
7.	Woodworking, Portable Powered Tools		243(a)	
H.	MACHINERY AND MACHINE GUARDING			
1.	Abrasive Wheel Machinery	O	215	
2.	Anchoring Fixed Machinery		212(b)	
3.	Cooperage Machinery		214	
4.	Forging Machines		218	
5.	General Requirements		212	
6.	Guarding Machines		212(a)	
7.	Mechanical Power Presses		217	
8.	Mechanical Power Transmission Apparatus		219	
9.	Mills and Calenders—Rubber and Plastics Industries		216	
10.	Other Machinery and Equipment			
	Alligator shears		212(a)(3)(iv)	
	Bakery equipment	R	263	
	Forming rolls	O	212(a)	
	Guilloting cutters		212(a)	
	Laundry equipment	R	264	
	Milling machines	O	212(a)	
	Revolving drums, barrels and containers		212(a)	
	Shears, power		212(a)	
	Textile equipment	R	262	
11.	Woodworking Machinery	O	213	
	Boring and mortising machines		217(l)	
	General requirements		213(a)&(b)	
	— guarding		212(a)	
			213(r)(4)	
	— inspection and maintenance		213(s)	
	— ventilation, exhaust hoods		213(r)(4)	

		Sub-part	Section	Page
	Jointers	O	213(j)	
	Other woodworking machines			
	— miscellaneous woodworking machines		213(r)	
	— pulp, paper and paperboard mills	R	261	
	— pulpwood logging		266	
	— sawmills		265	
	Planing, molding, sticking and matching	O	213(n)	
	Profile, swinghead lathes		213(o)	
	Sanding machines		213(p)	
	Saws			
	— bandsaws and band resaws		213(i)	
	— circular resaws		213(e)	
	— hand-fed crosscut table saws		213(d)	
	— hand-fed ripsaws		213(c)	
	— radial saws		213(h)	
	— self-feed circular saws		213(f)	
	— swing cutoff saws		213(g)	
	— veneer cutters and wringers		213(q)	
I.	MISCELLANEOUS EQUIPMENT USED IN GENERAL INDUSTRY			
1.	Manlifts	F	68	111-124
2.	Manually Propelled Mobile Ladder Stands and Scaffolds	D	29	
3.	Portable Metal Ladders	D	26	
4.	Portable Wood Ladders	D	25	
5.	Powered Platforms for Exterior Building Maintenance	F	66	101-110
6.	Vehicle-Mounted Work Platforms	F	67	
J.	MISCELLANEOUS EQUIPMENT USED IN SPECIAL INDUSTRIES			
1.	Bakery Equipment	R	263	
2.	Laundry Machine Operations		264	
3.	Pulp, Paper and Paperboard Mills		261	
4.	Pulpwood Logging		266	
5.	Sawmills		265	
6.	Textiles		262	
K.	TRUCKS			
1.	Powered Industrial Trucks	N	178	
	Application and general requirements		178(a)	
	Converted powered industrial trucks and operating locations		178(d)	
	Environmental controls			
	— lighting operating areas	N	178(h)	
	— noxious gases and fumes	N	178(i)	
		G	93	125-130
	Maintenance	N	178(q)	
	— fueling, fuel handling and storage		178(f)&(p)	
	— storage batteries, charging and changing		178(g)	
	Operation, traveling and loading		178(k),(m),(n)	
			(o)&(p)	
	Operator training and authorized operators		178(l)	
	Overhead guards for high-lift rider trucks		178(e)&(m)(9)	
	Restricted use in designated locations and hazardous atmospheres		178(b)&(c)	

MACHINES AND EQUIPMENT STANDARDS (Cont'd.)	**2** 29 CFR 1910		
		Sub-part	Section
2. Trucks, Other Types			
Ammonia systems mounted on farm vehicles		H	111(g)
Ammonia transporting tank motor vehicles			111(f)
Explosives transport			109(d)
Flammable liquids, tank vehicles			106(e)(4) &
			(g)(1)
LP-Gas systems mounted on commercial vehicles			110(g)
LP-Gas transport trucks			110(b)(15)
Personnel transport		R	266(e)(8)

Occupational Safety and Health Standards

Materials Standards

A HAZARDOUS MATERIALS

B HAZARDOUS LOCATIONS DUE TO MATERIALS

C MATERIALS HANDLING AND STORAGE

D MATERIALS HANDLING MACHINES AND EQUIPMENT

Occupational Safety and Health MATERIALS STANDARDS	**3**	29 CFR 1910		
		Sub-part	Section	Page
A. HAZARDOUS MATERIALS				125-130
1. Air Contaminants		G	93	129
Acceptable ceiling concentrations and 8-hour time weighted			93(h)	
averages (Table G-2)				125-128
Ceiling values and 8-hour time weighted averages (Table G-1)			93(a)	130
Mineral dusts 8-hour time weighted averages (Table G-3)			93(c)	125-130
Requirements and specifications			93	207
2. Anhydrous Ammonia, Storage and Handling		H	111	207
Basic rules			111(b)	
General requirements			111(a)	
Refrigerated storage systems			111(d)	
Systems mounted on farm vehicles, ammonia			111(h)	
Systems mounted on farm vehicles, other than ammonia			111(g)	
Systems utilizing portable DOT containers			111(e)	
Systems utilizing stationary, non-refrigerated storage containers			111(c)	
Tank motor vehicles for ammonia transport			111(f)	
3. Compressed Gases				
Acetylene		H	102	
General requirements			101	
Hydrogen			103	147-152
Nitrous oxide			105	
Oxygen			104	153-155
4. Explosives and Blasting Agents		H	109	197-203
Blasting agents			109(g)	
General requirements			109(b)	
Small arms ammunition, primers, propellants			109(j)	203
Storage of ammonium nitrate			109(i)	202-203
Storage of explosives			109(c)	197-201
Transportation of explosives			109(d)	
Use			109(e)	

		Sub-part	Section	Page
5.	Flammable and Combustible Liquids	H	106	156-190
	Bulk plants		106(f)	178-180
	Container and portable tank storage		106(d)	167-173
	Definitions		106(a)	156-157
	Industrial plants		106(e)	174-177
	Piping, valves and fittings		106(c)	
	Processing plants		106(h)	187-190
	Refineries, chemical plants and distilleries		106(i)	
	Service stations		106(g)	181-186
	Tank storage		106(b)	158-166
6.	Ionizing Radiation	G	96	145-146
7.	Storage and Handling of Liquefied Petroleum (LP) Gases	H	110	204-206
	Basic rules		110(b)	204-205
	Cylinder systems		110(c)	
	Motor fuel		110(e)	
	Service stations		110(h)	
	Storage of containers awaiting use or resale		110(f)	206
	System installations on commercial vehicles		110(g)	
	Systems using other than DOT containers		110(d)	
B.	HAZARDOUS LOCATIONS DUE TO MATERIALS			
1.	Class I Installations—Presence of Flammable Gases, Vapors or Liquids	S	309	235
2.	Class II Installations—Presence of Combustible Dusts		309	235
3.	Class III Installations—Presence of Easily Ignitable Fibers or Flyings		309	235
4.	General		309	235
C.	MATERIALS HANDLING AND STORAGE			
1.	General	N	176	
	Clearances, mechanical equipment		176(a)	
	Clearance limits and signs		176(e)	
	Drainage, storage areas		176(d)	
	Guarding open pits, vats and ditches		176(g)	
	Housekeeping, storage areas		176(c)	
	Rolling railroad cars		176(f)	
	Secure storage, materials		176(b)	
2.	Indoor Storage	N	177	
	Application and general requirements		177(b)	
	Building service equipment		177(f)	
	Fire protection		177(d)	
	Mechanical handling equipment		177(e)	
	Piling procedures and precautions		177(c)	
	Smoking restriction and signs		177(g)	
3.	Storage and Handling			
	Ammonium nitrate	H	109(i)	202-203
	Anhydrous ammonia	H	111(a)(1)	
	Batteries, industrial trucks	N	178(g)	
	Blasting agents	H	109(g)	
	Compressed gases		101(b)	
	Explosives		109(c)	197-201
	Flammable and combustible liquids		106(d)	167-173
	Flammable liquids		107(e)	
	Flammable liquids, dip tanks		108(d)	
	Flour	R	263	
	— dumpbins and blenders		263(d)(3)	
	— storage bins		263(d)(6)	

	Sub-part	Section	Page
Liquids, Classes I-III	H	106(f)	178-180
LP-Gas containers		110(f)	206
Pulpwood and pulp chips	R	261(c)	
— chemicals, tagged or drummed		261(h)(4)	
— chocking rolls		261(d)(4)	
— liquid chlorine		261(h)(3)	
Radioactive materials	G	96(j)	
Refrigerated storage	H	111(d)	
Sawmills			
— bins, bunkers and hoppers	R	265(c)(23)	
— log handling, sorting and storage		265(d)	
— lumber piling and storage		265(c)(27)	
Tanks			
— acid storage	R	261(g)(3)	
— flammable and combustible liquids	H	106(b)	158-166
D. MATERIALS HANDLING MACHINES AND EQUIPMENT			
1. Bakery Flour Handling Equipment			
Bag chutes and bag lifts	R	263(d)(2)	
Chain tackles		263(i)(12)	
Conveyors		263(i)(7)	
Flour elevators		263(d)(4)	
Hand trucks		263(i)(4)	
Overhead rail systems		263(i)(8)	
Racks		263(i)(6)	
Screw conveyors		263(d)(7)	
Troughs and other hoists		263(i)(13)	
2. Crawler, Locomotive and Truck Cranes	N	180	
3. Derricks		181	
4. Overhead and Gantry Cranes		179	
5. Powered Industrial Trucks		178	
6. Pulpwood and Pulp Chips	R	261(c)	
Banding of skids, cartons, cases		261(m)(3),(4)	
Conveyor belts		261(c)(15)	
Cranes		261(c)(8)	
Powered hand trucks		261(m)(2)	
Trucks and trailers		261(c)(7)	
7. Pulpwood Logging	R	266	
Skidding and prehauling		266(e)(6),(7)	
8. Sawmills—Log Handling Equipment	R	265	
Blowers, collecting and exhaust systems		265(c)(20)	
Mechanical stackers and unstackers		265(d)(26)	
Mobile equipment for sawmills, planing mills, storage and yard operations		265(c)(30)	

Occupational Safety and Health Standards

Employee Standards

A   IONIZING RADIATION PROTECTION

B   MEDICAL AND FIRST AID

C   PERSONNEL PROTECTION IN TANKS AND CONFINED SPACES

D   PERSONAL PROTECTIVE EQUIPMENT

E   SKILLS AND KNOWLEDGE

		29 CFR 1910	
4	Sub-part	Section	Page

		Sub-part	Section	Page
D.	PERSONAL PROTECTIVE EQUIPMENT			
1.	Application and General Requirements	I	132	
2.	Electrical (Personal) Protective Devices—Sawmills	I	137	
		R	265(c)(11)	
3.	Eye and Face Protection			
	Application and general requirements	I	133	
	Explosive actuated fastening tools	P	243(d)(1)	
	Pulp, paper and paperboard mills	R	261(b)(2)	
	— chemical processes, pulp making		261(g)(5)(14),(15)	
	Pulpwood logging		266(c)(1)	
	Sawmills		265(c)(17)&(g)	
4.	Foot Protection			
	General	I	136	
	Pulp, paper and paperboard mills	R	261(b)(2)	
	Pulpwood logging		266(c)(1)	
	Sawmills		265(g)	
5.	Head Protection			
	General	I	135	
	Pulp, paper and paperboard mills	R	261(b)(2)	
	Pulpwood logging		266(c)(1)	
	Sawmills		265(g)	
6.	Noise Exposure			
	General	G	95(b)(1)	144
	Pulpwood logging	R	266(c)(1)	
7.	Protective Clothing and Equipment			
	Acids, alkalis, caustics and heat	I	132(a)	
	Emergency showers, bubblers and eye fountains			
	— open-surface tank operations	G	94(d)(9)	143
	— pulp, paper and paperboard mills	R	261(g)(5)(15)	
	Open surface tank inspection and maintenance	G	94(d)(9)	
	Pulp, paper and paperboard mills	R	261(b)(2)	
	Pulpwood logging		266(c)(1)	
	Sawmills		265(g)	
	Textiles		266(qq)	
	Welding and burning	Q	252(e)(3)	
8.	Respiratory Protection			
	Abrasive blasting	G	94(a)(5)	
	Air quality	I	134(d)	
	Application, general and engineering controls	I	134(a)(1)	
	Asbestos	G	93a(d)	
	Gas mask canister identfication	I	134(g)	
	Open surface tank operations	G	94(d)(11)	
	Pulp, paper and paperboard mills	R	261(b)(2)	
	— bleaching, liquid chlorine		261(h)	
	— chemical processes		261(g)(2),(4),(10),(15)	
	— lead burning		261(g)(6)	
	Pulpwood logging		266(c)(1)	
	Respiratory protective programs	I	134(b)	
	Sawmills	R	265(g)	
	— chemicals handling, use and storage		265(c)(17)	
	Welding, brazing and cutting	Q	252(f)(2),(4),(5),(7)–(10)	

			29 CFR 1910	
		4	**Sub-part**	**Section**
9.	Safety Belts and Lifelines			
	Power platforms, exterior building maintenance		F	66(d)(8)
	Pulp, paper and paperboard mills		R	261(b)(5)&
				(g)(4),(15)
	Scaffolding			
	— boatswains' chairs		D	28(j)(4)
	— floats and ship scaffolds			28(u)(6)
	— needle beam scaffolds			28(n)(8)
	— roof work			
	- - crawling boards and chicken ladders			28(t)(2)
	- - sloping roofs			28(s)(3)
	Tank maintenance and repairs		G	94(d)(11)
	Welding		Q	252(e)(4)(iv)
E.	SKILLS AND KNOWLEDGE			
1.	Explosives		H	109(d)(3)
	Pulpwood logging		R	266(c)(7)
2.	Power Presses		O	217(e)(3) &
				(f)(1),(2)
3.	Powered Industrial Trucks		N	178(l)
4.	Welding		Q	252(b)(1) &
				(c)(1)

Occupational Safety and Health Standards

Power Source Standards

A   ELECTRICAL POWER
B   EXPLOSIVE ACTUATED POWER
C   HYDRAULIC POWER
D   PNEUMATIC POWER
E   STEAM POWER
F   MISCELLANEOUS POWER SOURCES USED IN SPECIAL INDUSTRIES

Occupational Safety and Health POWER SOURCE STANDARDS	**5**	29 CFR 1910		
		Sub-part	Section	Page
A. ELECTRICAL POWER				
1. National Electrical Code Adopted		S	309	235
B. EXPLOSIVE ACTUATED POWER				
1. Explosive Actuated Fastening Tools		P	243(d)	
C. HYDRAULIC POWER				
1. Forging Presses		O	218(f)(2)	
2. Jacks		P	244(a)	
3. Mechanical Power Presses		O	217(b)(11),(12)	
4. Sawmills		R	265(c)(13)	
D. PNEUMATIC POWER				
1. Air Lift Gravity Hammers		O	218(e)(1)	
2. Air Receivers		M	169	
3. Compressed Air Used for Cleaning		P	242(b)	
4. General		P	243(b)	
5. Mechanical Power Presses		O	217(b)(9),(10),(12)	
6. Pneumatic Powered Tools and Equipment		P	243(b)	
7. Spray Finishing and Spraying Containers		H	107(e)(5)	
E. STEAM POWER				
1. Steam Control Valves—Textiles		R	262(h)(1),(p)(1),(q)	
2. Steam Hammers		O	218(d)	
3. Steam Pipes				
Laundry operations		R	264(c)(4),(d)(2)	
Textiles			262(c)(9)	
Pulp, paper and paperboard mills			261(k)(11)	
F. MISCELLANEOUS POWER SOURCES USED IN SPECIAL INDUSTRIES				
1. Bakery Equipment		R	263	
2. Laundry Machinery Operations			264	
3. Pulpwood Logging			266	
4. Pulp, Paper and Paperboard Mills			261	
5. Sawmills			265	
6. Textiles			262	

Occupational Safety and Health Standards

Process Standards

A ABRASIVE BLASTING

B DRY GRINDING, POLISHING AND BUFFING, EXHAUST SYSTEMS

C PROCESS, DIP AND OPEN SURFACES TANKS

D PROCESSING PLANTS AND OPERATIONS

E SPECIAL INDUSTRIES AND RELATED PROCESSES

F SPRAY FINISHING

G WELDING, CUTTING AND BRAZING

Occupational Safety and Health PROCESS STANDARDS	**6**		29 CFR 1910	
		Sub-part	Section	Page
A. ABRASIVE BLASTING				
1. Air Supply and Air Compressors		G	94(a)(6)	
2. Blast Cleaning Enclosures, Construction			94(a)(3)	
3. Dust Hazards—Allowable Levels of Concentration, Limited Use of Combustible Abrasives, and Fire-Explosion Requirements			94(a)(2)	
4. Exhaust Ventilation Systems, Construction Maintenance and Inspection			94(a)(4)	
5. General Requirements			94(a)	
6. Operational Procedures and General Safety			94(a)(7)	
7. Personal Protective Equipment			94(a)(5)	
		I	132	
Eye and face protection		G	94(a)(5)	
		I	133	
Protective clothing, shoes and gloves		G	94(a)(5)	
Respirators, need, approvals and types		G	94(a)(5)	
Respiratory protection		I	134(a)&(b)	
8. Standards		G	94(a)(8)	
B. DRY GRINDING, POLISHING AND BUFFING, EXHAUST SYSTEMS				
1. Abrasive Wheel Machinery		O	215	
2. Application and Requirements		G	94(b)(2)	132
3. Exhaust System Design		G	94(b)(4)	132
4. Exhaust Ventilation		G	94(b)	132-139
Buffing and polishing wheels (Table G-5)				134
Grinding and abrasive cut-off wheels (Table G-4)				133
Grinding and polishing belts (Table G-9)				138
Horizontal double—spindle disk grinders (Table G-7)				136
Horizontal single—spindle disk grinders (Table G-6)				135
Vertical spindle disk grinders (Table G-8)				137
5. Hood Enclosure Design		G	94(b)(5)	132-139
6. Standards			94(b)(6)	

		Sub-part	Section	Page
C. PROCESS, DIP AND OPEN SURFACE TANKS				
1. Application and General Requirements		G	94(d)	
Washing, degreasing, pickling, quenching, dying, dipping, bleaching, stripping, rinsing, electroplating, anodizing, tanning and coating		H	108	195-196
2. Classification of Open Surface Tanks		G	94(d)(2)	142
Fire and explosion determination			94(d)(2)	142
Hazard potential determination			94(d)(2)	142
Toxic gas, fumes and mists, allowable concentrations (TLV)			93	125-130
3. Controls other than Ventilation			94(d)(6)	
4. Dip Tanks Containing Flammable or Combustible Liquids		H	108	195-196
Construction and design			108(c)	195
Fire extinguishing facilities			108(c)(15),(16) & (d) & (g)	
Storage of flammable liquids			108(d)&(g)	
Ventilation			108(b)	
5. Dip Tanks, Special Applications			108(h)	
Electrostatic coatings			108(h)(3)	
Flow coatings			108(h)(2)	
Hardening and tempering tanks			108(h)(1)	
Roll coatings			108(h)(4)	
6. Exhaust System Design		G	94(d)(7)	142
7. Exhaust Systems Operation and Maintenance			94(d)(8)	143
8. Fire Prevention and Protection		H	108(g)	
Extinguishing facilities (automatic)			108(c)(5)	
Ignition sources			108(e)	196
9. Installation, Maintenance and Inspection of Open Tanks		G	94(d)(11)	
10. Open Surface Tank Operations		G	94(d)(13)	
11. Operation, Maintenance and Inspection of Dip Tanks		H	108(f)	
12. Other Special Process Tanks				
Acid tanks—pulp, paper and paperboard mills		R	261(g)(4)	
Dissolving tanks—smelting			261(g)(18)	
Open mixing tanks—textiles			262(11)	
13. Personal Protection Against Acids, Corrosives and Irritating Contaminants		G	94(d)(9)	143
Chemical splashes, water flushing			94(d)(9)	143
Clothing, coats, jackets, sleeves, aprons			94(d)(9)	143
Cyanide, special precautions			94(d)(10)	
Emergency showers and bubblers		R	261(g)(18)	
Emergency situations		G	94(d)(9)	
-- hazardous concentration contaminants, respirators			94(d)(9)	
— oxygen deficient atmospheres, respirators			94(d)(9)	
— personal protective equipment		I	134	
Eye and face protection		G	94(d)(9)	
Foot protection, impervious types			94(d)(9)	131
Hand protection, impervious types			94(d)(9)	219
Hazard instruction, employee			94(d)(9)	143
Locker space or change rooms				
— asbestos workers		G	93a(d)(4)	
— general requirements		J	141(e)	
— open tank workers		G	94(d)(9)	
Medical examinations				
— asbestos workers		G	93a(j)	
— chromic acid workers			94(d)(9)	
Medical restrictions and treatment			94(d)(9)	

	6	**29 CFR 1910**		
		Sub-part	Section	Page
9. Operation and Maintenance		H	107(g)	
Cleaning solvents			107(g)(5)	
Clothing storage			107(g)(4)	
Hazardous material combinations			107(g)(6)	
Housekeeping, cleaning and waste disposal			107(g)(2),(3)	
10. Other Spraying Techniques				
Asbestos		G	93a	131
Automobile undercoating		H	107(k)	
Organic peroxides and dual component coatings			107(m)	
Powder coating			107(l)	
11. Spray Booths and Spray Rooms		G	94(c)(8)	140-141
Flammable and combustible materials		H	107(n)	
12. Spray Booths, Design and Construction		G	94(c)(3)	140
13. Spray Rooms, Design and Construction		G	94(c)(4)	140
14. Ventilation and Atmospheric Controls		G	94(c)(5)	141
Automobile undercoating		H	107(k)	
Electrostatic spraying, hand			107(i)	
Electrostatic spraying, mechanical			107(h)	
Spray finishing			107(d)	193
G. WELDING, CUTTING AND BRAZING				
1. Arc Welding and Cutting				
Equipment installation		Q	252(b)(3)	
— conductors and supply connectors			252(b)(3)	
— grounding of welding machines			252(b)(3)	
Equipment installation and operation			252(b)	
— employee qualifications and instructions			252(b)(1)	
— equipment selection, atmospheric and environmental considerations			252(b)(2)	
— voltage and design			252(b)(2)	
Equipment operation and maintenance			252(b)(4)	
2. Fire Prevention and Protection			252(d)	
Confined spaces, care of idle equipment			252(d)(4)	
Containers, welding and cutting			252(d)(3)	
Hazards, guards and restrictions			252(d)(1)	
Special precautions			252(d)(2)	
3. Fuel-Gas Systems Installation and Operation			252(a)	
Acetylene generators			252(a)(6)	
Calcium carbide storage			252(a)(7)	
Cylinders and containers, approval and identification			252(a)(2)	
General requirements			252(a)(1)	
Manifolding cylinders			252(a)(3)	
Oxygen-fuel gas systems			252(a)	
Public exhibitions and demonstrations			252(a)(8)	
Regulators, hoses, piping and protective devices			252(a)(5)	
Service piping systems			252(a)(4)	
Storage and operating procedures			252(a)(2)	
Storage of cylinders			252(a)(2)	
4. Health Protection and Ventilation			252(f)	
Application and general requirements for atmospheric contamination, ventilation, maximum allowable concentrations, warning labels, shielding and screening			252(f)(1)	

	Sub-part	Section	Page
Confined spaces	Q	252(f)(4)	
— air line respirators		252(f)(4)	
— air replacement		252(f)(4)	
— respiratory protection	I	134	
— self contained respirators	Q	252(f)(4)	
Exhaust hoods and booths		252(f)(3)	
First aid equipment requirements		252(f)(13)	
— medical and first aid	K	151	
Ventilation	Q	252(f)(2)	
Welding and cutting		252(f)	
— air contaminants	G	93	125-130
— beryllium	Q	252(f)(8)	
— cadmium		252(f)(9)	
— cleaning compounds		252(f)(11)	
— fluorine compounds		252(f)(5)	
— lead		252(f)(7)	
— mercury		252(f)(10)	
— stainless steel		252(f)(12)	
— zinc		252(f)(6)	
5. Protection of Personnel			
Eye, head and face protection	Q	252(e)(2)	
— eye and face protection	I	133	
— head protection	I	135	
— selection and specifications	Q	252(e)(2)	
— welding booths, screens and shields	Q	252(e)(2)	
Noise exposure	G	95	144
Protection against falls	Q	252(e)(1)	
Protective clothing, types and specifications	Q	252(e)(3)	
Respirators	Q	252(f)(4)	
— respiratory protection	I	134(2),(4),(5), (7)-(10)	
Welding cables and hoses	Q	252(e)(1)	
Work in confined spaces		252(e)(4)	
— ventilation, lifelines, warning signs, securing equipment			
Radiation			
— ionizing	G	96	145-146
— non-ionizing		97	
6. Resistance Welding	Q	252(c)	
Equipment installation, operation, guarding, and employee protection and qualifications		252(c)(1)	
Flash welding equipment		252(c)(4)	
— flash guards, fire curtains and ventilation			
Hazards evaluation		252(c)(5)	
Maintenance, inspection and records		252(c)(6)	
Portable welding machines		252(c)(3)	
— counterbalance, safety chains, switch guards, holders and grounding			
Spot and seam welding equipment, non-portable		252(c)(2)	
— guarding, interlocks, shielding, emergency stop buttons and grounding			

	Sub-part	Section	Page
7. Special Industrial Applications	Q	252(g)	
Mechanical piping		252(g)(2)	
Transmission pipelines		252(g)(1)	
X-ray inspections		252(g)(1)&(2)	
— ionizing radiation	G	96	145-146

Occupational Safety and Health

Administrative Regulations

A ADVISORY COMMITTEES ON STANDARDS

B INSPECTIONS, CITATIONS AND PROPOSED PENALITIES

C PROMULGATING, MODIFYING OR REVOKING OCCUPATIONAL
SAFETY AND HEALTH STANDARDS

D RECORDING AND REPORTING OCCUPATIONAL INJURIES
AND ILLNESSES

E RECORDS— EMPLOYEE EXPOSURE TO HAZARDOUS
SUBSTANCES OR CONDITIONS

F VARIANCES, LIMITATIONS, VARIATIONS, TOLERANCES AND
EXEMPTIONS

Occupational Safety and Health ADMINISTRATIVE REGULATIONS	**7**	**29 CFR**	
		Part	**Section**
A. ADVISORY COMMITTEES ON STANDARDS—Title 29 CFR Part 1912		1912	
1. Construction Safety Advisory Committee			.20
2. National Advisory Committee on Occupational Safety and Health			.3
3. Participation by Interested Persons			.29
4. Standing and Temporary Committees			.10
5. Subcommittees, Experts and Consultants			.28
B. INSPECTIONS, CITATIONS AND PROPOSED PENALTIES—Title 29 CFR			
Part 1903		1903	
1. Advance Notice of Inspections			.6
2. Authority for OSHA Inspections			.3
3. Citations			.14
4. Complaints by Employees			.7
5. Conduct of Inspections			.7
6. Employer and Employee Contests before OSHA Review Commission			.17
7. Failure to Correct a Cited Violation			.18
8. Informal Conferences with OSHA Regional Administrators to Discuss			.19
Citations			
9. Posting of Citations at or Near Site of Violation			.16
10. Posting of Notices, Availability of OSH Act, Regulations and Applicable			.2
Standards			
11. Proposed Penalties			.15
12. Representatives of Employers and Employees			.8
C. PROMULGATING, MODIFYING OR REVOKING OCCUPATIONAL SAFETY			
AND HEALTH STANDARDS—Title 29 CFR Part 1911		1911	
1. Construction Standards			.10
2. Emergency Standards			.12
3. Hearings			.15
4. Other Standards			.11
5. Petition for the Promulgation, Modification or Revocation of a			.3
Standard			

ADMINISTRATIVE REGULATIONS (Cont'd.)	7	29 CFR	
		Part	Section
D. RECORDING AND REPORTING OCCUPATIONAL INJURIES AND			
ILLNESSES—Title 29 CFR Part 1904		1904	
1. Annual Summary, Injuries and Illnesses Posting			.5
2. Employer Completion of Survey Form			.21
3. Falsification and Failure to Keep Records or Reports			.9
4. Log of Occupational Injuries and Illnesses			.2
5. Reporting Fatalities or Multiple Hospitalization Accidents within			.8
48 Hours			
6. Retention of Records			.6
7. Supplementary Records			.4
E. RECORDS — EMPLOYEE EXPOSURE TO HAZARDOUS SUBSTANCES OR			
CONDITIONS—Title 29 CFR Part 1910		1910	
1. Asbestos		G	93a
Medical records			93a(f)
Monitoring			93a(j)(6)
2. Ionizing Radiation			
Notification of incidents		G	96(l)
Personnel monitoring			96(d)
Records			96(n)
Reports of overexposure			96(m)
F. VARIANCES, LIMITATIONS, VARIATIONS, TOLERANCES AND EXEMP-			
TIONS—Title 29 CFR Part 1905		1905	
1. Limitations, Variations, Tolerances or Exemptions under Section 16 of			.12
OSH Act (National Defense)			
2. Modification, Revocation and Renewal of Rules or Orders			.13
3. Requests for Hearings			.15
4. Variances and Other Relief Under Section 6(b)(6)(A) of OSH Act			.10
5. Variances and Other Relief Under Section 6(d) of OSH Act			.11

THREE

How to Use This Book

The regulations promulgated under the OSHA Act are published under Title 29 of the Code of Federal Regulations (CFR). Chapter XVII of same covers OSHA and includes the following:

Part

1901	Procedures for State agreements
1902	State plans for the development and enforcement of State Standards
1903	Inspections, citations, and proposed penalties
1904	Recording and reporting occupational injuries and illnesses
1905	Rules of practice for variances, limitations, variations, tolerances, and exemptions under the Williams-Steiger Occupational Safety and Health Act of 1970.
1910	Occupational safety and health standards
1911	Rules of procedure for promulgating, modifying, or revoking occupational safety or health standards
1912	Advisory committees on standards
1915	Safety and health regulations for ship repairing
1916	Safety and health regulations for shipbuilding
1917	Safety and health regulations for shipbreaking
1918	Safety and health regulations for longshoring
1919	Gear certification
1920	Procedure for variations from safety and health regulations under Longshoremen's and Harbor Workers' Compensation Act.
1921	Rules of practice in enforcement proceedings under Section 41 of the Longshoremen's and Harbor Workers' Compensation Act
1922	Investigational hearings under Section 41 of the Longshoremen's and Harbor Workers' Compensation Act
1923	Safety and health provisions for federal agencies
1924	Safety standards applicable to workshops and rehabilitation facilities assisted by grants

1925	Safety and health standards for federal service contracts
1926	Safety and health regulations for construction
1950	Development and planning grants for occupational safety and health

Of the above sections, Part 1910 is the one containing data of most concern to building designers. Part 1926 concerns itself with the actual process of construction and is, therefore, of primary interest to contractors and subcontractors. The pertinent administrative regulations appear in Parts 1903, 1904, 1905, 1911, and 1912 and are of only fleeting interest to most architects.

An architect who undertakes the design of a building where people are employed, or a plant manager who is responsible for operating virtually any type of facility (except such special uses as shipyards), is concerned with Part 1910 of OSHA. Since this book is intended as a handbook of OSHA requirements for building designers, its content is therefore limited almost entirely to Part 1910.

Textual material in this book has been kept deliberately brief, relying, wherever possible, on graphic illustrations instead. It is recognized that the illustrations and/or abbreviated text may not be applicable to every condition possible. The author has attempted to cover most frequently encountered situations, but he is aware that every possible situation may not have been covered. This has been done for reasons other than brevity. A deliberate attempt has been made not to interpret the regulations beyond portraying graphic presentation and organization of an otherwise lengthy text, because, in the final analysis, only the Department of Labor can provide a definitive interpretation of the regulations. A cautionary note is therefore extended: *the graphic material shown is the author's version of the written text and has neither official nor implied governmental approval.* Users are therefore advised not to use these illustrations verbatim, but to use them merely as a guide toward solving their own particular design problem. To assist in this, most illustrations are accompanied by a few descriptive words extracted from the OSHA text. Most importantly, the detailed numerical reference to the actual text of the subpart has been included for each illustration. Some portions of the OSHA regulations do not readily lend themselves to illustrations, but are, in the author's view, sufficiently important to be included herein, either in full text or in abbreviated form. The architect and engineer are therefore encouraged to refer to the actual text of the regulations to determine for themselves what may be the most appropriate design for a particular situation. The full text of such regulations may be obtained from area or regional OSHA offices.

Some of the material shown may appear to be inconsistent with other drawings, in conflict with other governmental regulations or codes, or, indeed, just plain wrong. Again, no judgmental values have been made in the illustrations; they are simply the author's translation of the written word into graphic content.

Chapter 2 of this book consists of a "Designer's Quick-Reference Guide to OSHA." This Guide will be most helpful not only in determining the appropriate OSHA standards as they may relate to a particular problem, but also in giving the page number in Chapter 4 of this book where the particular standard has been included. The Guide follows the same general format of the "General Industry Guide for Applying Safety and Health Standards" as published by the U.S. Government Printing Office.

A typical sheet with an explanation of its contents has been reproduced on the following page. In this example, the architect who is designing for a floor opening cover other than as illustrated, or who needs some other clarification, would look up Section 1910.23 entitled "Guarding Floor and Wall Openings and Holes." Subparagraph (e) of this paragraph is entitled "Railing, toe boards, and cover specifications." Sub-subparagraph (2) thereunder contains the descriptive language of the regulation which the architect is researching. By comparing the full OSHA text with the appropriate illustration and notes in the book it will be seen that the latter provides an easy-to-follow guide to the former.

The OSHA standards include many existing national consensus standards (such as the National Electric Code) not otherwise detailed in Part 1910. Appendix B lists these adopted standards and the addresses of the standards organizations. It is hoped that this reference material will be of value to the designer who wishes to undertake further research into his particular design problem.

(e) (7) (iii)

Sub-paragraph of Section ↗

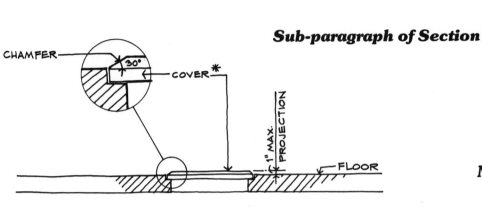

FLOOR OPENING COVER

SECTION

Notes ⤵

NOTE:
*Cover may be of any material that meets the strength requirements.
All hinges, handles, bolts, or other parts shall set flush with the floor or cover surface.

(e) (8)

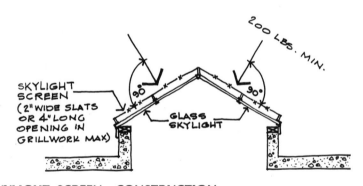

SKYLIGHT SCREEN—CONSTRUCTION

NOTE:
Screen construction and mounting—
1. Capable of withstanding minimum of 200 lb at any area on the screen.
2. Shall not deflect downward sufficiently to break glass.

(e) (9)

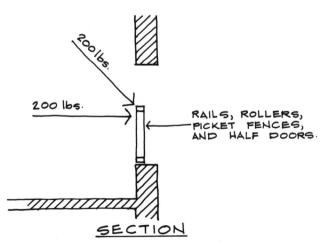

WALL OPENING BARRIER—CONSTRUCTION

NOTE:
Barrier shall be capable of withstanding a load of a minimum of 200 lb in any direction (except upward) at any point on the top rail or corresponding member.

FOUR

Occupational Safety and Health Standards—
Part 1910

NOTE: The above list is complete as published in the *Federal Register* of October 18, 1972, as amended. The following pages illustrate only those sections which, in the author's opinion, are of most frequent use to architects and engineers. For complete text of all sections, refer to the *Federal Register*.

(a) (1)

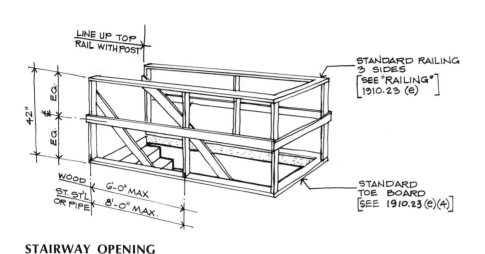

STAIRWAY OPENING

NOTE:

For infrequently used stairways where traffic across the opening prevents the use of fixed standard railing, the guard shall consist of a hinged floor opening cover and removable standard railings on all exposed sides (except entrance to stairs).

(a) (2)

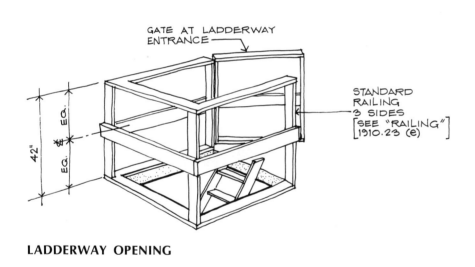

LADDERWAY OPENING

NOTE:

This requirement also applies to ladderway platforms.

(a) (3)

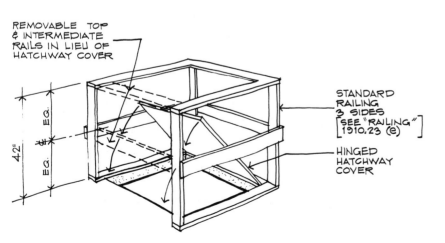

HATCHWAY OR CHUTE OPENING

NOTE:

1. When hatchway or chute not in use—close cover or replace removable railing.

2. Alternate—Removable railing on not more than two sides of opening and fixed standard railings with toe board on remaining sides.

GUARDING FLOOR AND WALL OPENINGS AND HOLES

(a) (4)

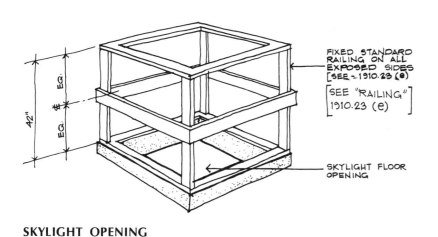

SKYLIGHT OPENING

FIXED STANDARD RAILING ON ALL EXPOSED SIDES [SEE-1910.23 (e)]

[SEE "RAILING" 1910.23 (e)]

SKYLIGHT FLOOR OPENING

NOTE:
 Standard skylight screen may be substituted for standard railing.

(a) (5)

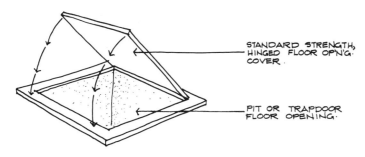

PIT OR TRAPDOOR OPENING

STANDARD STRENGTH, HINGED FLOOR OP'N'G. COVER.

PIT OR TRAPDOOR FLOOR OPENING.

NOTE:
 When cover is not in place—
 1. Attendant required, or
 2. Removable standard railings installed.
 See "Railing," Sec. 1910.23 (e).

(a) (6)

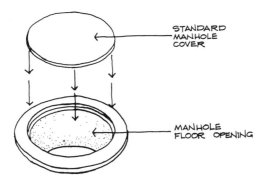

MANHOLE OPENING

STANDARD MANHOLE COVER

MANHOLE FLOOR OPENING

NOTE:
 When cover is not in place—
 1. Attendant required, or
 2. Removable standard railings installed.
 See "Railing," Sec. 1910.23 (e).

47

(a) (7)

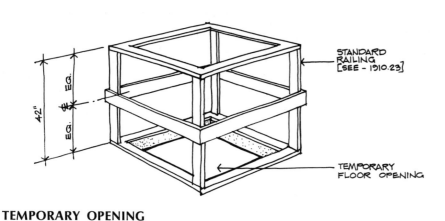

TEMPORARY OPENING

NOTE:
Alternate—Opening may be attended constantly in lieu of installation of standard railing.

(a) (9)

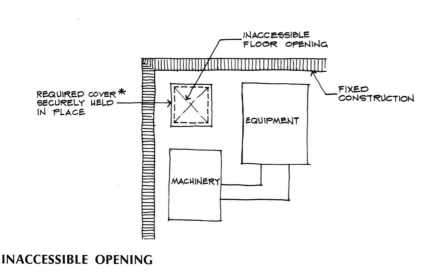

INACCESSIBLE OPENING

NOTE:
* No opening more than 1 in. wide in cover.

(a) (10)

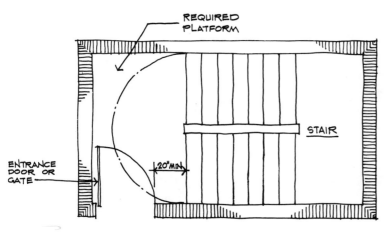

STAIRWAY OPENING WITH DOOR OR GATE

GUARDING FLOOR AND WALL OPENINGS AND HOLES

(b) (1) (i) and (b) (2)

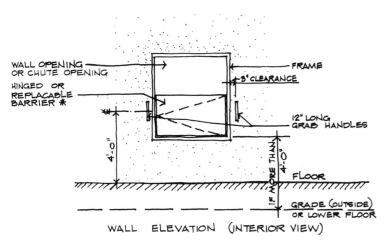

WALL OPENING OR CHUTE OPENING — FRAME — 3" CLEARANCE

HINGED OR REPLACABLE BARRIER *

12" LONG GRAB HANDLES

4'-0"

IF MORE THAN 4'-0"

FLOOR

GRADE (OUTSIDE) OR LOWER FLOOR

WALL ELEVATION (INTERIOR VIEW)

WALL OR CHUTE OPENING

NOTE:
* Barrier may be:
1. Railing
2. Roller
3. Picket Fence
4. Half Door
For specs. see "Wall Opening Screens," 1910.23 (e) (11).

(b) (1) (i)

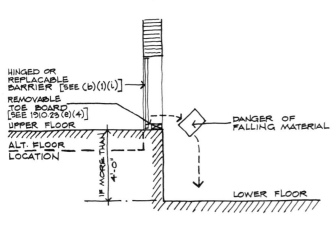

HINGED OR REPLACABLE BARRIER [SEE (b)(1)(i)]

REMOVABLE TOE BOARD [SEE 1910.23 (e)(4)]

UPPER FLOOR

ALT. FLOOR LOCATION

IF MORE THAN 4'-0"

DANGER OF FALLING MATERIAL

LOWER FLOOR

EXPOSURE TO FALLING MATERIAL

NOTE:
Alternate—
See (b) (1) (i) this page.

(b) (1) (ii)

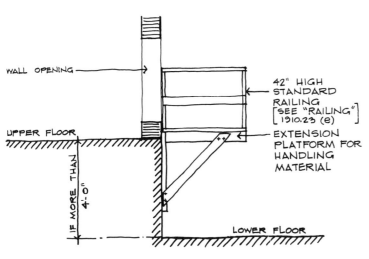

WALL OPENING

42" HIGH STANDARD RAILING [SEE "RAILING" 1910.23 (e)]

EXTENSION PLATFORM FOR HANDLING MATERIAL

UPPER FLOOR

IF MORE THAN 4'-0"

LOWER FLOOR

EXTENSION PLATFORM

NOTE:
If materials handling platform is not needed at wall opening, use barrier.
See (b) (1) (i) this page.

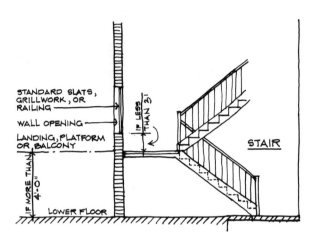

STAIR WALL OPENING

(b) (3)

NOTE:
For specs. see "Wall Opening Screens," 1910.23 (e) (11).
When sill is below landing, add toe board at landing.

(b) (4)

TEMPORARY OPENING

NOTE:
Temporary wall openings—
Shall have adequate guards but need not be of standard construction.

(b) (5)

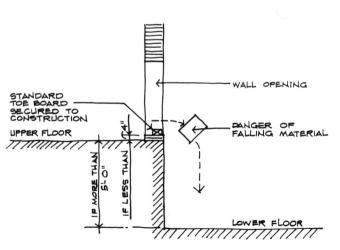

HAZARD OF FALLING MATERIAL

NOTE:
Alternate—Enclosure screen either solid construction or as described in Sec. 1910.23; (e) (11) may be used in lieu of toe board.

(c) (1)

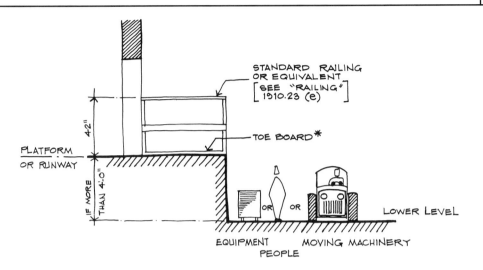

PLATFORM OR OPEN-SIDED FLOOR

NOTE:
*Provide toe board whenever, beneath the open sides:
1. Persons can pass
2. There is moving machinery, or
3. There is equipment with which falling materials could create a hazard.

(c) (2)

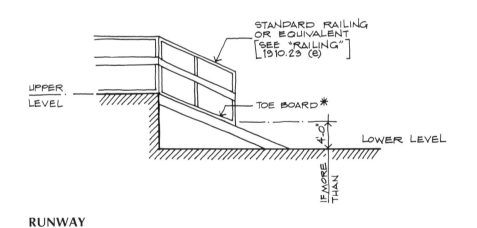

RUNWAY

NOTE:
*Provide toe board on each exposed side, wherever tools, machine parts, or materials are likely to be used on the runway.

(c) (2)

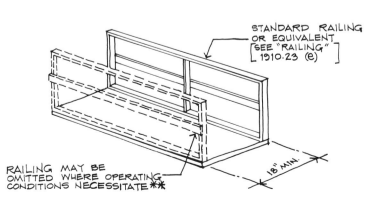

SPECIAL-PURPOSE RUNWAY*

NOTE:
Special-Purpose Runways
*Used exclusively for purposes such as oiling, shafting, or filling tank cars.
**Additional guarding may be essential where persons entering upon runways are exposed to dangers other than to a falling hazard, such as machinery or electrical equipment.

(c) (3)

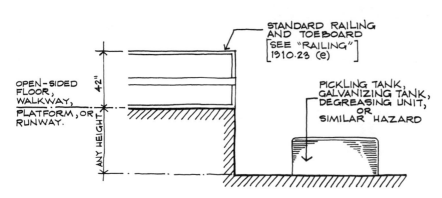

OPEN-SIDED FLOOR, WALKWAY, PLATFORM, OR RUNWAY.

42"

ANY HEIGHT

STANDARD RAILING AND TOEBOARD [SEE "RAILING" 1910.23 (e)]

PICKLING TANK, GALVANIZING TANK, DEGREASING UNIT, OR SIMILAR HAZARD

HAZARD BELOW OR ADJACENT

GUARDING FLOOR AND WALL OPENINGS AND HOLES

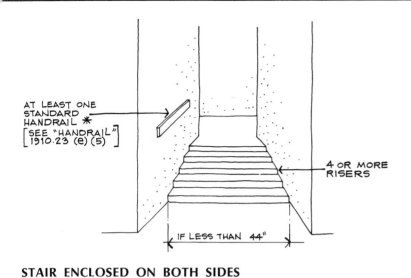

AT LEAST ONE STANDARD HANDRAIL ✳
[SEE "HANDRAIL" 1910.23 (e) (5)]

4 OR MORE RISERS

IF LESS THAN 44"

STAIR ENCLOSED ON BOTH SIDES

(d) (1) (i)

NOTE:
*Preferably on the right side descending.

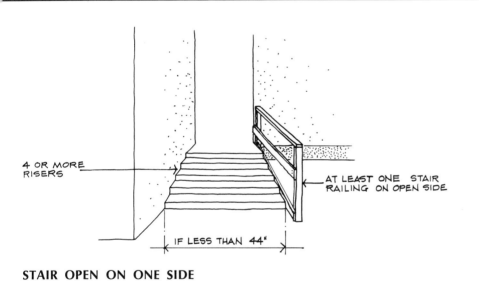

4 OR MORE RISERS

AT LEAST ONE STAIR RAILING ON OPEN SIDE

IF LESS THAN 44"

STAIR OPEN ON ONE SIDE

(d) (1) (ii)

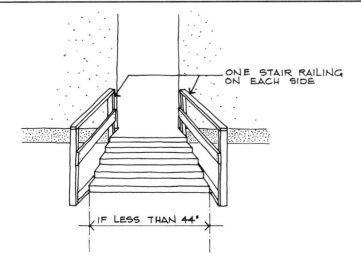

ONE STAIR RAILING ON EACH SIDE

IF LESS THAN 44"

STAIR OPEN ON BOTH SIDES

(d) (1) (iii)

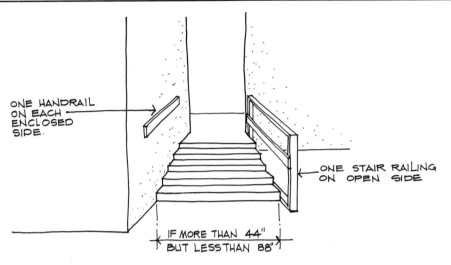

ONE HANDRAIL ON EACH ENCLOSED SIDE.

ONE STAIR RAILING ON OPEN SIDE

IF MORE THAN 44" BUT LESS THAN 88"

INTERMEDIATE-WIDTH STAIR

(d) (1) (iv)

NOTE:
See Sec. 1910.23 (e) (2) for Stair Railing.
See Sec. 1910.23 (e) (5) for Handrail.

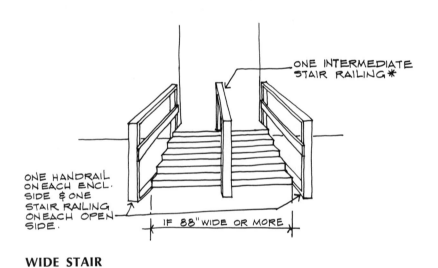

ONE INTERMEDIATE STAIR RAILING ✳

ONE HANDRAIL ON EACH ENCL. SIDE & ONE STAIR RAILING ON EACH OPEN SIDE.

IF 88" WIDE OR MORE

WIDE STAIR

(d) (1) (v)

NOTE:
 *To be located approximately midway of the width.
See Sec. 1910.23 (e) (5) (i) for Handrail.

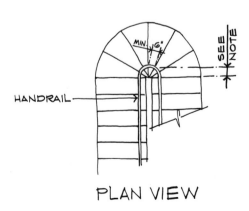

MIN. 6"

SEE NOTE

HANDRAIL

PLAN VIEW

WINDING STAIR

(d) (2)

NOTE:
 Offset rail to prevent walking on portions of treads less than 6 in. wide.

(e) (1)

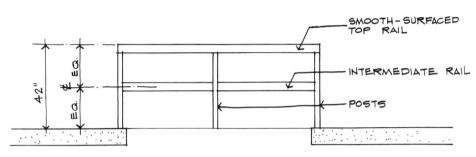

STANDARD RAILING—ELEVATION

NOTE:
    The ends of the rails shall not overhang the terminal posts except where it does not create a hazard.
    See Sec. 1910.23 (e) (3) (i) through (v) for construction.

(e) (2)

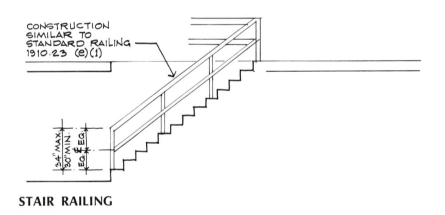

STAIR RAILING

(e) (3) (i)

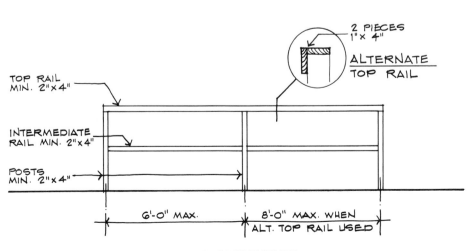

WOOD RAILINGS—MINIMUM REQUIREMENTS

NOTE:
    Dimensions specified are based on the "U.S. Dept. of Agriculture Wood Handbook," No. 72, 1955 (No. 1 [S4S], Southern Yellow Pine [Modulus of Rupture 7,400 P.S.I.]).

(e) (3) (ii)

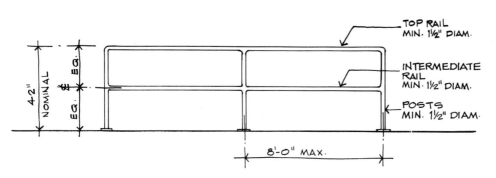

PIPE RAILINGS—MINIMUM REQUIREMENTS

NOTE:
Dimensions specified are based on ANSI B125.1–1970 American National Standard Specifications for Welded and Seamless Steel Pipe.
1½-in. diameter shown refers to outside diameter.

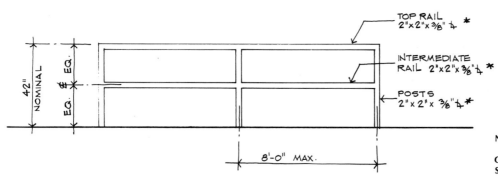

STRUCTURAL STEEL RAILINGS—MINIMUM REQUIREMENTS

NOTE:
Dimensions Specified are based on ANSI G41.5–1970 American National Standard Specifications for Structural Steel.
*Or other metal shapes of equivalent bending strength.

(e) (3) (iv)

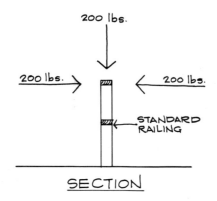

ANCHORING OF POSTS AND FRAMING MEMBERS

NOTE:
Anchoring—shall be of such construction that the complete structure shall be capable of withstanding 200-lb load applied in any direction at the top rail.

(e) (3) (v)

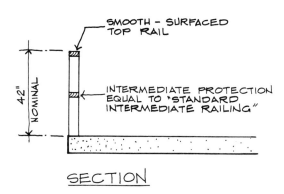

SECTION

OTHER ACCEPTABLE TYPES OF RAILING CONSTRUCTION

NOTE:
A minimum strength capable of withstanding 200 lb of pressure. Overhanging ends of top rail—only if they do not constitute a hazard.

(e) (4)

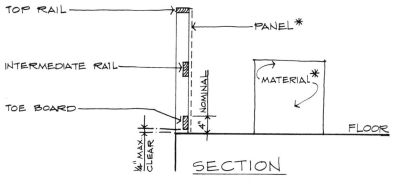

SECTION

STANDARD TOE BOARD

NOTE:
Toe board may be made of any substantial material either solid or with openings not over 1 in.
*Where material is piled higher than toe board can provide protection—install paneling to intermediate or top rail as required.

(e) (5) (i)

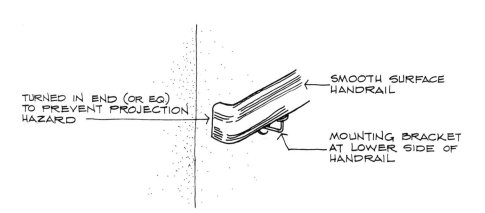

NOTE:
Section of handrail shall be rounded or other shape that will furnish adequate handhold for anyone grasping it to avoid falling.

HANDRAIL

(e) (5) (ii)

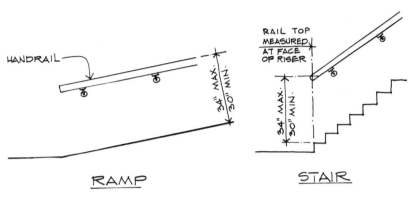

RAMP

STAIR

HANDRAIL — HEIGHTS

(e) (5) (iii)

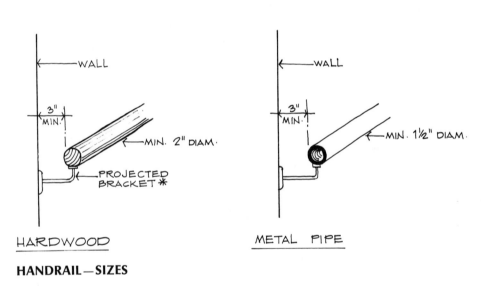

HARDWOOD

METAL PIPE

HANDRAIL — SIZES

NOTE:
*Maximum bracket spacing = 8 ft.

(e) (5) (iv)

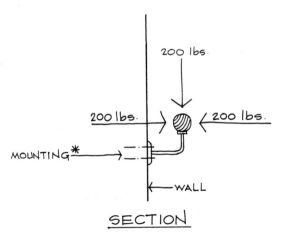

SECTION

HANDRAIL — MOUNTING

NOTE:
*Mounting shall be such that the completed structure is capable of withstanding 200 lb applied in any direction at any point on the rail.

(e) (6)

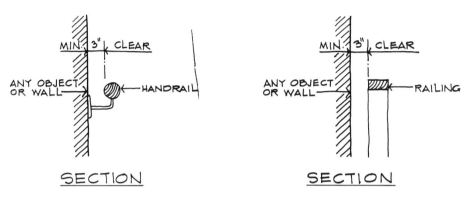

HANDRAIL AND RAILING CLEARANCE

(e) (7) (i)

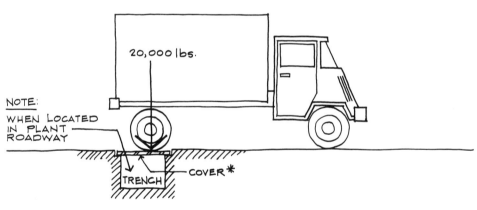

TRENCH OR CONDUIT COVERS

NOTE:
*Cover and supports—designed to withstand truck rear-axle load of 20,000 lb minimum (or local standard highway requirements, if any).

(e) (7) (ii)

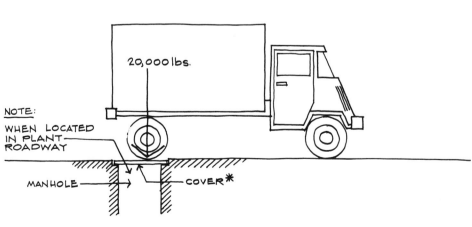

MANHOLE COVERS

NOTE:
*Cover and Support—shall comply with local standard highway requirements, if any; otherwise designed to carry truck rear-axle load of at least 20,000 lb.

(e) (7) (iii)

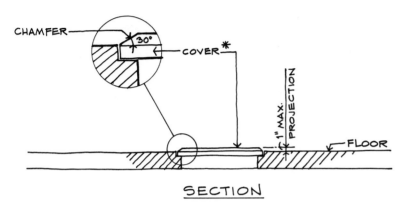

FLOOR OPENING COVER

NOTE:
  *Cover may be of any material that meets the strength requirements.
  All hinges, handles, bolts, or other parts shall set flush with the floor or cover surface.

(e) (8)

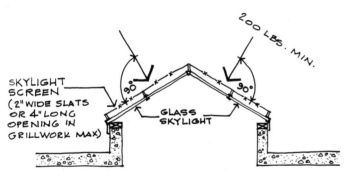

SKYLIGHT SCREEN—CONSTRUCTION

NOTE:
  Screen construction and mounting—
  1. Capable of withstanding minimum of 200 lb at any area on the screen.
  2. Shall not deflect downward sufficiently to break glass.

(e) (9)

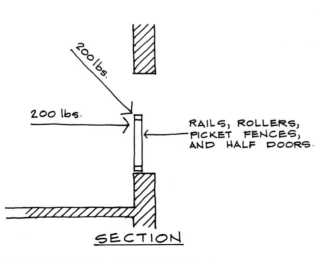

WALL OPENING BARRIER—CONSTRUCTION

NOTE:
  Barrier shall be capable of withstanding a load of a minimum of 200 lb in any direction (except upward) at any point on the top rail or corresponding member.

(e) (10)

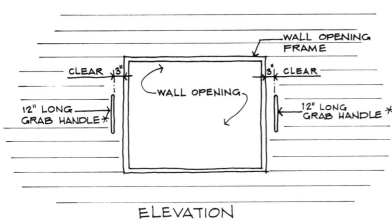

ELEVATION

WALL OPENING—GRAB HANDLES

NOTE:
*Grab Handles—size, material, and anchoring of completed structure shall withstand a minimum load of 200 lb applied in any direction at any point on the handles.

(e) (11)

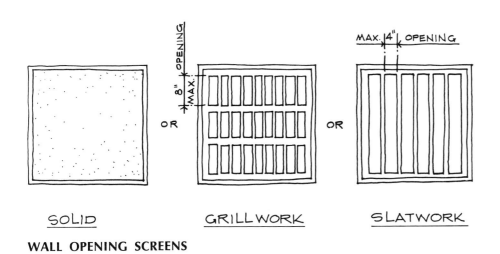

SOLID   GRILLWORK   SLATWORK

WALL OPENING SCREENS

NOTE:
Construction and Mounting—shall be capable of withstanding a load of a minimum 200 lb applied horizontally at any point on the near side of the screen.

(a)

FIXED GENERAL INDUSTRIAL STAIRS

NOTE:
Fixed General Industrial Stairs includes interior and exterior stairs around machinery tanks and other equipment, and stairs leading to or from floors, platforms, or pits.

(a)

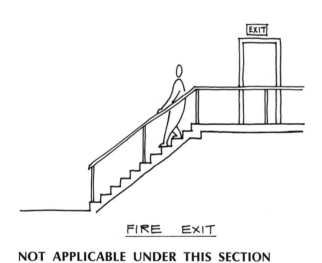

FIRE EXIT

NOT APPLICABLE UNDER THIS SECTION

(a)

NOTE:
Fixed General Industrial Stairs—Does not apply to:
1. Construction operations to private residences.
2. Articulated Stairs, such as installed on floating roof tanks and dock facilities.

NOT APPLICABLE UNDER THIS SECTION

FIXED INDUSTRIAL STAIRS

(b)

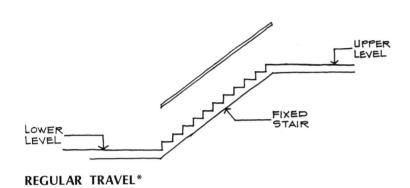

REGULAR TRAVEL*

NOTE:
* Where operations necessitate regular travel between levels.

(b)

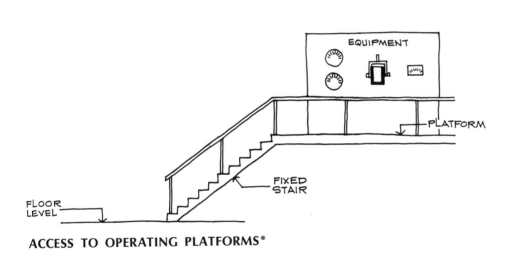

ACCESS TO OPERATING PLATFORMS*

NOTE:
* At any equipment which requires attention routinely during operations.

(b)

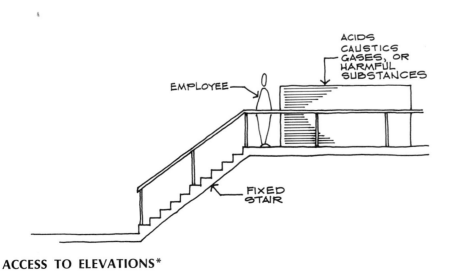

ACCESS TO ELEVATIONS*

NOTE:
* Where access is daily or at each shift for purposes as gauging, inspection, regular maintenance, etc.

(b)

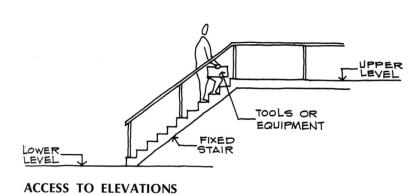

ACCESS TO ELEVATIONS

NOTE:
   Fixed stairs do not preclude the use of fixed ladders to elevated tanks, towers, and similar structures, overhead traveling cranes, etc., where the use of fixed ladders is common practice.

(b)

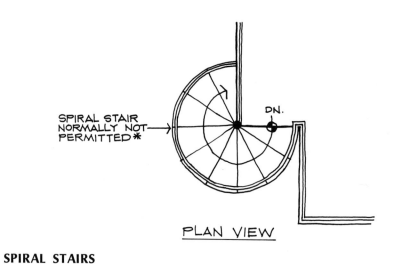

PLAN VIEW

SPIRAL STAIRS

NOTE:
   *Only for special limited usage and secondary access situations where it is not practical to provide a conventional stairway.

(b)

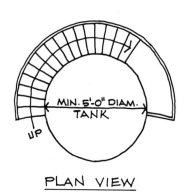

PLAN VIEW

WINDING STAIRS*

NOTE:
   *May be installed on tanks and similar round structures where diam. of structure is not less than 5 ft 0 in.

(c)

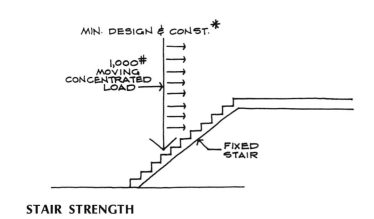

STAIR STRENGTH

NOTE:
* Fixed stairway shall be designed and constructed to carry a load of five times the normal live load anticipated but not less than 1,000 lb.

(d)

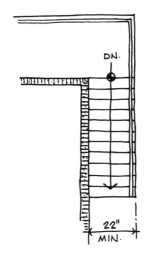

STAIR WIDTH

(e)

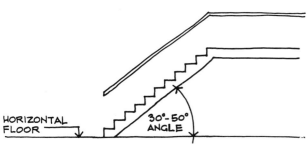

ANGLE OF STAIRWAY RISE

NOTE:
Any uniform combination of rise/tread dimensions that will result in stairway angle shown. See table (next page) for suggested rise/tread dimensions.

65

(f)

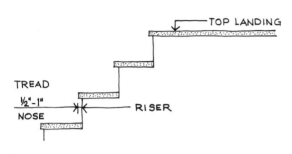

TOP LANDING

TREAD

½"-1"

NOSE

RISER

STAIR TREADS

NOTE:

1. Noses should have an even leading edge.
2. All treads shall be reasonably slip-resistant and the nosings shall be of nonslip finish.

(f)

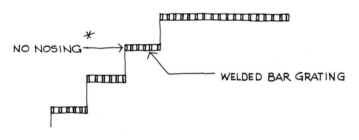

* NO NOSING

WELDED BAR GRATING

ACCEPTABLE ALTERNATE

NOTE:
* Treads without nosing are acceptable provided the leading edge can be readily identified by personnel descending and provided the tread is serrated or is of definite nonslip design.

(e) (f)

ANGLE TO HORIZONTAL	RISE (INCHES)	TREAD (INCHES)
30°35'-------------	6 1/2	11
32°08'-------------	6 3/4	10 3/4
33°41'-------------	7	10 1/2
35°16'-------------	7 1/4	10 1/4
36°52'-------------	7 1/2	10
38°29'-------------	7 3/4	9 3/4
40°08'-------------	8	9 1/2
41°44'-------------	8 1/4	9 1/4
43°22'-------------	8 1/2	9
45°00'-------------	8 3/4	8 3/4
46°38'-------------	9	8 1/2
48°16'-------------	9 1/4	8 1/4
49°54'-------------	9 1/2	8

NOTE:
Rise height and tread width shall be uniform throughout any flight. Rise/tread combinations are not limited to those given in the table.

SUGGESTED RISE/TREAD TABLE

(g)

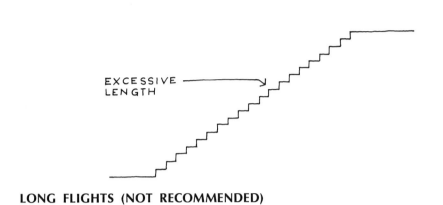

LONG FLIGHTS (NOT RECOMMENDED)

NOTE:
  Long flights, unbroken by landings or intermediate platforms, should be avoided.

(g)

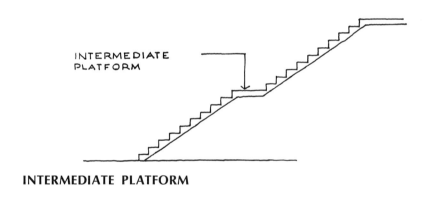

INTERMEDIATE PLATFORM

NOTE:
  Intermediate platforms should be provided where such stairways are in frequent use.

(g)

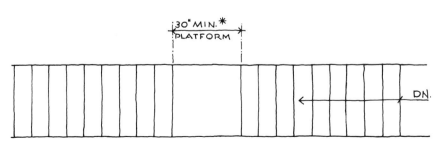

PLATFORM WIDTH

NOTE:
  * Stairway platforms shall be no less than the width of stairway and a minimum of 30 in. in length measured in the direction of travel.

(h)

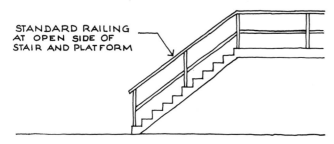

EXPOSED STAIR

NOTE:
   Stair railings shall be installed in accordance with the provisions of Section 1910.23.

(h)

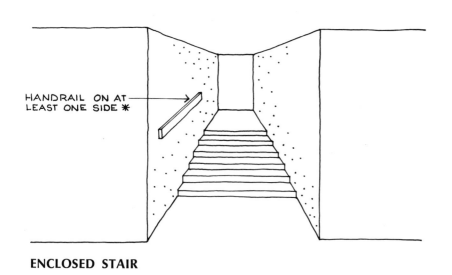

ENCLOSED STAIR

NOTE:
   *Preferably on right side descending. Handrails shall be installed in accordance with the provisions of Section 1910.23.

(i)

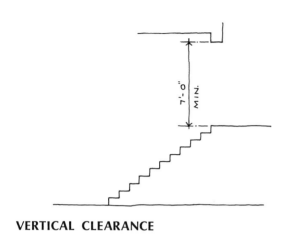

VERTICAL CLEARANCE

NOTE:
Vertical clearance above any stair tread to an overhead obstruction shall be measured from the leading edge of the tread.

(j)

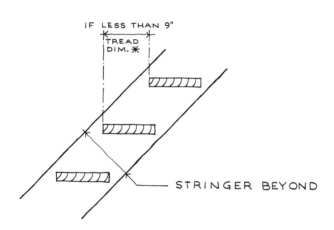

IF LESS THAN 9"

TREAD DIM. ✳

STRINGER BEYOND

OPEN RISERS

NOTE:
✳ Stairs with treads of less than 9-in. width should have open risers.

(k)

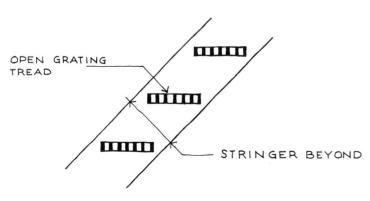

OPEN GRATING TREAD

STRINGER BEYOND

OPEN-GRATING TREADS

NOTE:
Open-grating-type treads are desirable for outside stairs.

FIXED LADDERS

(a) (i) and (ii)

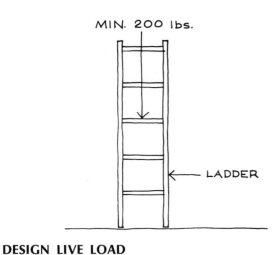

MIN. 200 lbs.

← LADDER

DESIGN LIVE LOAD

NOTE:
Minimum-design live load = single concentrated load of 200 lb.
Additional concentrated live-load units of 200 lb each for anticipated usage shall also be considered in the design.

(a) (iii)

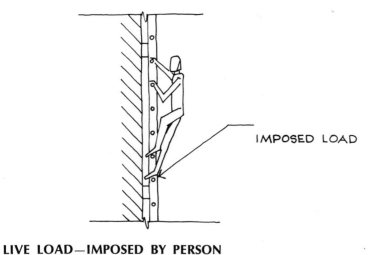

IMPOSED LOAD

LIVE LOAD—IMPOSED BY PERSON

NOTE:
Live load imposed by persons occupying the ladder shall be considered to be concentrated at such points as will cause the maximum stress in the structural member being considered.

(a) (iv)

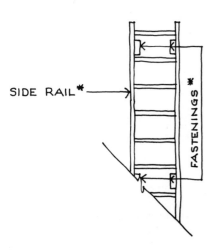

SIDE RAIL*→

FASTENINGS*

DESIGN OF RAILS AND FASTENINGS

NOTE:
*The weight of the ladder and attached appurtenances and live load shall be considered in the design of rails and fastenings.

(a) (2)

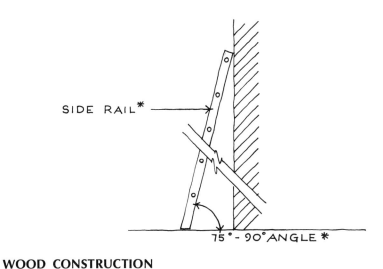

SIDE RAIL*

75° - 90° ANGLE *

WOOD CONSTRUCTION

NOTE:
  * If intended for use by no more than one person per section, then a single ladder no longer than 30 ft tall may be used.

(a) (2)

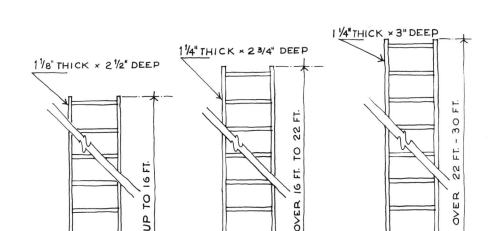

1 1/8" THICK × 2 1/2" DEEP

1 1/4" THICK × 2 3/4" DEEP

1 1/4" THICK × 3" DEEP

UP TO 16 FT.

OVER 16 FT. TO 22 FT.

OVER 22 FT. - 30 FT.

MINIMUM DIMENSIONS OF SIDE RAILS FOR WOOD LADDERS

NOTE:
  Smaller side rails will be acceptable in all ladders when reinforced by a steel wire, rod, or strap running the length of the side rails and adequately secured thereto.

(a) (2)

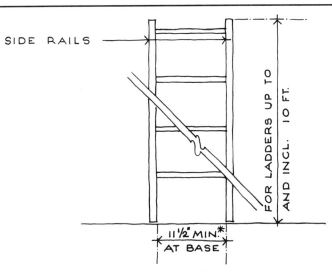

SIDE RAILS

FOR LADDERS UP TO AND INCL. 10 FT.

11 1/2" MIN* AT BASE

MINIMUM WIDTH FOR WOOD LADDERS

NOTE:
  *Minimum width of inside rails shall be increased at least 1/4 in. for each additional 2 ft of length.

(b) (1) (i) and (ii)

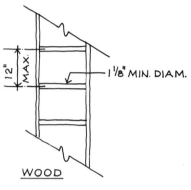
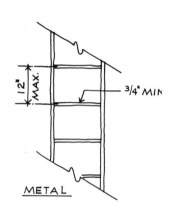

RUNGS AND CLEATS

NOTE:
*1 in. minimum diameter when metal rungs are imbedded in concrete for access to pits, etc., or paint or treat to resist corrosion and rusting.

(b) (1) (iii) and (iv)

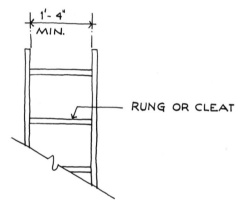

MINIMUM CLEAR LENGTH OF RUNGS AND CLEATS

NOTE:
Rungs, cleats, and steps shall be free of splinters, sharp edges, burrs, or projections which may be a hazard.

(b) (1) (v)

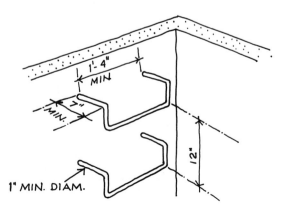

INDIVIDUAL RUNG LADDERS

NOTE:
The rungs shall be so designed that the foot cannot slide off the end.

(b) (2)

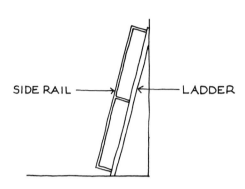

SIDE RAILS

NOTE:
   Side rails which might be used as a climbing aid shall be of such cross sections as to
afford adequate gripping surface without
sharp edges, splinters, or burrs.

(b) (7) (i), (ii), and (iii)

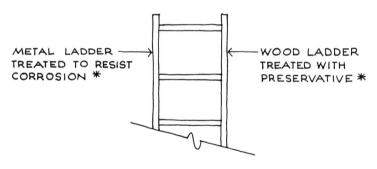

METAL LADDER
TREATED TO RESIST
CORROSION *

WOOD LADDER
TREATED WITH
PRESERVATIVE *

PROTECTION FROM DETERIORATION

NOTE:
   *When location demands.
   1. For wood ladders details shall be such
as to prevent or minimize the accumulation
of water on wood parts.
   2. When different types of materials are
used, they shall be so treated so as to have
no deleterious effect one upon the other.

(c) (1)

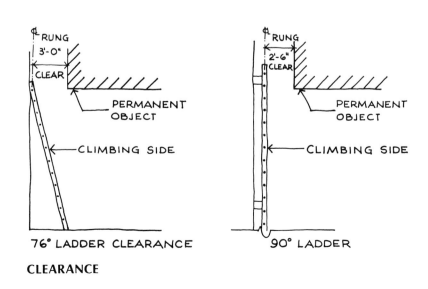

76° LADDER CLEARANCE

90° LADDER

CLEARANCE

NOTE:
   Minimum clearances for intermediate
pitches shall vary between these two limits
in proportion to the slope.
   See Sec. 1910. 27 (c) (3) for exceptions.

(c) (2)

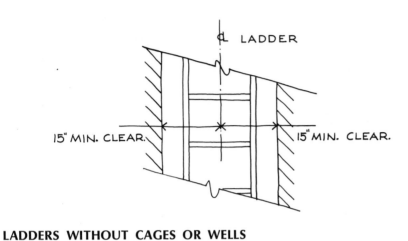

LADDERS WITHOUT CAGES OR WELLS

NOTE:
See Sec. 1910. 27 (c) (3) for exceptions.

(c) (3)

NOTE:
Ladders equipped with cage or basket are excepted from the provisions of Subsection 1910. 27 (c) (1) and (c) (2), but shall conform to Subsection 1910.27 (d) (1) (v). Fixed ladders in smooth-walled wells are excepted from the provisions of Subsection 1910.27 (c) (1), but shall conform to Subsection 1910.27 (d) (1) (vi).

LADDERS WITH CAGES OR BASKETS

(c) (4)

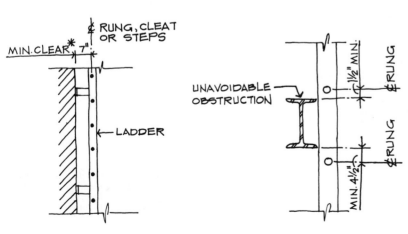

NOTE:
* Except when unavoidable obstructions are encountered at rear of ladder.

CLEARANCE IN BACK OF LADDER

FIXED LADDERS

(c) (5)

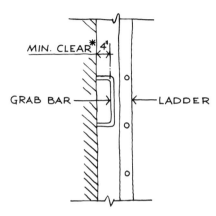

CLEARANCE IN BACK OF GRAB BARS

NOTE:
* Grab bars shall not protrude on the climbing side beyond the rungs of the ladder which they serve.

(c) (6)

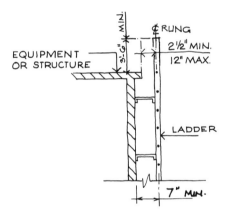

STEP-ACROSS DISTANCE

(c) (7)

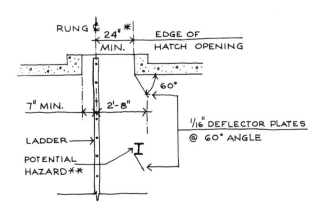

HATCH

NOTE:
* For offset well only (offset well shown), 30 in. minimum for straight wells.
** Potential hazards within 30 in. of rung or cleat center line shall be fitted with deflector plates.

(c) (7)

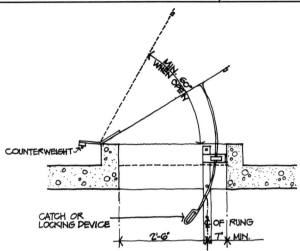

COUNTERWEIGHT

MIN. 60° WHEN OPEN

CATCH OR LOCKING DEVICE

¢ OF RUNG

2'-6"

7" MIN.

HATCH COVER—SIDE VIEW

(c) (7)

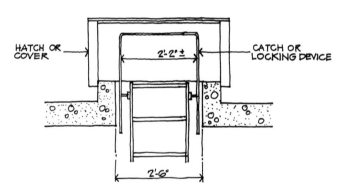

HATCH OR COVER

CATCH OR LOCKING DEVICE

2'-2" ±

2'-6"

HATCH COVER—FRONT VIEW

(d) (1) (i)

NOTE:
Cages or wells (except on chimney ladders) shall be built as shown in the following illustrations, or of equivalent construction.

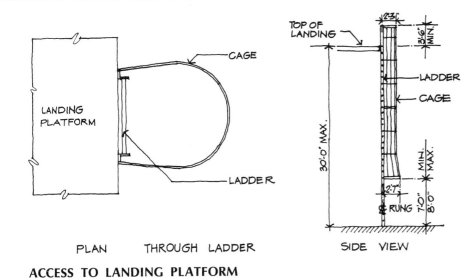

PLAN   THROUGH LADDER

SIDE VIEW

ACCESS TO LANDING PLATFORM

(d) (1) (ii) and (iii)

NOTES:
Cages shall be provided on ladders of more than 20 ft to a maximum unbroken length of 30 ft.

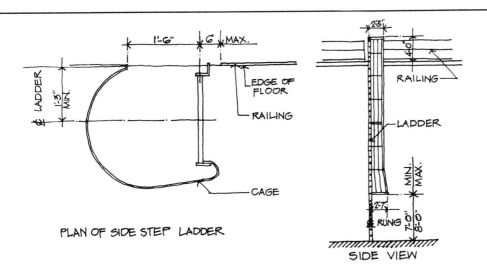

PLAN OF SIDE STEP LADDER

SIDE VIEW

ACCESS LATERALLY FROM LADDER

(d) (1) (i), (ii), and (iv)

NOTE:
Cages shall extend a minimum of 42 in. above the top of landing, unless otherwise acceptable protection is provided.

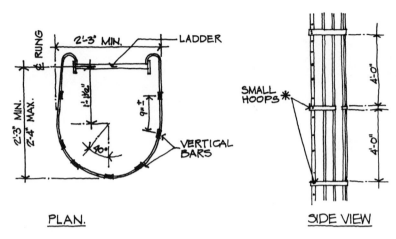

PLAN.

SIDE VIEW

CAGES FOR LADDERS MORE THAN 20 FEET HIGH

(d) (1) (v)

NOTE:
1. All hoops shall be riveted or welded to vertical bars.
2. Inside of cage shall be clear of projections.
* Top and bottom hoops shall be 3 in. wide as well as every 20 ft 0 in. maximum spacing vertically.

(d) (7) (vi)

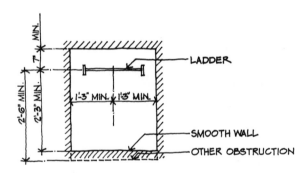

FIXED LADDER IN WELL

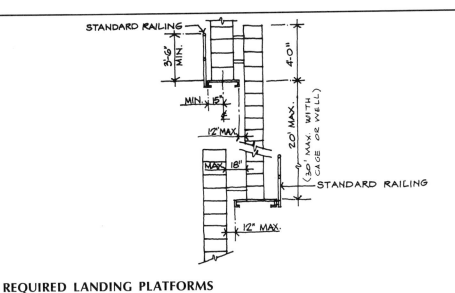

REQUIRED LANDING PLATFORMS

(d) (2)

NOTE:
1. When platforms are required, each ladder section shall be offset from adjacent sections.
2. Even for short, unbroken lengths, where installation conditions require that adjacent ladder sections be offset, landing platforms shall be provided at each offset.

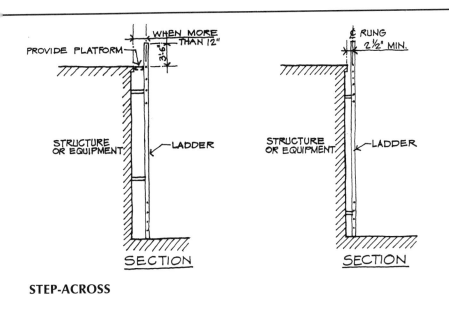

STEP-ACROSS

(d) (2) (i)

(d) (2) (ii)

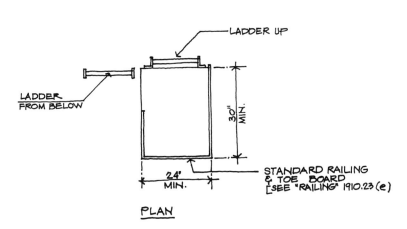

PLAN

LANDING PLATFORM

NOTE:
1. Landing Platforms shall be equipped with standard railing and toe board, so arranged as to give safe access to the ladder.

(d) (2) (iii)

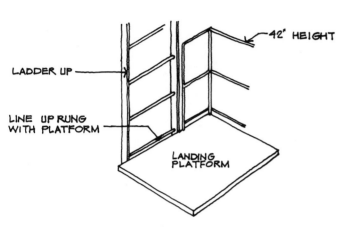

RUNG LOCATIONS

(d) (2) (iii)

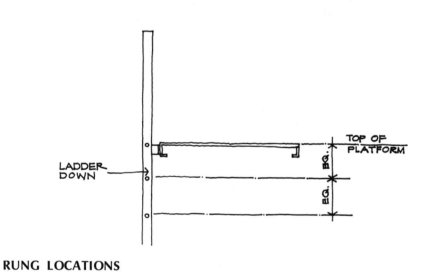

RUNG LOCATIONS

(d) (3)

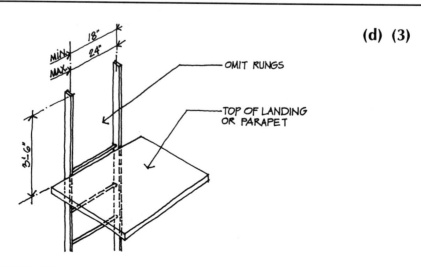

THROUGH-LADDER EXTENSIONS

(d) (3)

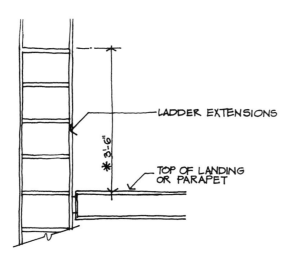

LADDER EXTENSIONS—SIDE STEP

NOTE:
    *For side step or offset fixed ladder sections, at landings, the side rails and rungs shall be carried to the next regular rung beyond or above the 3½-ft minimum.

(d) (4)

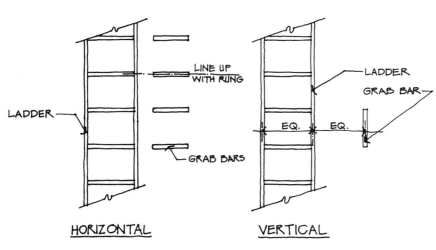

HORIZONTAL   VERTICAL

GRAB BARS

NOTE:
    Grab-bar diameters shall be the equivalent of the round-rung diameters.

(d) (5)

TOWER OR WATER TANK   CHIMNEY

LADDER SAFETY DEVICES

NOTE:
    * May be used in lieu of cage protection for ladders over 20 ft in unbroken length for towers, water tanks, and chimneys.
    Ladder safety devices incorporating lifebelts, friction brakes, and sliding attachments shall meet design requirements of the ladders which they serve.

(e) (1)

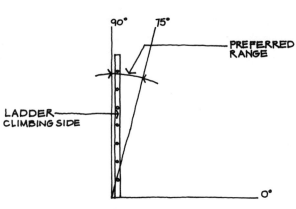

PREFERRED PITCH

(e) (2)

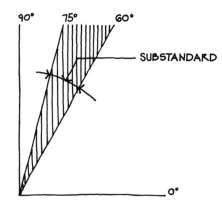

SUBSTANDARD PITCH

NOTE:
 Substandard fixed ladders are permitted only where it is found necessary to meet conditions of installation. This substandard pitch range shall be considered as a critical range to be avoided, if possible.

(e) (4)

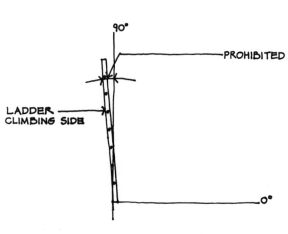

PITCH GREATER THAN 90 DEGREES

NOTE:
 Ladders having a pitch in excess of 90 degrees with the horizontal are prohibited.

As used in this subpart (Sections 1910.35 through 1910.40):

(a) *Means of egress.* A means of egress is a continuous and unobstructed way of exit travel from any point in a building or structure to a public way and consists of three separate and distinct parts: the way of exit access, the exit, and the way of exit discharge. A means of egress comprises the vertical and horizontal ways of travel and shall include intervening room spaces, doorways, hallways, corridors, passageways, balconies, ramps, stairs, enclosures, lobbies, escalators, horizontal exits, courts, and yards.

(b) *Exit access.* Exit access is that portion of a means of egress which leads to an entrance to an exit.

(c) *Exit.* Exit is that portion of a means of egress which is separated from all other spaces of the building or structure by construction or equipment as required in this subpart to provide a protected way of travel to the exit discharge.

(d) *Exit discharge.* Exit discharge is that portion of a means of egress between the termination of an exit and a public way.

(e) *Low-hazard contents.* Low-hazard contents shall be classified as those of such low combustibility that no self-propagating fire therein can occur and that consequently the only probable danger requiring the use of emergency exits will be from panic, fumes, or smoke, or fire from some external source.

(f) *High-hazard contents.* High-hazard contents shall be classified as those which are liable to burn with extreme rapidity or from which poisonous fumes or explosions are to be feared in the event of fire.

(g) *Ordinary hazard contents.* Ordinary hazard contents shall be classified as those which are liable to burn with moderate rapidity and to give off a considerable volume of smoke but from which neither poisonous fumes nor explosions are to be feared in case of fire.

(h) *Approved.* For the purposes of this subpart approved shall mean listed or approved equipment by a nationally recognized testing laboratory.

(b) (1)

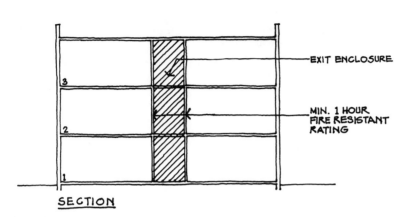

SECTION

THREE STORIES OR LESS

EXIT ENCLOSURE

MIN. 1 HOUR FIRE RESISTANT RATING

NOTE:
   This applies whether the stories connected are above or below the story at which exit discharge begins.

(b) (2)

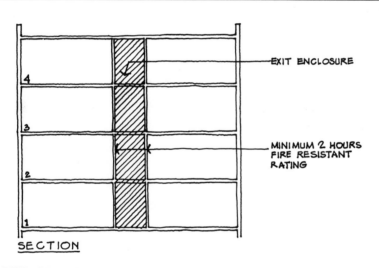

SECTION

FOUR STORIES OR MORE

EXIT ENCLOSURE

MINIMUM 2 HOURS FIRE RESISTANT RATING

NOTE:
   This applies whether the stories connected are above or below the story at which exit discharge begins.

(b) (3) and (4)

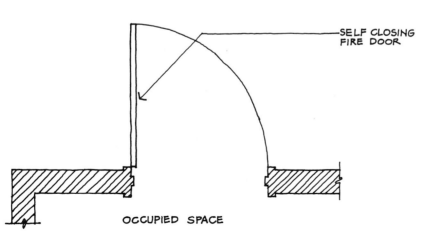

SELF CLOSING FIRE DOOR

OCCUPIED SPACE

OPENINGS IN EXIT ENCLOSURES

NOTE:
   Openings in exit enclosures shall be confined to those necessary for access to the enclosure from normally occupied spaces and for egress from the enclosure.

(c) (1) (i)

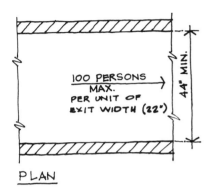

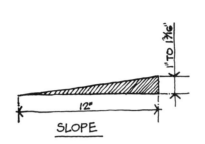

PLAN

LEVEL EGRESS COMPONENTS*

NOTE:
No limit in height between landings.
* Including Class "A" ramps.

(c) (1) (ii)

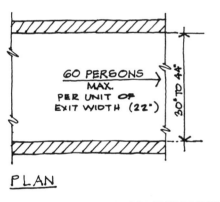

PLAN

INCLINED EGRESS COMPONENTS*

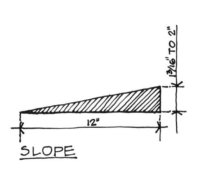

NOTE:
Maximum height between landings-12 ft.
* Including Class "B" ramps.

(c) (1) (iii)

	CLASS A	CLASS B
WIDTH	44 inches and greater.	30 to 44 inches.
SLOPE	1 to 1 3/16 inches in 12 inches.	1 3/16 to 2 inches in 12 inches.
MAXIMUM HEIGHT BETWEEN LANDINGS	No limit	12 feet

RAMP DESIGNATION TABLE

(c) (2)

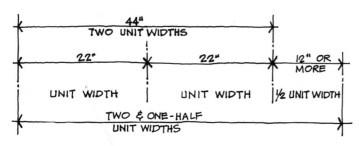

UNITS OF EXIT WIDTH

NOTE:
Fractions of a unit shall not be counted, except that 12 in. added to one or more full units shall be counted as one-half a unit of exit width.

(c) (3)

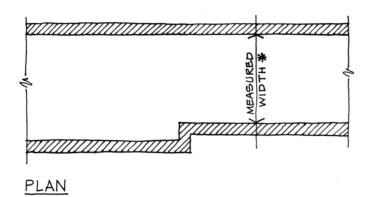

PLAN

NARROWEST POINT

NOTE:
* Units of exit width shall be measured in the clear at the narrowest point of the means of egress.

(c) (3)

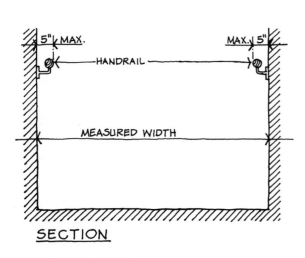

SECTION

HANDRAIL PROJECTION

NOTE:
A handrail may project inside the measured width not more than 15 in.

(c) (3)

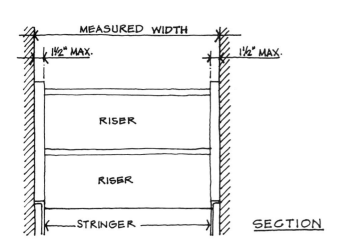

MEASURED WIDTH

1½" MAX.   1½" MAX.

RISER

RISER

STRINGER   SECTION

STRINGER PROJECTION

NOTE:
A stringer may project inside the measured width not more than 1½ in.

(c) (3)

AISLE OR PASSAGEWAY

MIN. WIDTH REQUIRED

EXIT OR EXIT ACCESS DOOR

PLAN

EXIT OR EXIT ACCESS DOOR

NOTE:
An exit or exit access door swinging into an aisle or passageway shall not restrict the effective width thereof at any point during its swing to less than the minimum width.

(d) (1)

NOTE:
The capacity of means of egress for any floor, balcony, tier, or other occupied space shall be sufficient for the occupant load thereof. The occupant load shall be the maximum number of persons that may be in the space at any time.

GENERAL

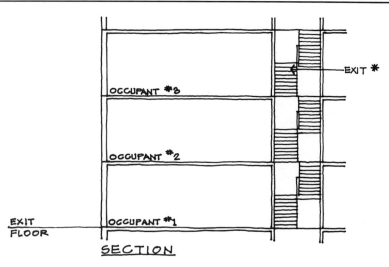

OCCUPANT #3

OCCUPANT #2

EXIT
FLOOR   OCCUPANT #1

SECTION

MULTIPLE FLOOR

EXIT *

(d) (2)

NOTE:
*Where exits serve more than one floor, only the occupant load of each floor considered individually need be used in computing the capacity of the exits at that floor, provided that exit capacity shall not be decreased in the direction of exit travel.

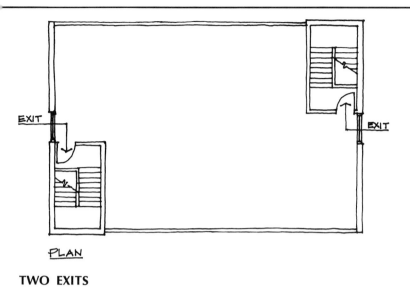

PLAN

TWO EXITS

(e)

NOTE:
When more than one exit is required from a story at least two of the exits shall be remote from each other and so arranged as to minimize any possibility that both may be blocked by any one fire or other emergency condition.

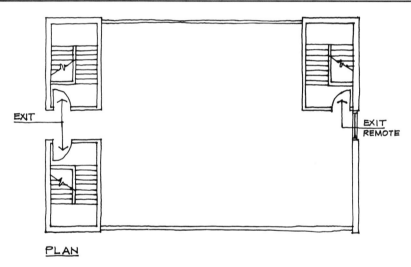

PLAN

THREE OR MORE EXITS

(e)

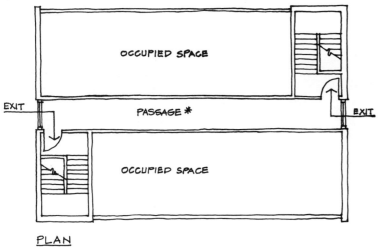

PLAN

EXITS NOT ACCESSIBLE FROM OPEN AREA

(f) (1)

NOTE:
Exits and exit access shall be readily accessible at all times.
*Safe and continuous passageways, aisles, or corridors providing convenient access for each occupant to at least two exits.

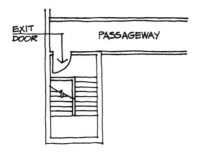

EXIT DOOR

(f) (2)

NOTE:
A door from a room to an exit or to a way of exit access shall be of the side-hinged, swinging type.

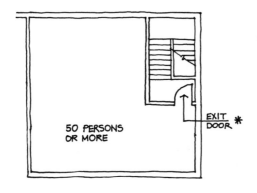

DOOR SWING

(f) (2)

NOTE:
*Exit access shall swing in the direction of exit travel when the room is occupied by more than fifty persons or used for a high-hazard occupancy.

(f) (3)

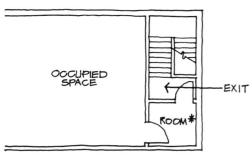

ACCESS—NOT PERMITTED

NOTE:
*In no case shall access to an exit be through a bathroom, or other room subject to locking, except where the exit is required to serve only the room subject to locking.

(f) (4)

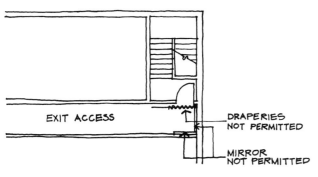

CLEAR RECOGNITION

NOTE:
Ways of exit access and exit doors shall be clearly recognizable. Mirrors not permitted on exit doors or on adjacent walls.

(f) (5)

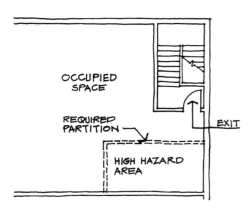

ACCESS THROUGH HIGH-HAZARD AREA

NOTE:
It shall not be necessary to travel toward high-hazard occupancy in order to reach the nearest exit, unless path of travel is shielded by suitable partitions or other physical barriers.

(f) (6)

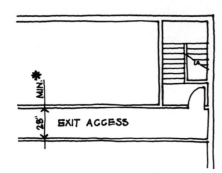

MINIMUM WIDTH—ONE DIRECTION

NOTE:
   *Where a single way of exit access leads to an exit, its minimum width shall be equal to the required capacity of the exit to which it leads.
   See "Width and Capacity," Sec. 1910.37 (c) (1).

(f) (6)

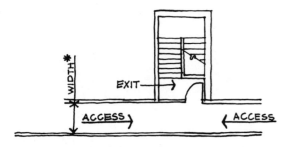

MINIMUM WIDTH—MORE THAN ONE DIRECTION

NOTE:
   *Where more than one way of exit access leads to an exit, each shall have a width adequate for the number of persons it must accommodate.
   See "Width and Capacity," Sec. 1910.37 (c) (1).

(g) (1)

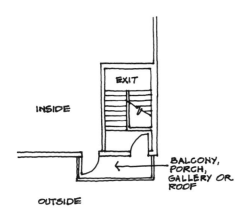

EXTERIOR ACCESS

NOTE:
Access to an exit may be by means of any exterior balcony, porch, gallery, or roof that conforms to this section.

(g) (2)

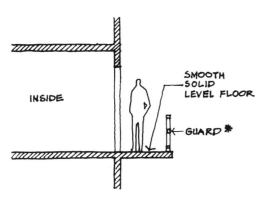

EXTERIOR ACCESS

NOTE:
*Guards on unenclosed sides.

(g) (3)

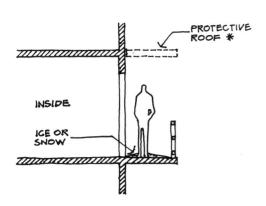

ICE OR SNOW ACCUMULATION

NOTE:
*Where accumulation of ice or snow is likely, a protective roof shall be provided, unless way of exit access serves as the sole means of access to the rooms or spaces served. Then it is assumed snow and ice will be regularly removed.

93

(g) (4)

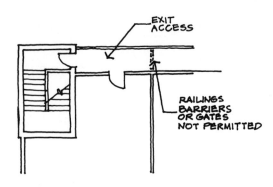

PATH OF TRAVEL

NOTE:
Maintain reasonably straight path of travel over exterior way of exit access, without obstruction by railings, barriers, or gates. Where furniture or other movable objects obstruct path of travel, they may be required to be fastened out of the way or other permanent barriers may be required to protect path of travel against encroachment.

(g) (5)

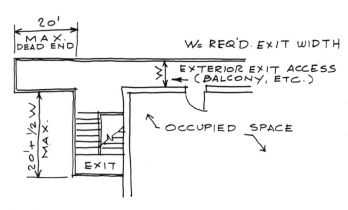

DEAD ENDS AND UNENCLOSED EXITS

(g) (6)

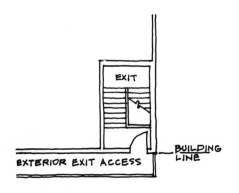

EXTERIOR EXIT ACCESS—PROJECTION

NOTE:
Any gallery, balcony, bridge, porch, or other exterior exit access that projects beyond the outside wall of the building shall comply with the requirements of this section as to width and arrangement.

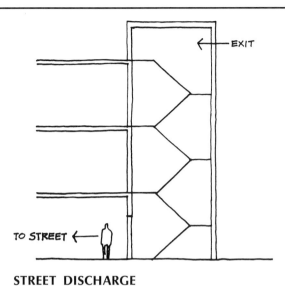

STREET DISCHARGE

(h) (1)

NOTE:
All exits shall discharge directly to the street, or to a yard, court, or other open space that gives safe access to a public way.
Street width shall be adequate to accommodate all persons leaving the building.

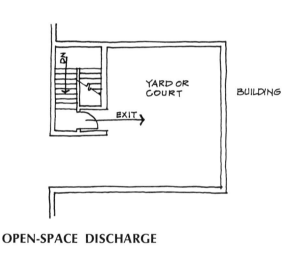

OPEN-SPACE DISCHARGE

(h) (1)

NOTE:
Yards, courts, or other open spaces to which exits discharge shall be of adequate width and size to provide all persons leaving the building with ready access to the street.

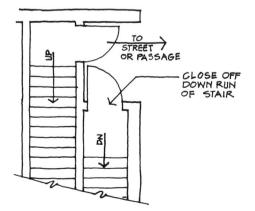

PLAN—STREET LEVEL

(h) (2)

NOTE:
Stairs and other exits shall be so arranged as to make the direction of egress to the street clear.

(i)

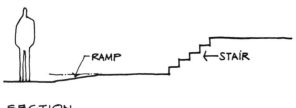

SECTION

HEADROOM

(j)

SECTION

CHANGES IN ELEVATION

NOTE:
   Where a means of egress is not substantially level, such differences in elevation shall be negotiated by stairs or ramps.

(k) (1)

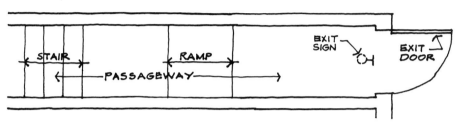

CONSTRUCTION

NOTE:
All components of means of egress shall be of substantial, reliable construction and shall be built or installed in a workmanlike manner.

(k) (2)

MAINTENANCE

NOTE:
Means of egress shall be continuously maintained free of all obstructions or impediments to full instant use in case of fire or other emergency.

(k) (3)

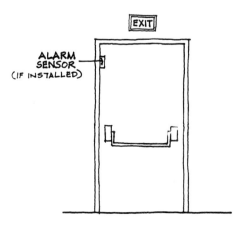

RESTRICTIVE DEVICES

NOTE:
Any device or alarm installed to restrict the improper use of an exit shall be so designed and installed that it cannot, even in case of failure, impede or prevent emergency use of such exit.

(l) (1)

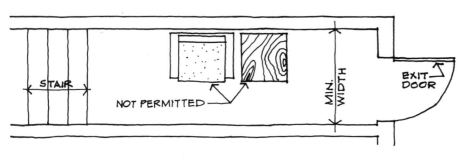

PLAN

OBSTRUCTIONS

NOTE:
No furnishings, decorations, or other objects shall be so placed as to obstruct exits, access thereto, egress therefrom, or visibility thereof.

(l) (2)

FURNISHINGS OR DECORATIONS

NOTE:
No furnishings or decorations of an explosive or highly flammable character shall be used in any occupancy.

(m)

NOTE:
Continuously maintain all automatic sprinkler systems in reliable operating condition. Periodic tests shall be made to assure proper maintenance.

AUTOMATIC SPRINKLER SYSTEMS

(q) (1)

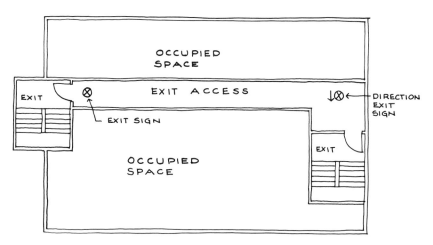

VISIBLE SIGNS

NOTE:
   Exits shall be marked by readily visible signs. Access to exits shall be marked by readily visible signs where exit or way to reach it is not readily visible to occupants.

(q) (2)

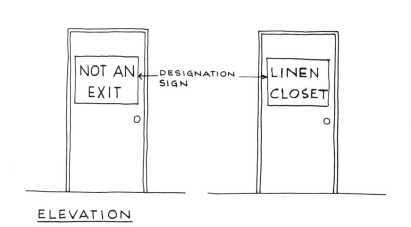

ELEVATION

DESIGNATION OF NON-EXITS

NOTE:
   When any door, passage, or stairway is neither an exit nor a way of exit access and likely to be mistaken for an exit, identify by a sign reading "Not an Exit" or similarly, or sign indicating its actual character, such as "To Basement," "Linen Closet," etc.

(q) (3)

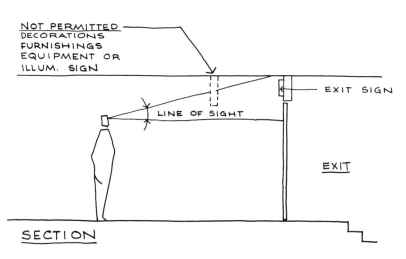

SECTION

LOCATION OF EXIT SIGNS

NOTE:
   Required exit signs or way of exit access signs shall be located and of such size, color, and design as to be readily visible. Decorations, furnishings, other brightly illuminated signs, displays, etc., shall not detract attention from exit signs.

(q) (4)

EXIT RECOGNITION

NOTE:
Every exit sign shall be distinctive in color and shall provide contrast with decorations, interior finish, or other signs.

(q) (5)

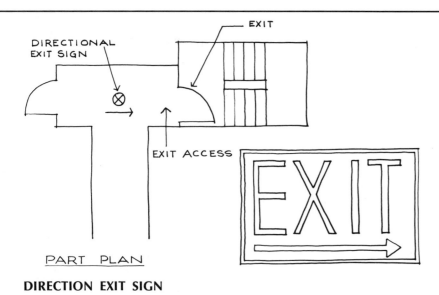

DIRECTIONAL EXIT SIGN

EXIT

EXIT ACCESS

PART PLAN

DIRECTION EXIT SIGN

NOTE:
A sign reading "EXIT" or similar designation, with an arrow indicating the direction, shall be placed in every location where the direction of the travel to reach the nearest exit is not immediately apparent.

(q) (6), (7), and (8)

NOTE:
Every exit sign shall be suitably illuminated by a reliable light source giving a value of not less than 5 foot-candles on the illuminated surface. Artificial lights giving illumination to exit signs other than the internally illuminated types shall have screens, discs, or lenses of not less than 25 sq in. area made of translucent material to show red or other specified designating color on the side of the approach.

Each internally illuminated exit sign shall be provided in all occupancies where reduction of normal illumination is permitted.

Every exit sign shall have the word "EXIT" in plainly legible letters not less than 6 in. high, with the principal strokes of letters not less than ¾ in. wide.

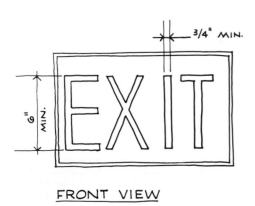

3/4" MIN.

6" MIN.

MIN. 5 FOOT CANDLES

FRONT VIEW

SECTION

ILLUMINATED SIGNS

POWER PLATFORMS FOR EXTERIOR BUILDING MAINTENANCE

(b)

APPLICATION

NOTE:
   The requirements of this section do not apply to temporary equipment used for construction work, or to devices which are raised and lowered manually. The purpose of this standard is to provide for the safety of life and limb of users and others who may be exposed to exterior powered platforms, such as window cleaning, metal polishing, general exterior building maintenance or repairs, etc., and which are electrically powered.

(b) (5) (ii)

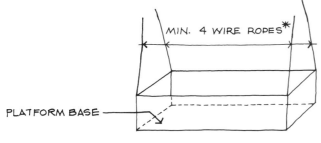

TYPE F PLATFORM

NOTE:
   *Type F powered platform shall have at least four wire ropes so that failure of any one rope will not substantially alter the normal position of the platform. Comply with Part II of ANSI A120.1-1970, "American National Standard Safety Requirements for Powered Platforms for Exterior Building Maintenance."

(b) (5) (ii)

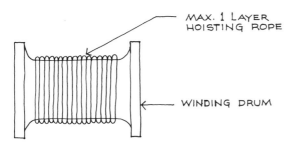

TYPE F PLATFORM

NOTE:
   Type F powered platforms may be either roof-powered or self-powered.

(b) (5) (iii)

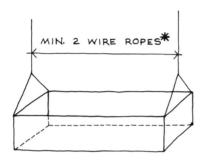

TYPE T PLATFORM

NOTE:

* Type T powered platforms shall have at least two wire ropes so that failure of one rope would upset its normal position but not fall to the ground. Employees must wear safety belts attached by lifelines to working platform or building structure. Comply with Part III of ANSI A120.1–1970, "American National Safety Requirements for Powered Platforms for Exterior Building Maintenance."

(b) (5) (iv)

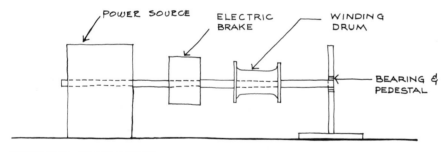

HOISTING EQUIPMENT

NOTE:

The requirements of this section apply to powered platforms with winding-drum-type hoisting machines. It is not the intent of this section to prohibit powered platforms using other types of hoisting machines, such as, but not limited to, traction-drum hoisting machines, air-powered machines, hydraulic-powered machines, and internal combustion machines. Installation of powered platforms with other types of hoisting machines is permitted, provided adequate protective devices are used, and provided reasonable safety of life and limb to users of the equipment and to others who may be exposed is assured.

(c) (1) (i)

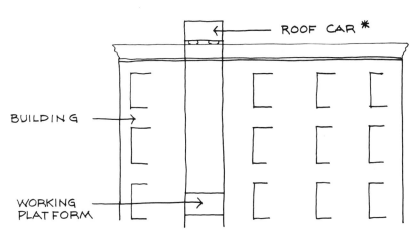

BUILDING

WORKING PLATFORM

ROOF CAR — GENERAL

NOTE:
 * A roof car shall be provided whenever it is necessary to move the working platform horizontally to working or storage positions.

(c) (1) (ii)

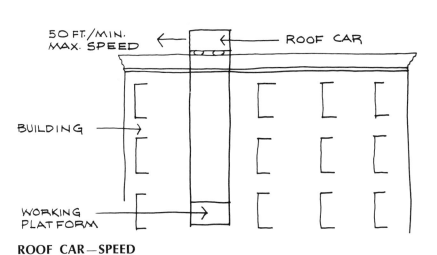

50 FT./MIN. MAX. SPEED

BUILDING

WORKING PLATFORM

ROOF CAR — SPEED

(c) (2) (i)

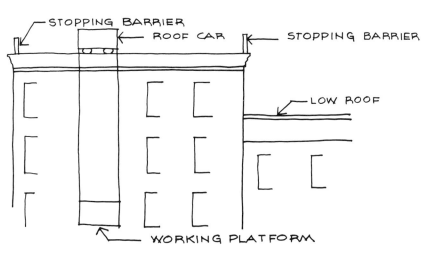

ROOF CAR — PROTECTION

NOTE:
 Provision shall be made to protect against having the roof car leave the roof or enter roof areas not designed for travel.

(c) (2) (ii)

ROOF CAR—HORIZONTAL MOTION

NOTE:
The horizontal motion of the roof cars shall be positively controlled so as to ensure proper movement and positioning of the roof car.

(c) (2) (iii) and (iv)

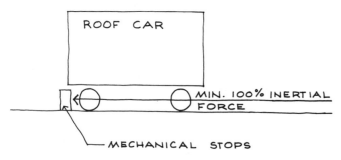

ROOF CAR—POSITIONING DEVICES AND STOPS

NOTE:
Roof car-positioning devices shall be provided to ensure that the working platform is placed and retained in proper position for vertical travel and during storage.
Mechanical stops shall be provided to prevent the traversing of the roof car beyond its normal limits of travel. Such stops shall be capable of withstanding a force equal to 100 percent of the inertial effect of the roof car in motion with traversing power applied.

(c) (2) (v)

NOTE:
The operating device of a power-operated roof car for traversing shall be located on the roof car, the working platform, or both, and shall be of the continuous-pressure, weatherproof, electric type.
The operating device shall be so connected that it is not operable until:
(1) The working platform is located at its uppermost position of travel and is not in contact with the building face or fixed vertical guides in the face of the building; and
(2) All protective devices and interlocks are in a position for traversing.
* If more than one operating device is provided, they shall be so arranged that traversing is possible only from one operating device at a time.

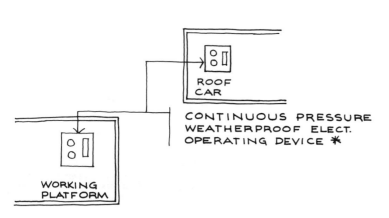

ROOF CAR—OPERATING DEVICES

POWER PLATFORMS FOR EXTERIOR BUILDING MAINTENANCE

(c) (3)

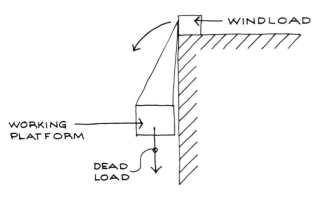

ROOF CAR—STABILITY

NOTE:

Determine roof car stability by the greater of (i) or (ii) below:

(i) The roof car shall be continuously stable, considering overturning moment as determined by 125 percent rated load, plus maximum dead load and the prescribed wind loading.

(ii) The roof car and its anchorages shall resist accidental over-tensioning of the wire ropes suspending the working platform, and this calculated value shall include the effect of one and one-half times the value. For this calculation, the simultaneous effect of one-half wind load shall be included and the design stresses shall not exceed those referred to in Parts II and III of ANSI A120.1–1970.

(c) (4)

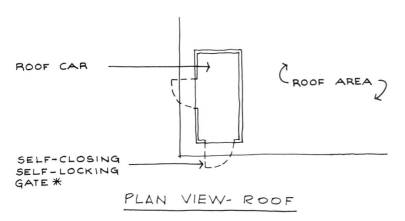

PLAN VIEW- ROOF

ROOF CAR—ACCESS

NOTE:

*Provide safe access to the roof car and from the roof car to the working platform. If the access to the roof car at any point of its travel is not over the roof area or where otherwise necessary for safety, self-closing, self-locking gates conforming to ANSI A12.1–1967 shall be provided.

(c) (5)

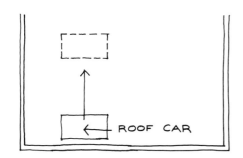

PLAN VIEW - ROOF

ROOF CAR—MAINTENANCE, REPAIR, AND STORAGE

NOTE:

Provide means to run the roof car away from the roof perimeter, where necessary, and to provide a safe area for maintenance, repairs, and storage. Provisions shall be made to secure the machine in the stored position.

(c) (6)

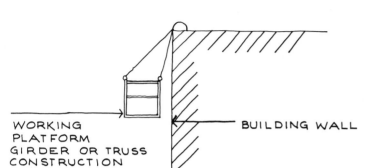

WORKING PLATFORM—CONSTRUCTION

NOTE:
Construction shall be adequate to support its rated load under any position of loading, and comply with the provisions set forth in Section 10 of ANSI A120.1–1970.

(c) (7)

LOAD-RATING PLATE

NOTE:
Each working platform shall bear a manufacturer's load-rating plate, conspicuously posted, stating the maximum permissible rated load.

(c) (8)

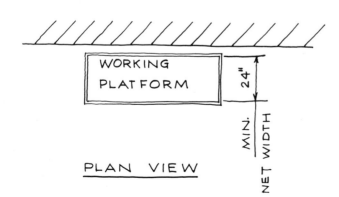

MINIMUM SIZE

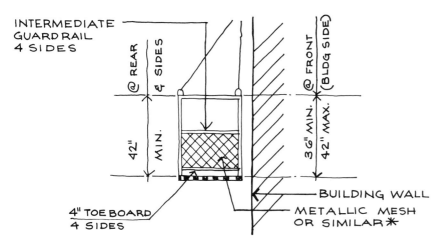

WORKING PLATFORM—REQUIREMENTS

(c) (9), (10), and (11)

NOTE:
* Mesh to reject a ball 1 in. in diameter. Mesh shall be capable of withstanding a load of 100 lb applied horizontally over any area of 144 sq in. If space between platform and building face is 8 in. or less, the mesh may be omitted on the front (building) side.

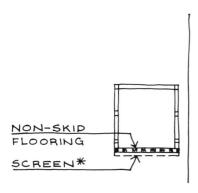

SECTION

WORKING PLATFORM—FLOORING

(c) (12)

NOTE:
*If flooring is of open construction, it shall reject a $\%_{16}$-in.-diameter ball, or be provided with a screen below the floor to reject a $\%_{16}$-in.-diameter ball.

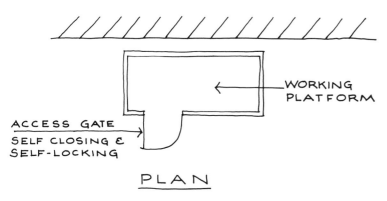

PLAN

WORKING PLATFORM—ACCESS GATES

(c) (13)

NOTE:
Where access gates are provided, they shall be self-closing and self-locking.

(c) (14)

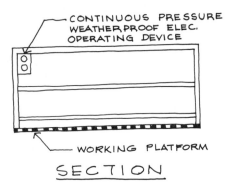

CONTINUOUS PRESSURE WEATHERPROOF ELEC. OPERATING DEVICE

WORKING PLATFORM

SECTION

OPERATING DEVICE FOR VERTICAL MOVEMENT

NOTE:
The normal operating device for the working platform shall be located on the working platform.

The operating device shall be operable only when all electrical protective devices and interlocks on the working platform are in position for normal service, and the roof car, if provided, is at an established operating point.

(c) (15)

FOR EMERGENCY OPERATION ONLY. ESTABLISH COMMUNICATION WITH PERSONNEL ON WORKING PLATFORM BEFORE USE

LEGEND MOUNTED NEAR HOISTING MACHINE

EMERGENCY ELECTRICAL OPERATIVE DEVICE

NOTE:
In addition, on roof-powered platforms, an emergency electrical operating device shall be provided near the hoisting machine for use in the event of failure of the normal operating device for the working platform, or failure of the traveling cable system. The emergency operating device shall be mounted in a locked compartment.

A key for unlocking the compartment housing the emergency operating device shall be mounted in a break-glass receptacle located near the emergency operating device.

(c) (16)

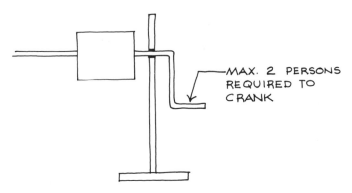

MAX. 2 PERSONS REQUIRED TO CRANK

NOTE:
Emergency operation of the main-drive machine may be provided to allow manual cranking. The access to this provision shall include a means to automatically make the machine inoperative electrically while under the emergency manual operation. The design shall be such that the emergency brake is operative at or below governor-tripping speed during manual operation.

MANUAL CRANKING FOR EMERGENCY OPERATION

(c) (17), (18) (i)

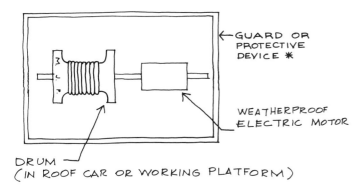

GUARD OR PROTECTIVE DEVICE *

WEATHERPROOF ELECTRIC MOTOR

DRUM
(IN ROOF CAR OR WORKING PLATFORM)

GUARDING OF HOISTING EQUIPMENT

NOTE:
* Provide protective device wherever rotating shafts or other mechanisms or gears expose personnel to a hazard. Belt- or chain-driven machines are prohibited. Do not use friction devices or clutches to connect main driving mechanism to drum.

(c) (19)

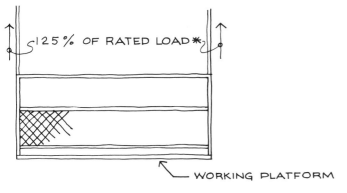

125% OF RATED LOAD *

WORKING PLATFORM

BRAKES

NOTE:
* Hoisting machine shall have two independent braking means, each designed to hold and stop working platform with 125 percent of rated load.

(c) 20 (i), (ii), (iii), and (iv)

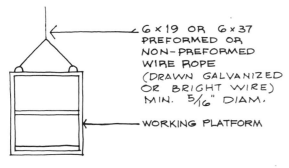

6 × 19 OR 6 × 37 PREFORMED OR NON-PREFORMED WIRE ROPE (DRAWN GALVANIZED OR BRIGHT WIRE) MIN. 5/16" DIAM.

WORKING PLATFORM

HOISTING ROPES

NOTE:
Winding drums to have a minimum of three turns of rope with platform at lowest point of travel.

(c) (20) (vii) and (viii)

SHACKLE RODS AT NONDRUM ENDS

REVERSE BENDS*

HOISTING ROPES

NOTE:
  * Avoid reverse bends in rope. More than two reverse bends in each rope are prohibited.
  Shackle rod requirement applies to Type T powered platforms only if the working platform is suspended by more than two wire ropes.

(c) (21) (i) and (ii)

a. DIAM. IN INCHES
b. CONSTRUCTION CLASSIFICATION
c. NON PREFORMED OR PREFORMED
d. GRADE OF MATERIAL USED
e. MANUF. RATED BREAKING STRENGTH
f. MANUF. NAME
g. MONTH & YEAR ROPES INSTALLED
h. NAME OF INSTALLER

← NON CORROSIVE METAL

METAL DATA TAG

MIN. 1/16" HIGH LETTERS STAMPED OR ETCHED

ROPE TAG DATA

(c) 22 (i), (23)

NOTE:
  All electrical equipment and wiring shall conform to National Electric Code, NFPA 70–1971; ANSI C1–1971 (Rev. of 1968) except as modified by ANSI A120.1-1970, "American National Standard Safety Requirements for Exterior Building Maintenance." Provide emergency two-way communication between personnel on roof and personnel on stalled platform via telephone or an approved two-way radio system.

ELECTRIC WIRING AND EQUIPMENT AND EMERGENCY COMMUNICATION

(b) (1)

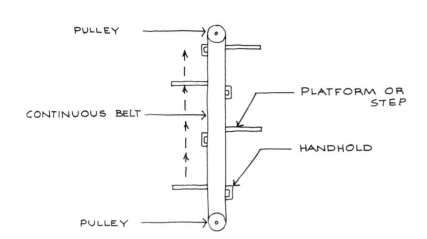

PULLEY

CONTINUOUS BELT

PULLEY

PLATFORM OR STEP

HANDHOLD

APPLICATION

NOTE:
Manlifts operate vertically in one direction only, and are intended for conveyance of persons only. This section does not cover moving stairways, elevators with enclosed platforms, gravity lifts, or conveyors used only for conveying material.

(b) (3) and (4)

NOTE:
All new manlifts shall comply with "American National Safety Standard of Manlifts," ANSI A90.1–1969, and this section. Other applicable codes: ANSI B15.1–1953 (R 1958); NFPA 70–1971; ANSI C1–1971 (Rev. of 1968); ANSI A14.3–1956; ANSI A12.1–1967. Other applicable Subparts of OSHA (Part 1910): Subparts D, S, and O.

DESIGN REQUIREMENTS

(b) (5)

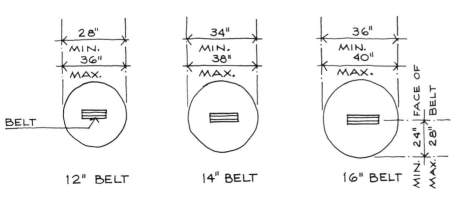

28" MIN.
36" MAX.

34" MIN.
38" MAX.

36" MIN.
40" MAX.

BELT

FACE OF BELT

MIN. 24"
MAX. 28"

12" BELT   14" BELT   16" BELT

NOTE:
Floor openings shall be uniform in size, approximately circular, and each shall be located vertically above the opening below it.

FLOOR OPENINGS (FOR UP AND DOWN RUNS)

(b) (6) (i)

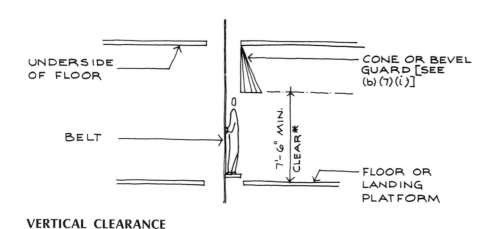

VERTICAL CLEARANCE

NOTE:
* Where this clearance cannot be obtained, no access to the manlift shall be provided and the manlift runway shall be enclosed where it passes through such floor.

(b) (6) (ii)

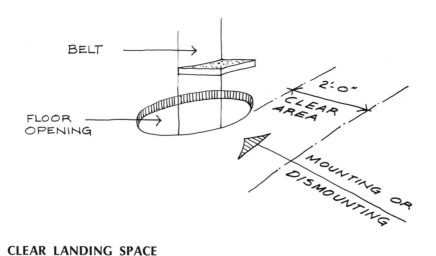

CLEAR LANDING SPACE

NOTE:
The landing space adjacent to the floor openings shall be free from obstruction and kept clear at all times.

(b) (6) (iii)

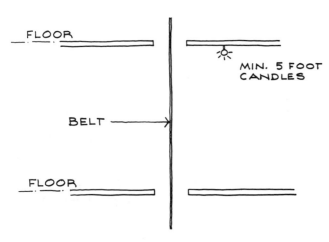

NOTE:
Adequate lighting shall be provided at each floor landing at all times when the lift is in operation.

LIGHTING

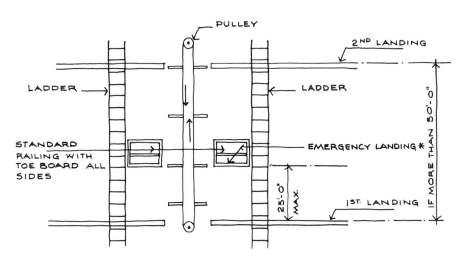

EMERGENCY LANDINGS

NOTE:
*Platforms constructed to give access to bucket elevators or other equipment for the purpose of inspection, lubrication, and repair may also serve as emergency landings under this rule. All such platforms will then be considered part of the emergency landing and shall be provided with standard railings and toe boards.

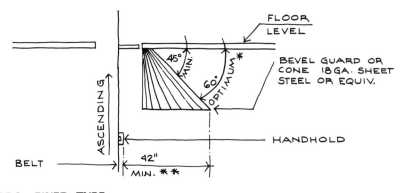

GUARDS—FIXED TYPE

NOTE:
*An angle of 60 degrees or greater shall be used where ceiling heights permit.
**Lower edge shall not project beyond upper surface of the floor above. Lower edge shall be rolled to a minimum diameter of ½ in. and interior shall be smooth with no rivets, bolts, or screws protruding.

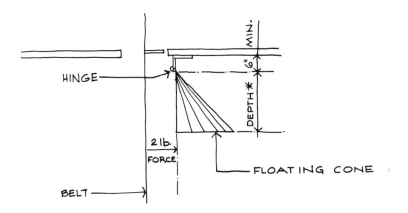

GUARDS—FLOATING TYPE

NOTE:
In lieu of the fixed guards a floating-type safety cone may be used, such floating cones to be mounted on hinges at least 6 in. below the underside of the floor and so constructed as to actuate a limit switch should a force of 2 lb be applied on the edge of the cone closest to the hinge.
*The depth of this floating cone need not exceed 12 in.

(b) (8) (i) and (v)

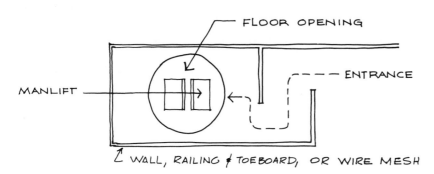

STAGGERED RAILINGS

PROTECTION OF ENTRANCES AND EXITS

NOTE:
  Except where building layout prevents, entrances at all landings shall be in the same relative position.

(b) (8) (i) and (ii)

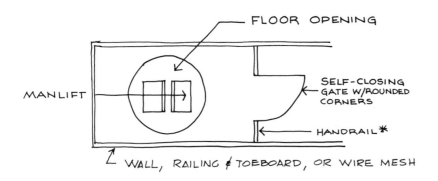

SELF-CLOSING GATE

PROTECTION OF ENTRANCES AND EXITS (ALTERNATE)

NOTE:
  *Rails shall be standard guard rails complying with Sec. 1910.23 and ANSI A12. 1–1967.

(b) (8) (vi)

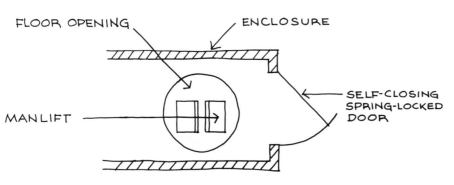

IN BUILDINGS WITH PUBLIC ACCESS

NOTE:
  If located in buildings to which the public has access, such manlift or manlifts shall be located in an enclosure protected by self-closing spring-locked doors. Keys to such doors shall be limited to authorized personnel.

(b) (9)

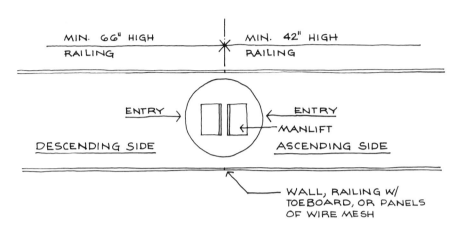

GUARDS FOR OPENINGS

(b) (10) (i) and (ii)

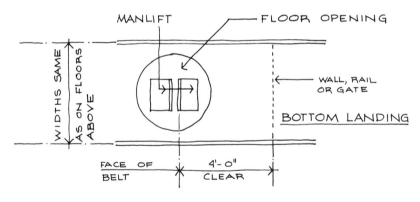

BOTTOM ARRANGEMENT

NOTE:
The lower (boot) pulley shall be installed so that it is supported by the lowest landing served. The sides of the pulley support shall be guarded to prevent contact with the pulley or the steps.

(b) (10) (iii) and (iv)

NOTE:
A mounting platform shall be provided in front or to one side of the up run at the lowest landing, unless the floor level is such that the following requirement can be met: The floor or platform shall be at or above the point at which the upper surface of the ascending step completes its turn and assumes a horizontal position.

*To guard against persons walking under a descending step, the area on the downside of the manlift shall be guarded with a guard rail.

**To guard against a person getting between the mounting platform and an ascending step, the area between the belt and the platform shall be protected by a guard rail.

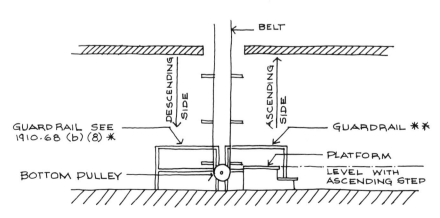

BOTTOM ARRANGEMENT

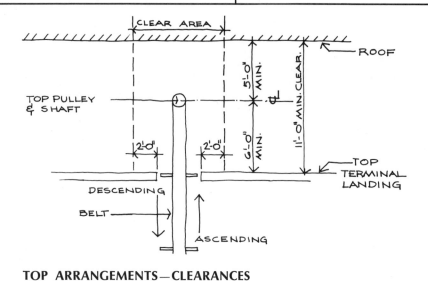

TOP ARRANGEMENTS—CLEARANCES

(b) (11) (i) and (ii)

NOTE:
Maintain minimum top clearance of 11 ft through a vertical cylindrical plane leaving a diameter 2 ft greater than diameter of floor opening to ceiling of up-running belt. Do not encroach within this space with structural or machine-supporting members.

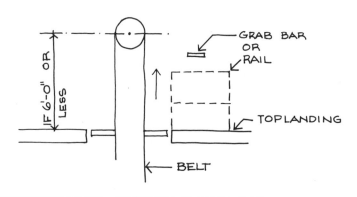

TOP ARRANGEMENTS—EMERGENCY GRAB RAIL

(b) (11) (iii)

NOTE:
Provide grab rail or railing to permit rider to swing free should emergency stops become inoperative.

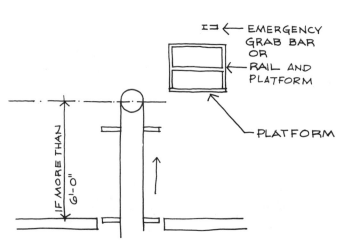

TOP ARRANGEMENTS—EMERGENCY GRAB RAIL

(b) (11) (iii)

NOTE:
Platforms to be provided at lead pulley.

(b) (12)

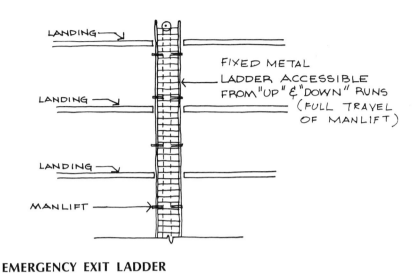

EMERGENCY EXIT LADDER

NOTE:
Ladder to conform to ANSI A14.3–1956 and OSHA Section 1910.27.

(b) (13)

NOTE:
Manlift rails shall be secured in a manner as to avoid spreading, vibration, and misalignment.

SUPERSTRUCTURE BRACING

(b) (14)

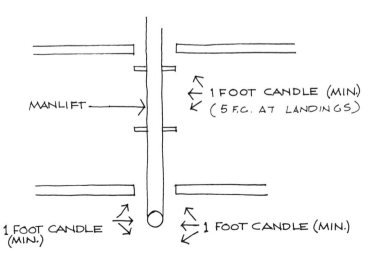

1 FOOT CANDLE (MIN.)
(5 F.C. AT LANDINGS)

MANLIFT

1 FOOT CANDLE (MIN.)

1 FOOT CANDLE (MIN.)

NOTE:
Illuminate both runs of manlift when lift is in operation. Lighting of manlift runways shall be by means of circuits permanently tied in to the building circuits (no switches) or shall be controlled by switches at each landing. Where separate switches are provided at each landing, any switch shall turn on all lights necessary to illuminate the entire runway.

ILLUMINATION

(c) (1) (i)

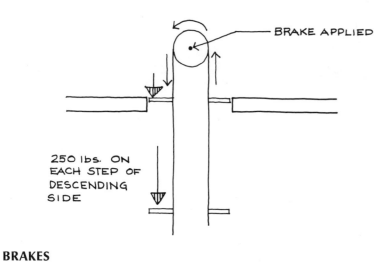

250 lbs. ON EACH STEP OF DESCENDING SIDE

BRAKE APPLIED

BRAKES

NOTE:
Brake shall be electrically released, and shall be applied to the motor shaft for belt-driven units. Brake shall be capable of holding manlift when descending side is loaded with 250 lb on each step.

(c) (1) (ii) (a)

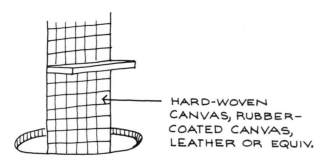

HARD-WOVEN CANVAS, RUBBER-COATED CANVAS, LEATHER OR EQUIV.

BELT CONSTRUCTION

NOTE:
Strength to comply with ANSI A90.1–1969, with coefficient of friction such that when used in conjunction with an adequate tension device it will meet the brake test (c) (1) (i) above.

(c) (1) (ii), (b) and (c)

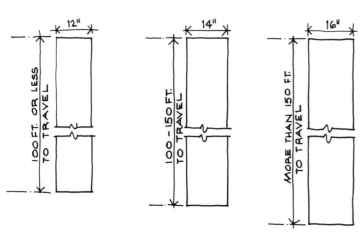

12"   14"   16"

100 FT. OR LESS TO TRAVEL   100 – 150 FT. TO TRAVEL   MORE THAN 150 FT. TO TRAVEL

MINIMUM BELT WIDTHS

NOTE:
A belt that has become torn while in use on a manlift shall not be spliced and put back in service.

(c) (2)

SPEED

(c) (3) (i), (ii), and (iii)

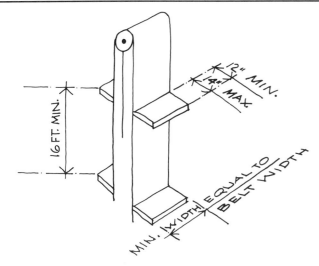

STEPS OR PLATFORMS

NOTE:
    Steps shall be equally spaced.

(c) (3) (iv)

DOWN   UP

90°   90°

ANGLE OF STEP

(c) (3) (v)

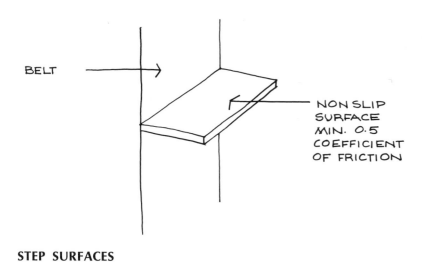

STEP SURFACES

NOTE:
   Nonslip characteristic may be inherent or nonslip tread securely fastened to step.

(c) (3) (vi)

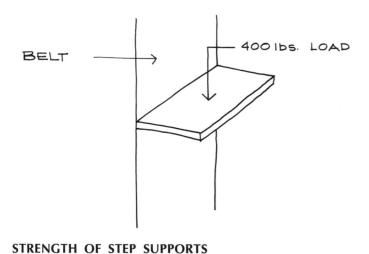

STRENGTH OF STEP SUPPORTS

NOTE:
   When subjected to a load of 400 lb applied at the approximate center of the step, step frames, or supports and their guides, shall be of adequate strength to:
   (a) Prevent the disengagement of any step roller.
   (b) Prevent any appreciable misalignment.
   (c) Prevent any visible deformation of the step or its support.

(c) (3) (vii) and (c) (4)

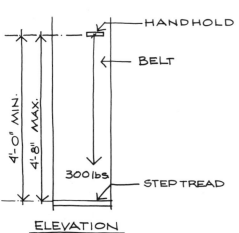

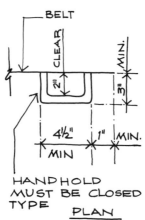

HANDHOLDS

NOTE:
   Steps without corresponding handholds, and handholds without corresponding steps, are prohibited. Handholds shall be available for both "up" and "down" run of belt, shall support 300 lb parallel to run of belt, and shall be fastened not less than 1 in. from edge of belt.

(c) (5) (i)

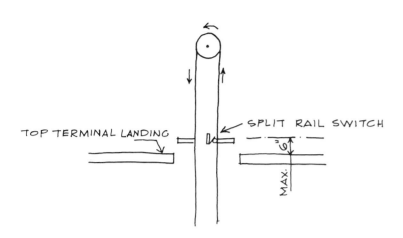

UP LIMIT STOPS

NOTE:
Provide two separate automatic stop devices. One of these shall be a split-rail switch as shown. The second device may consist of any of the following:
(a) Any split-rail switch placed 6 in. above and on the side opposite the first limit switch.
(b) An electronic device.
(c) A switch actuated by a lever, rod, or plate, the latter to be placed on the "up" side of the head pulley so as to just clear a passing step.

(c) (5) (ii)

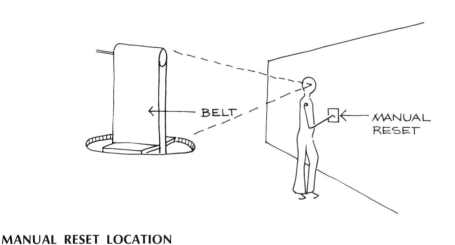

MANUAL RESET LOCATION

NOTE:
To reset after the manlift has been stopped by a stop device, the person shall have to be off the step or platform and have a clear view of the "up" and "down" runs.

(c) (5) (iii)

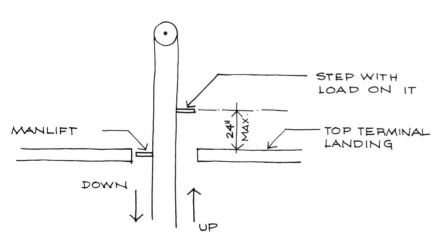

CUTOFF POINT

NOTE:
The initial-limit stop device described in (c) (5) (i) above shall function so that the manlift will be stopped before the loaded step has reached a point 24 in. above the top terminal landing.

(c) (5) (iv)

ELECTRICAL REQUIREMENTS

NOTE:

1. Where switches open main motor directly, they shall be of the multipole type.

2. Electronic devices, where used, shall shut off power to the driving motor in case of failure.

3. Where flammable vapors or dusts are present, conform to NFPA 70–1971; ANSI C1–1971 (Rev. of 1968) for such locations.

4. Controller contacts carrying main motor current shall be copper to carbon, or equal, except where circuit is broken simultaneously at two or more points, or unless of the oil-immersed type.

(c) (6) (i) and (ii)

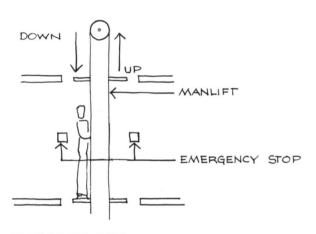

EMERGENCY STOP

NOTE:

Provide an emergency stop means within easy reach of the ascending and descending runs of the belt.

(c) (6) (iv)

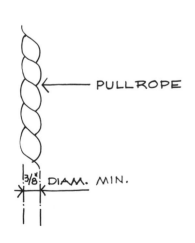

EMERGENCY STOP-ROPE

NOTE:

If rope is used, it shall not be less than ⅜ in. diameter. Wire rope, unless marlin-covered, shall not be used.

(c) (7) (i)

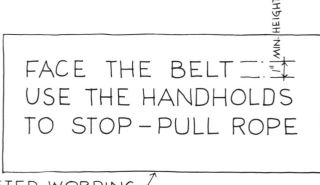

FACE THE BELT
USE THE HANDHOLDS
TO STOP — PULL ROPE

MIN. HEIGHT

SUGGESTED WORDING
SUGGESTED COLORS:
(BLACK ON WHITE)   (BLACK ON GREY)
(WHITE ON BLACK)   (YELLOW ON BLACK)

INSTRUCTION SIGNS AT LANDING OR BELTS

NOTE:
Signs giving instructions for the use of the manlift shall be posted at each landing or stenciled on the belt.

(c) (7) (ii)

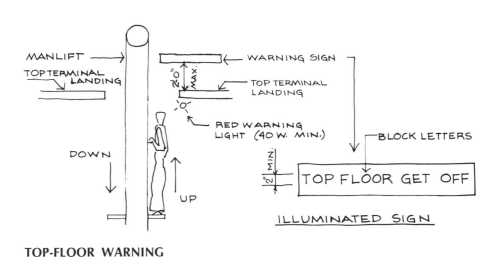

MANLIFT
TOP TERMINAL LANDING
WARNING SIGN
TOP TERMINAL LANDING
2'-0" MAX.
RED WARNING LIGHT (40 W. MIN.)
BLOCK LETTERS
DOWN
UP
2" MIN.
TOP FLOOR GET OFF

ILLUMINATED SIGN

TOP-FLOOR WARNING

NOTE:
Top-floor warning sign shall be located within easy view of an ascending passenger. Locate red warning light immediately below the upper landing terminal so as to shine in the passenger's face.

(c) (7) (iii)

BLOCK LETTERS

AUTHORIZED PERSONNEL ONLY

2" MIN. HEIGHT

SIGN — DISPLAYED AT EACH LANDING

NOTE:
Sign shall be conspicuous and of a color offering high contrast with the background color.

VISITOR WARNING

(d) (1)

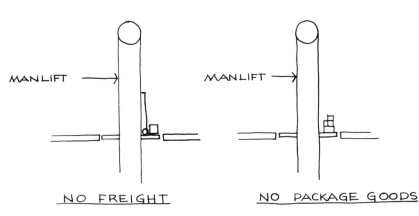

PROPER USE OF MANLIFTS

(d) (1)

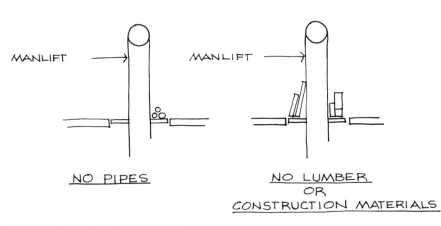

PROPER USE OF MANLIFTS

(e) (1) and (3)

NOTE:

All manlifts shall be inspected by a competent designated person at intervals of not more than 30 days. Limit switches shall be checked weekly. Manlifts found to be unsafe shall not be operated until properly repaired. Maintain a written record of findings at each inspection.

PERIODIC INSPECTION

To achieve compliance with paragraph (a) through (d) of this section, administrative or engineering controls must first be determined and implemented whenever feasible. When such controls are not feasible to achieve full compliance, protective equipment or any other protective measures shall be used to keep the exposure of employees to air contaminants within the limits prescribed in this section. Any equipment and/or technical measures used for this purpose must be approved for each particular use by a competent industrial hygienist or other technically qualified person.

An employee's exposure to any material listed in table G–1, G–2, or G–3 of this section shall be limited in accordance with the requirements of the following paragraphs of this section.

(a) Table G–1:

(1) Materials with names preceded by "C"—ceiling values. An employee's exposure to any material in table G–1, the name of which is preceded by a "C" (e.g., C Boron trifluoride), shall at no time exceed the ceiling value given for that material in the table.

(2) Other materials—8-hour time weighted averages. An employee's exposure to any material in table G–1, the name of which is not preceded by "C", in any 8-hour work shift of a 40-hour work week, shall not exceed the 8-hour time weighted average given for that material in the table.

TABLE G–1

Substance	p.p.m.[a]	mg./M^3 [b]
Acetaldehyde	200	360
Acetic acid	10	25
Acetic anhydride	5	20
Acetone	1,000	2,400
Acetonitrile	40	70
Acetylene dichloride, see 1, 2-Dichloroethylene		
Acetylene tetrabromide	1	14
Acrolein	0.1	0.25
Acrylamide—Skin		0.3
Acrylonitrile—Skin	20	45
Aldrin—Skin		0.25
Allyl alcohol—Skin	2	5
Allyl chloride	1	3
**C Allyl glycidyl ether (AGE)	10	45
Allyl propyl disulfide	2	12
2-Aminoethanol, see Ethanolamine		
2-Aminopyridine	0.5	2
**Ammonia	50	35
Ammonium sulfamate (Ammate)		15
n-Amyl acetate	100	525
sec-Amyl acetate	125	650
Aniline—Skin	5	19
Anisidine (o, p-isomers)—Skin		0.5

[a] Parts of vapor or gas per million parts of contaminated air by volume at 25° C. and 760 mm. Hg pressure.

[b] Approximate milligrams of particulate per cubic meter of air.

(No footnote "c" is used to avoid confusion with ceiling value notations.)

[d] An atmospheric concentration of not more than 0.02 p.p.m., or personal protection may be necessary to avoid headache.

[e] As sampled by method that does not collect vapor.

[f] For control of general room air, biologic monitoring is essential for personnel control.

Antimony and compounds (as Sb)		0.5
ANTU (alpha naphthyl thiourea)		0.3
Arsenic and compounds (as As)		0.5
Arsine	0.05	0.2
Azinphos-methyl—Skin		0.2
Barium (soluble compounds)		0.5
p-Benzoquinone, see Quinone		
Benzoyl peroxide		5
Benzyl chloride	1	5
Biphenyl, see Diphenyl		
Bisphenol A, see Diglycidyl ether		
Boron oxide		15
C Boron trifluoride	1	3
Bromine	0.1	0.7
Bromoform—Skin	0.5	5
Butadiene (1, 3-butadiene)	1,000	2,200
Butanethiol, see Butyl mercaptan		
2-Butanone	200	590
2-Butoxy ethanol (Butyl Cellosolve)—Skin	50	240
Butyl acetate (n-butyl acetate)	150	710
sec-Butyl acetate	200	950
tert-Butyl acetate	200	950
Butyl alcohol	100	300
sec-Butyl alcohol	150	450
tert-Butyl alcohol	100	300
C Butylamine—Skin	5	15
C tert-Butyl chromate (as CrO$_3$)—Skin		0.1
n-Butyl glycidyl ether (BGE)	50	270
*Butyl mercaptan	10	35
p-tert-Butyltoluene	10	60
Calcium arsenate		1
Calcium oxide		5
**Camphor	2	
Carbaryl (Sevin ®)		5
Carbon black		3.5
Carbon dioxide	5,000	9,000
Carbon monoxide	50	55
Chlordane—Skin		0.5
Chlorinated camphene—Skin		0.5
Chlorinated diphenyl oxide		0.5
*Chlorine	1	3
Chlorine dioxide	0.1	0.3
C Chlorine trifluoride	0.1	0.4
C Chloroacetaldehyde	1	3
α-Chloroacetophenone (phenacylchloride)	0.05	0.3
Chlorobenzene (monochlorobenzene)	75	350
o-Chlorobenzylidene malononitrile (OCBM)	0.05	0.4
Chlorobromomethane	200	1,050
2-Chloro-1,3-butadiene, see Chloroprene		
Chlorodiphenyl (42 percent Chlorine)—Skin		1
Chlorodiphenyl (54 percent Chlorine)—Skin		0.5
1-Chloro,2,3-epoxypropane, see Epichlorhydrin		

125

TABLE G–1—Continued

Substance	p.p.m.[a]	mg./M³ [b]
2-Chloroethanol, see Ethylene chlorohydrin		
Chloroethylene, see Vinyl chloride		
C Chloroform (trichloromethane)	50	240
1-Chloro-1-nitropropane	20	100
Chloropicrin	0.1	0.7
Chloroprene (2-chloro-1,3-butadiene)—Skin	25	90
Chromium, sol. chromic, chromous salts as Cr		0.5
Metal and insol. salts		1
Coal tar pitch volatiles (benzene soluble fraction) anthracene, BaP, phenanthrene, acridine, chrysene, pyrene		0.2
Cobalt, metal fume and dust		0.1
Copper fume		0.1
Dusts and Mists		1
Cotton dust (raw)		1
Crag® herbicide		15
Cresol (all isomers)—Skin	5	22
Crotonaldehyde	2	6
Cumene—Skin	50	245
Cyanide (as CN)—Skin		5
Cyclohexane	300	1,050
Cyclohexanol	50	200
Cyclohexanone	50	200
Cyclohexene	300	1,015
Cyclopentadiene	75	200
2, 4-D		10
DDT—Skin		1
DDVP, see Dichlorvos		
Decaborane—Skin	0.05	0.3
Demeton®—Skin		0.1
Diacetone alcohol (4-hydroxy-4-methyl-2-pentanone)	50	240
1,2-diaminoethane, see Ethylenediamine		
Diazomethane	0.2	0.4
Diborane	0.1	0.1
Dibutylphthalate		5
C o-Dichlorobenzene	50	300
p-Dichlorobenzene	75	450
Dichlorodifluoromethane	1,000	4,950
1,3-Dichloro-5,5-dimethyl hydantoin		0.2
1,1-Dichloroethane	100	400
1,2-Dichloroethylene	200	790
C Dichloroethyl ether—Skin	15	90
Dichloromethane, see Methylenechloride		
Dichloromonofluoromethane	1,000	4,200
C 1,1-Dichloro-1-nitroethane	10	60
1,2-Dichloropropane, see Propylenedichloride		
Dichlorotetrafluoroethane	1,000	7,000
Dichlorvos (DDVP)—Skin		1
Dieldrin—Skin		0.25
Diethylamine	25	75
Diethylamino ethanol—Skin	10	50
Diethylether, see Ethyl ether		
Difluorodibromomethane	100	860
C Diglycidyl ether (DGE)	0.5	2.8
Dihydroxybenzene, see Hydroquinone		
Diisobutyl ketone	50	290
Diisopropylamine—Skin	5	20
Dimethoxymethane, see Methylal		
Dimethyl acetamide—Skin	10	35
Dimethylamine	10	18
Dimethylaminobenzene, see Xylidene		
Dimethylaniline(N-dimethyl-aniline)—Skin	5	25
Dimethylbenzene, see Xylene		
Dimethyl 1,2-dibromo-2,2-dichloroethyl phosphate, (Dibrom)		3
Dimethylformamide—Skin	10	30
2,6-Dimethylheptanone, see Diisobutyl ketone		
1,1-Dimethylhydrazine—Skin	0.5	1
Dimethylphthalate		5
Dimethylsulfate—Skin	1	5
Dinitrobenzene (all isomers)—Skin		1
Dinitro-o-cresol—Skin		0.2
Dinitrotoluene—Skin		1.5
Dioxane (Diethylene dioxide)—Skin	100	360
Diphenyl	0.2	1
Diphenylmethane diisocyanate (see Methylene bisphenyl isocyanate (MDI))		
Dipropylene glycol methyl ether—Skin	100	600
Di-sec, octyl phthalate (Di-2-ethylhexylphthalate)		5
Endrin—Skin		0.1
Epichlorhydrin—Skin	5	19
EPN—Skin		0.5
1,2-Epoxypropane, see Propyleneoxide		
2,3-Epoxy-1-propanol, see Glycidol		
Ethanethiol, see Ethylmercaptan		
Ethanolamine	3	6
2-Ethoxyethanol—Skin	200	740
2-Ethoxyethylacetate (Cellosolve acetate)—Skin	100	540
Ethyl acetate	400	1,400
Ethyl acrylate—Skin	25	100
Ethyl alcohol (ethanol)	1,000	1,900
Ethylamine	10	18
Ethyl sec-amyl ketone (5-methyl-3-heptanone)	25	130
Ethyl benzene	100	435
Ethyl bromide	200	890
Ethyl butyl ketone (3-Heptanone)	50	230
Ethyl chloride	1,000	2,600
Ethyl ether	400	1,200
Ethyl formate	100	300
C Ethyl mercaptan	10	25
Ethyl silicate	100	850
Ethylene chlorohydrin—Skin	5	16
Ethylenediamine	10	25
Ethylene dibromide, see 1,2-Dibromoethane		
Ethylene dichloride, see 1,2-Dichloroethane		
C Ethylene glycol dinitrate and/or Nitroglycerin—Skin	[d] 0 2	1

TABLE G-1—Continued

Substance	p.p.m.[a]	mg./M³[b]
Ethylene glycol monomethyl ether acetate, see Methyl cellosolve acetate		
Ethylene imine—Skin	0.5	1
Ethylene oxide	50	90
Ethylidine chloride, see 1,1-Dichloroethane		
N-Ethylmorpholine—Skin	20	94
Ferbam		15
Ferrovanadium dust		1
Fluoride (as F)		2.5
Fluorine	0.1	0.2
Fluorotrichloromethane	1,000	5,600
Formic acid	5	9
Furfural—Skin	5	20
Furfuryl alcohol	50	200
Glycidol (2,3-Epoxy-1-propanol)	50	150
Glycol monoethyl ether, see 2-Ethoxyethanol		
Guthion ®, see Azinphos-methyl		
Hafnium		0.5
Heptachlor—Skin		0.5
Heptane (n-heptane)	500	2,000
Hexachloroethane—Skin	1	10
Hexachloronaphthalene—Skin		0.2
Hexane (n-hexane)	500	1,800
2-Hexanone	100	410
Hexone (Methyl isobutyl ketone)	100	410
sec-Hexyl acetate	50	300
Hydrazine—Skin	1	1.3
Hydrogen bromide	3	10
C Hydrogen chloride	5	7
Hydrogen cyanide—Skin	10	11
Hydrogen peroxide (90%)	1	1.4
Hydrogen selenide	0.05	0.2
Hydroquinone		2
C Iodine	0.1	1
Iron oxide fume		10
Isoamyl acetate	100	525
Isoamyl alcohol	100	360
Isobutyl acetate	150	700
Isobutyl alcohol	100	300
Isophorone	25	140
Isopropyl acetate	250	950
Isopropyl alcohol	400	980
Isopropylamine	5	12
Isopropylether	500	2,100
Isopropyl glycidyl ether (IGE)	50	240
Ketene	0.5	0.9
Lead arsenate		0.15
Lindane—Skin		0.5
Lithium hydride		0.025
L.P.G. (liquified petroleum gas)	1,000	1,800
Magnesium oxide fume		15
Malathion—Skin		15
Maleic anhydride	0.25	1
C Manganese		5
Mesityl oxide	25	100
Methanethiol, see Methyl mercaptan		
Methoxychlor		15
2-Methoxyethanol, see Methyl cellosolve		
Methyl acetate	200	610
Methyl acetylene (propyne)	1,000	1,650

Substance	p.p.m.[a]	mg./M³[b]
Methyl acetylene-propadiene mixture (MAPP)	1,000	1,800
Methyl acrylate—Skin	10	35
Methylal (dimethoxymethane)	1,000	3,100
Methyl alcohol (methanol)	200	260
Methylamine	10	12
Methyl amyl alcohol, see Methyl isobutyl carbinol		
Methyl (n-amyl) ketone (2-Heptanone)	100	465
C Methyl bromide—Skin	20	80
Methyl butyl ketone, see 2-Hexanone		
Methyl cellosolve—Skin	25	80
Methyl cellosolve acetate—Skin	25	120
Methyl chloroform	350	1,900
Methylcyclohexane	500	2,000
Methylcyclohexanol	100	470
o-Methylcyclohexanone—Skin	100	460
Methyl ethyl ketone (MEK), see 2-Butanone		
Methyl formate	100	250
Methyl iodide—Skin	5	28
Methyl isobutyl carbinol—Skin	25	100
Methyl isobutyl ketone, see Hexone		
Methyl isocyanate—Skin	0.02	0.05
C Methyl mercaptan	10	20
Methyl methacrylate	100	410
Methyl propyl ketone, see 2-Pentanone		
C α Methyl styrene	100	480
C Methylene bisphenyl isocyanate (MDI)	0.02	0.2
Molybdenum:		
Soluble compounds		5
Insoluble compounds		15
Monomethyl aniline—Skin	2	9
C Monomethyl hydrazine—Skin	0.2	0.35
Morpholine—Skin	20	70
Naphtha (coaltar)	100	400
Naphthalene	10	50
Nickel carbonyl	0.001	0.007
Nickel, metal and soluble cmpds, as Ni		1
Nicotine—Skin		0.5
Nitric acid	2	5
Nitric oxide	25	30
p-Nitroaniline—Skin	1	6
Nitrobenzene—Skin	1	5
p-Nitrochlorobenzene—Skin		1
Nitroethane	100	310
Nitrogen dioxide	5	9
Nitrogen trifluoride	10	29
Nitroglycerin—Skin	0.2	2
Nitromethane	100	250
1-Nitropropane	25	90
2-Nitropropane	25	90
Nitrotoluene—Skin	5	30
Nitrotrichloromethane, see Chloropicrin		
Octachloronaphthalene—Skin		0.1
*Octane	500	2,350
*Oil mist, mineral		5
Osmium tetroxide		0.002
Oxalic acid		1
Oxygen difluoride	0.05	0.1
Ozone	0.1	0.2
Paraquat—Skin		0.5
Parathion—Skin		0.1 1
Pentaborane	0.005	0.01

TABLE G–1—Continued

Substance	p.p.m.ᵃ	mg./M³ᵇ
Pentachloronaphthalene—Skin		0.5
Pentachlorophenol—Skin		0.5
*Pentane	1,000	2,950
2-Pentanone	200	700
Perchloromethyl mercaptan	0.1	0.8
Perchloryl fluoride	3	13.5
Petroleum distillates (naphtha)	500	2,000
Phenol—Skin	5	19
p-Phenylene diamine—Skin		0.1
Phenyl ether (vapor)	1	7
Phenyl ether-biphenyl mixture (vapor)	1	7
Phenylethylene, see Styrene		
Phenyl glycidyl ether (PGE)	10	60
Phenylhydrazine—Skin	5	22
Phosdrin (Mevinphos ®)—Skin		0.1
Phosgene (carbonyl chloride)	0.1	0.4
Phosphine	0.3	0.4
Phosphoric acid		1
Phosphorus (yellow)		0.1
Phosphorus pentachloride		1
Phosphorus pentasulfide		1
Phosphorus trichloride	0.5	3
Phthalic anhydride	2	12
Picric acid—Skin		0.1
Pival ® (2-Pivalyl-1,3-indandione)		0.1
Platinum (Soluble Salts) as Pt		0.002
Propargyl alcohol—Skin	1	
Propane	1,000	1,800
n-Propyl acetate	200	840
Propyl alcohol	200	500
n-Propyl nitrate	25	110
Propylene dichloride	75	350
Propylene imine—Skin	2	5
Propylene oxide	100	240
Propyne, see Methylacetylene		
Pyrethrum		5
Pyridine	5	15
Quinone	0.1	0.4
RDX—Skin		1.5
Rhodium, Metal fume and dusts, as Rh		0.1
Soluble salts		0.001
Ronnel		10
Rotenone (commercial)		5
Selenium compounds (as Se)		0.2
Selenium hexafluoride	0.05	0.4
Silver, metal and soluble compounds		0.01
Sodium fluoroacetate (1080)—Skin		0.05
Sodium hydroxide		2
Stibine	0.1	0.5
*Stoddard solvent	500	2,950
Strychnine		0.15
Sulfur dioxide	5	13
Sulfur hexafluoride	1,000	6,000
Sulfuric acid		1
Sulfur monochloride	1	6
Sulfur pentafluoride	0.025	0.25
Sulfuryl fluoride	5	20
Systox, see Demeton ®		
2,4,5T		10
Tantalum		5
TEDP—Skin		0.2
Tellurium		0.1

Substance	p.p.m.ᵃ	mg./M³ᵇ
Tellurium hexafluoride	0.02	0.2
TEPP—Skin		0.05
C Terphenyls	1	9
1,1,1,2-Tetrachloro-2,2-difluoro-ethane	500	4,170
1,1,2,2-Tetrachloro-1,2-difluoro-ethane	500	4,170
1,1,2,2-Tetrachloroethane—Skin	5	35
Tetrachloroethylene, see Perchloroethylene		
Tetrachloromethane, see Carbon tetrachloride		
Tetrachloronaphthalene—Skin		2
Tetraethyl lead (as Pb)—Skin		0.075
Tetrahydrofuran	200	590
Tetramethyl lead (as Pb)—Skin		0.07
Tetramethyl succinonitrile—Skin	0.5	3
Tetranitromethane	1	8
Tetryl (2,4,6-trinitrophenyl-methylnitramine)—Skin		1.5
Thallium (soluble compounds)—Skin as Tl		0.1
Thiram		5
Tln (inorganic cmpds, except oxides		2
Tin (organic cmpds)		0.1
C Toluene-2,4-diisocyanate	0.02	0.14
o-Toluidine—Skin	5	22
Toxaphene, see Chlorinated camphene		
Tributyl phosphate		5
1,1,1-Trichloroethane see Methyl chloroform		
1,1,2-Trichloroethane—Skin	10	45
Titaniumdioxide		15
Trichloromethane, see Chloroform		
Trichloronaphthalene—Skin		5
1,2,3-Trichloropropane	50	300
1,1,2-Trichloro 1,2,2-trifluoro-ethane	1,000	7,600
Triethylamine	25	100
Trifluoromonobromomethane	1,000	6,100
2,4,6-Trinitrophenol, see Picric acid		
2,4,6-Trinitrophenylmethyl-nitramine, see Tetryl		
Trinitrotoluene—Skin		1.5
Triorthocresyl phosphate		0.1
Triphenyl phosphate		3
Turpentine	100	560
Uranium (soluble compounds)		0.05
Uranium (insoluble compounds)		0.25
C Vanadium:		
V₂O₅ dust		0.5
V₂O₅ fume		0.1
Vinyl benzene, see Styrene		
**C Vinyl chloride	500	1,300
Vinylcyanide, see Acrylonitrile		
Vinyl toluene	100	480
Warfarin		0.1
Xylene (xylol)	100	435
Xylidine—Skin	5	25
Yttrium		1
Zinc chloride fume		1
Zinc oxide fume		5
Zirconium compounds (as Zr)		5

*1970 Addition.

(b) Table G–2:

(1) **8-hour time weighted averages.** An employee's exposure to any material listed in table G–2, in any 8-hour work shift of a 40-hour work week, shall not exceed the 8-hour time weighted average limit given for that material in the table.

(2) **Acceptable ceiling concentrations.** An employee's exposure to a material listed in table G–2 shall not exceed at any time during an 8-hour shift the acceptable ceiling concentration limit given for the material in the table, except for a time period, and up to a concentration not exceeding the maximum duration and concentration allowed in the column under "acceptable maximum peak above the acceptable ceiling concentration for an 8-hour shift."

(3) **Example.** During an 8-hour work shift, an employee may be exposed to a concentration of Benzene above 25 p.p.m. (but never above 50 p.p.m.) only for a maximum period of 10 minutes. Such exposure must be compensated by exposures to concentrations less than 10 p.p.m. so that the cumulative exposure for the entire 8-hour work shift does not exceed a weighted average of 10 p.p.m.

TABLE G–2

Material	8-hour time weighted average	Acceptable ceiling concentration	Acceptable maximum peak above the acceptable ceiling concentration for an 8-hour shift.	
			Concentration	Maximum duration
Benzene (Z37.4–1969)	10 p.p.m.	25 p.p.m.	50 p.p.m.	10 minutes.
Beryllium and beryllium compounds (Z37.29–1970).	2 μg./M³	5 μg./M³	25 μg./M³	30 minutes.
Cadmium fume (Z37.5–1970)	0.1 mg./M³	3 mg./M³		
Cadmium dust (Z37.5–1970)	0.2 mg./M³	0.6 mg./M³		
Carbon disulfide (Z37.3–1968)	20 p.p.m.	30 p.p.m.	100 p.p.m.	Do.
Carbon tetrachloride (Z37.17–1967)	10 p.p.m.	25 p.p.m.	200 p.p.m.	5 minutes in any 4 hours.
Ethylene dibromide (Z37.31–1970)	20 p.p.m.	30 p.p.m.	50 p.p.m.	5 minutes.
Ethylene dichloride (Z37.21–1969)	50 p.p.m.	100 p.p.m.	200 p.p.m.	5 minutes in any 3 hours.
Formaldehyde (Z37.16–1967)	3 p.p.m.	5 p.p.m.	10 p.p.m.	30 minutes.
Hydrogen fluoride (Z37.28–1969)	do			
Fluoride as dust (Z37.28–1969)	2.5 mg./M³			
Lead and its inorganic compounds (Z37.11–1969).	0.2 mg./M³			
Methyl chloride (Z37.18–1969)	100 p.p.m.	200 p.p.m.	300 p.p.m.	5 minutes in any 3 hours.
Methylene Chloride (Z37.3–1969)	500 p.p.m.	1,000 p.p.m.	2,000 p.p.m.	5 minutes in any 2 hours.
Organo (alkyl) mercury (Z37.30–1969)	0.01 mg./M³	0.04 mg./M³		
Styrene (Z37.15–1969)	100 p.p.m.	200 p.p.m.	600 p.p.m.	5 minutes in any 3 hours.
Trichloroethylene (Z37.19–1967)	do	do	300 p.p.m.	5 minutes in any 2 hours.
Tetrachloroethylene (Z37.22–1967)	do	do	do	5 minutes in any 3 hours.
Toluene (Z37.12–1967)	200 p.p.m.	300 p.p.m.	500 p.p.m.	10 minutes.
Hydrogen sulfide (Z37.2–1966)		20 p.p.m.	50 p.p.m.	10 minutes once only if no other measurable exposure occurs.
Mercury (Z37.8–1971)		1 mg./10M³		
Chromic acid and chromates (Z37.7–1971)		do³		

(c) Table G–3: An employee's exposure to any material listed in table G–3, in any 8-hour work shift of a 40-hour work week, shall not exceed the 8-hour time weighted average limit given for that material in the table.

TABLE G–3—MINERAL DUSTS

Substance	Mppcf [e]	Mg/M³
Silica:		
Crystalline:		
Quartz (respirable)	250 [f]	10mg/M³ [m]
	$\frac{250}{\%SiO_2+5}$	$\frac{10mg/M^3}{\%SiO_2+2}$
Quartz (total dust)		$\frac{30mg/M^3}{\%S_2O_2+2}$
Cristobalite: Use ½ the value calculated from the count or mass formulae for quartz.		
Tridymite: Use ½ the value calculated from the formulae for quartz.		
Amorphous, including natural diatomaceous earth	20	$\frac{80mg/M^3}{\%SiO_2}$
Silicates (less than 1% crystalline silica):		
Mica	20	
Soapstone	20	
Talc (non-asbestos-form)	20 [n]	
Talc (fibrous). Use asbestos limit		
Tremolite (see talc, fibrous)		
Portland cement	50	
Graphite (natural)	15	
Coal dust (respirable fraction less than 5% SiO₂)		2.4mg/M³ or
For more than 5% SiO₂		$\frac{10mg/M^3}{\%SiO_2+2}$
Inert or Nuisance Dust:		
Respirable fraction	15	5mg/M³
Total dust	50	15mg/M³

NOTE: Conversion factors—
mppcf×35.3=million particles per cubic meter
=particles per c.c.
[e] Millions of particles per cubic foot of air, based on impinger samples counted by light-field technics.
[f] The percentage of crystalline silica in the formula is the amount determined from air-borne samples, except in those instances in which other methods have been shown to be applicable.
[j] As determined by the membrane filter method at 430×phase contrast magnification.
[m] Both concentration and percent quartz for the application of this limit are to be determined from the fraction passing a size-selector with the following characteristics:
[n] Containing < 1% quartz; if > 1% quartz, use quartz limit.

(d) Computation formulae:

(1)

(i) The cumulative exposure for an 8-hour work shift shall be computed as follows:

$$E = \frac{C_aT_a + C_bT_b + \ldots C_nT_n}{8}$$

where:

E is the equivalent exposure for the working shift.
C is the concentration during any period of time T where the concentration remains constant.
T is the duration in hours of the exposure at the concentration C.

The value of E shall not exceed the 8-hour time weighted average limit in table G–1, G–2, or G–3 for the material involved.

(ii) To illustrate the formula prescribed in subdivision (i) of this subparagraph, note that isoamyl acetate has an 8-hour time weighted average limit of 100 p.p.m. (table G–1). Assume that an employee is subject to the following exposure:

Two hours exposure at 150 p.p.m.
Two hours exposure at 75 p.p.m.
Four hours exposure at 50 p.p.m.

Substituting this information in the formula, we have

$$\frac{2 \times 150 + 2 \times 75 + 4 \times 50}{8} = 81.25 \text{ p.p.m.}$$

Since 81.25 p.p.m. is less than 100 p.p.m., the 8-hour time weighted average limit, the exposure is acceptable.

(2)

(i) In case of a mixture of air contaminants an employer shall compute the equivalent exposure as follows:

$$E_m = \frac{C_1}{L_1} + \frac{C_2}{L_2} + \ldots \frac{C_n}{L_n}$$

where:
E_m is the equivalent exposure for the mixture.
C is the concentration of a particular contaminant.
L is the exposure limit for that contaminant, from table G–1, G–2, or G–3.

The value of E_m shall not exceed unity (1).

(b) (1), (2), and (3)

NOTE:
8-hour-time weighted-average airborne concentration to which any employee may be exposed shall not exceed five fibers (two fibers, effective July 1, 1976), longer than 5 micrometers, per cubic centimeter of air. Ceiling concentration:—exposure at any time—ten fibers longer than 5 micrometers per cubic centimeter of air.

PERMISSIBLE EXPOSURE

(d) (4) (i) and (ii)

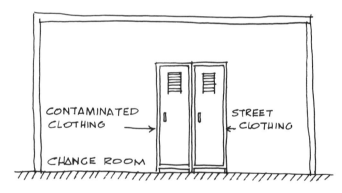

NOTE:
At fixed place of employment where airborne concentrations exceed those noted in (b) above, provide change rooms and two separate lockers or containers, separated or isolated to prevent contamination of street clothes from work clothes.

CHANGE ROOMS AND LOCKERS

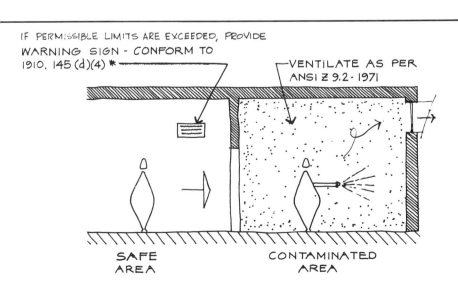

IF PERMISSIBLE LIMITS ARE EXCEEDED, PROVIDE WARNING SIGN - CONFORM TO 1910, 145 (d)(4) *

VENTILATE AS PER ANSI Z 9.2 - 1971

SAFE AREA

CONTAMINATED AREA

(g) (l) (i) and (ii)

NOTE:
* Mark and letter signs as follows:

Legend	Notation
Asbestos	1 in. Sans Serif, Gothic or Block.
Dust Hazard	¾ in. San Serif. Gothic or Block.
Avoid Breathing Dust	¼ in. Gothic.
Wear Assigned Protective Equipment.	¼ in. Gothic.
Do Not Remain In Area Unless Your Work Requires It.	¼ in. Gothic
Breathing Asbestos Dust May Be Hazardous To Your Health.	14 point Gothic.

CAUTION SIGNS

(b)

Exhaust systems for grinding, polishing, and buffing operations should be designed in accordance with American Standard Fundamentals Governing the Design and Operation of Local Exhaust Systems, Z9.2–1960.

Portable grinding operations, whenever the nature of the work permits, shall be conducted within a partial enclosure. The opening in the enclosure shall be no larger than is actually required in the operation and an average face air velocity of not less than 200 feet per minute shall be maintained.

It is the dual function of grinding and abrasive cutting-off wheel hoods to protect the operator from the hazards of bursting wheels as well as to provide a means for the removal of dust and dirt generated. All hoods shall be not less in structural strength than specified in the American National Standard Code for the Use, Care, and Protection of Abrasive Wheels, B7.1–1970.

Due to the variety of work and types of grinding machines employed, it is necessary to develop hoods adaptable to the particular machine in question, and such hoods shall be located as close as possible to the operation.

NOTE:

These general notes apply to exhaust hood enclosures and systems in removing dust, dirt, fumes, and gases (shown on this and the following pages) generated through the grinding, polishing, or buffing of ferrous and nonferrous metals.

(b) (3) (viii)
(b) (5) (vi)

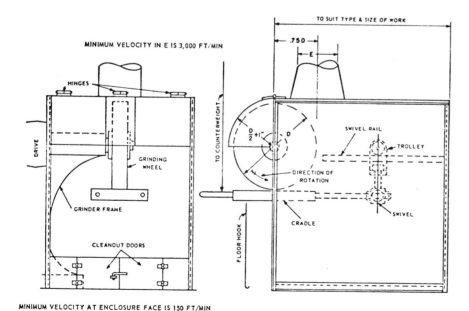

MINIMUM VELOCITY IN E IS 3,000 FT/MIN

TO SUIT TYPE & SIZE OF WORK

.750

E

HINGES

TO COUNTERWEIGHT

DRIVE

GRINDING WHEEL

SWIVEL RAIL

TROLLEY

$\frac{D}{2}$+1"   D

DIRECTION OF ROTATION

GRINDER FRAME

FLOOR HOOK

SWIVEL

CRADLE

CLEANOUT DOORS

MINIMUM VELOCITY AT ENCLOSURE FACE IS 150 FT/MIN

Fig. G-5

Entry loss = 0.45 velocity pressure for tapered takeoff

NOTE:

Where cradles are used for handling the parts to be ground, polished, or buffed, requiring large partial enclosures to house the complete operation, a minimum average air velocity of 150 ft/min shall be maintained over the entire opening of the enclosure. Swing-frame grinders shall also be exhausted in the same manner as provided for cradles.

CRADLE POLISHING OR GRINDING ENCLOSURE

(b) (3) (ii)

TABLE G-4—GRINDING AND ABRASIVE CUTTING-OFF
WHEELS

Wheel diameter (inches)	Wheel width (inches)	Minimum exhaust volume (feet³/min.)
To 9	1½	220
Over 9 to 16	2	390
Over 16 to 19	3	500
Over 19 to 24	4	610
Over 24 to 30	5	880
Over 30 to 36	6	1,200

GRINDING WHEELS—HOOD AND BRANCH PIPING

NOTE:

Recommended duct velocity is 4,500 ft per minute in branch and 3,500 ft/min in main. For wheels wider than diameters in Table G-4, increase volume by the ratio of the new width to the width shown. Example: If wheel width = 4½ in. then

$$\frac{4.5}{4} \times 610 = 686 \text{ (rounded to 690)}$$

(b) (5) (ii)

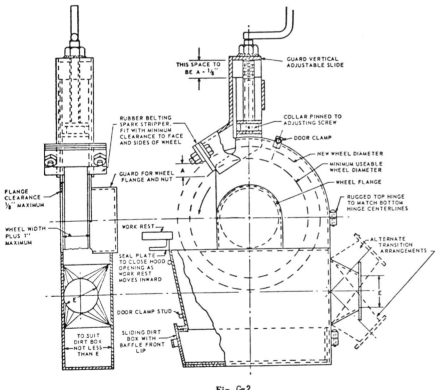

Fig. G-2

Wheel Dimension			Exhaust Outlet, Inches	Volume of Air at 4,500 ft/min
Diameter, Inches		Width, Inches		
Min = d	Max = D	Max	E	
	9	1½	3	220
Over 9	16	2	4	390
Over 16	19	3	4½	500
Over 19	24	4	5	610
Over 24	30	5	6	880
Over 30	36	6	7	1,200

Entry loss = 0.45 velocity pressure for tapered takeoff
0.65 velocity pressure for straight takeoff

STANDARD GRINDER HOOD

(b) (iii)

TABLE G-5—BUFFING AND POLISHING WHEELS

Wheel diameter (inches)	Wheel width (inches)	Minimum exhaust volume (feet³/min.)
To 9	2	300
Over 9 to 16	3	500
Over 16 to 19	4	610
Over 19 to 24	5	740
Over 24 to 30	6	1,040
Over 30 to 36	6	1,200

SCRATCH BRUSH, BUFFING AND POLISHING WHEELS—HOOD AND BRANCH PIPING

(b) (5) (v)

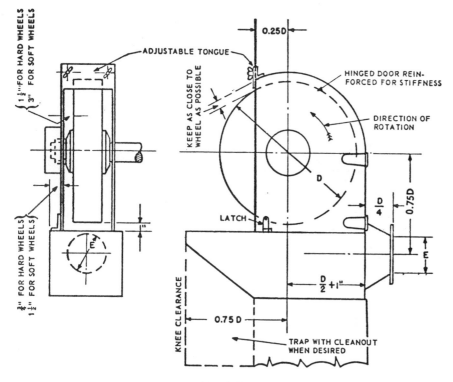

Fig. G-4

Wheel Dimension, Inches			Exhaust Outlet, Inches	Volume of Air at 4,500 ft/min
Diameter		Width		
Min = d	Max = D	Max	E	
	9	2	3½	300
Over 9	16	3	4	500
Over 16	19	4	5	610
Over 19	24	5	5½	740
Over 24	30	6	6½	1,040
Over 30	36	6	7	1,200

Entry loss = 0.15 velocity pressure for tapered takeoff
0.65 velocity pressure for straight takeoff

STANDARD BUFFING AND POLISHING HOOD

(b) (3) (iv)

TABLE G–6—HORIZONTAL SINGLE-SPINDLE DISC GRINDER

	Exhaust volume
Disc diameter (inches) :	(ft. 3/min.)
Up to 12	220
Over 12 to 19	390
Over 19 to 30	610
Over 30 to 36	880

HORIZONTAL SINGLE-SPINDLE DISC GRINDER—HOOD AND BRANCH PIPING

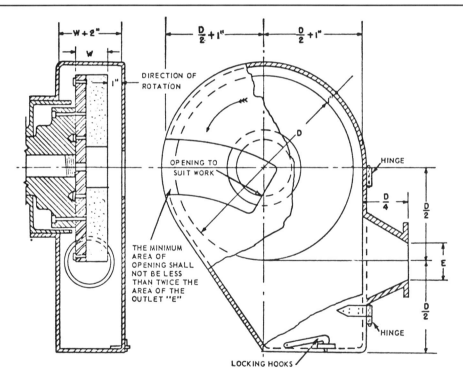

(b) (5) (vii)

Fig. G–6

Dia D. Inches		Exhaust E	Volume Exhausted at 4.500 ft/min
Min	Max	Dia. Inches	ft³/min
	12	3	220
Over 12	19	4	390
Over 19	30	5	610
Over 30	36	6	880

NOTE: If grinding wheels are used for disc grinding purposes, hoods must conform to structural strength and materials as described in 9.1.

Entry loss = 0.45 velocity pressure for tapered takeoff

NOTE:
Provide at least 1 in. space around periphery of wheel for suction. Opening on side of disc must be at least twice the area of the branch outlet.

HORIZONTAL SINGLE-SPINDLE DISC GRINDER EXHAUST HOOD

(b) (3) (v)

TABLE G–7—HORIZONTAL DOUBLE-SPINDLE DISC GRINDER

Disc diameter (inches):	Exhaust volume (ft. 3/min.)
Up to 19	610
Over 19 to 25	880
Over 25 to 30	1,200
Over 30 to 53	1,770
Over 53 to 72	6,280

HORIZONTAL DOUBLE-SPINDLE DISC GRINDER—HOOD AND BRANCH PIPING

(b) (5) (viii)

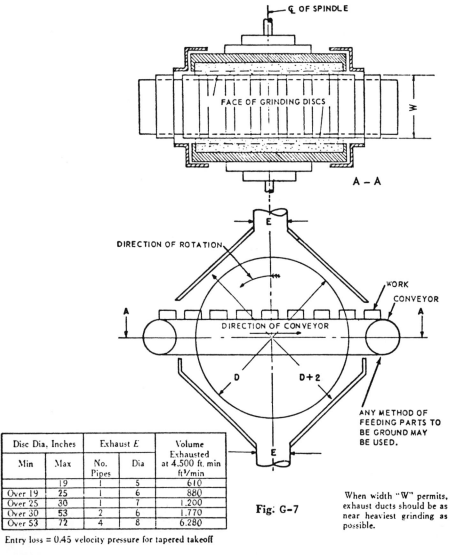

Fig. G-7

Disc Dia, Inches		Exhaust E		Volume Exhausted at 4,500 ft. min ft³/min
Min	Max	No. Pipes	Dia	
	19	1	5	610
Over 19	25	1	6	880
Over 25	30	1	7	1,200
Over 30	53	2	6	1,770
Over 53	72	4	8	6,280

Entry loss = 0.45 velocity pressure for tapered takeoff

When width "W" permits, exhaust ducts should be as near heaviest grinding as possible.

NOTE:
Opening for passing work into grinding chamber shall be at least twice the area of the branch outlets.

HORIZONTAL DOUBLE-SPINDLE DISC GRINDER EXHAUST HOOD

VENTILATION

1910.94

Grinding, Polishing, and Buffing
Operations

TABLE G-8—VERTICAL SPINDLE DISC GRINDER

(b) (3) (vi)

Disc diameter (inches)	One-half or more of disc covered		Disc not covered	
	Number [1]	Exhaust foot³/min.	Number [1]	Exhaust foot³/min.
Up to 20	1	500	2	780
Over 20 to 30	2	780	2	1,480
Over 30 to 53	2	1,770	4	3,530
Over 53 to 72	2	3,140	5	6,010

[1] Number of exhaust outlets around periphery of hood, or equal distribution provided by other means.

**VERTICAL-SPINDLE DISC GRINDER—
HOOD AND BRANCH PIPING**

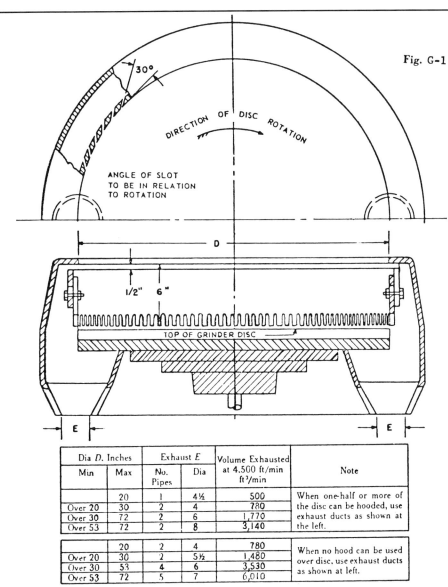

Fig. G-1

(b) (5) (ix)

Dia D. Inches		Exhaust E		Volume Exhausted at 4.500 ft/min ft³/min	Note
Min	Max	No. Pipes	Dia		
	20	1	4½	500	When one-half or more of the disc can be hooded, use exhaust ducts as shown at the left.
Over 20	30	2	4	780	
Over 30	72	2	6	1,770	
Over 53	72	2	8	3,140	

	20	2	4	780	When no hood can be used over disc, use exhaust ducts as shown at left.
Over 20	30	2	5½	1,480	
Over 30	53	4	6	3,530	
Over 53	72	5	7	6,010	

NOTE:
Hood shall be constructed so that heavy dust is drawn off a surface of the disc and the lighter dust exhausted through a continuous slot at the top of the hood.
Entry loss = 1.0 slot velocity pressure + 0.5 branch velocity pressure.
Minimum slot velocity = 2,000 ft/min—½ in. slot width.

VERTICAL-SPINDLE DISC GRINDER EXHAUST HOOD

137

(b) (3) (vii)

TABLE G-9—GRINDING AND POLISHING BELTS

Belts width (inches):	Exhaust volume (ft.³/min.)
Up to 3	220
Over 3 to 5	300
Over 5 to 7	390
Over 7 to 9	500
Over 9 to 11	610
Over 11 to 13	740

GRINDING AND POLISHING BELTS—
HOOD AND BRANCH PIPING

(b) (5) (x)

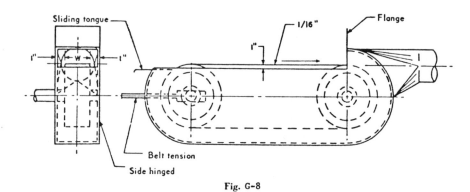

Fig. G-8

Belt Width W, Inches	Exhaust Volume, ft³/min
up to 3	220
3 to 5	300
5 to 7	390
7 to 9	500
9 to 11	610
11 to 13	740

Minimum duct velocity = 4,500 ft/min branch, 3,500 ft/min main
Entry loss = 0.45 velocity pressure for tapered takeoff
0.65 velocity pressure for straight takeoff

NOTE:
Provide 1-in.-wide opening between belt and hood.

A TYPICAL HOOD FOR A BELT OPERATION

(b) (3) (viii)
(b) (5) (iii)

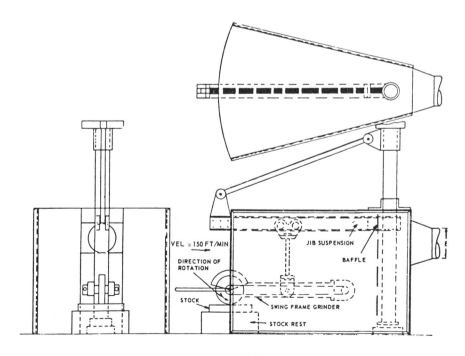

VEL = 150 FT/MIN

DIRECTION OF ROTATION

STOCK

JIB SUSPENSION

BAFFLE

SWING FRAME GRINDER

STOCK REST

Fig. G-3

NOTE:
Where cradles are used for handling the parts to be ground, polished, or buffed, requiring large partial enclosures to house the complete operation, a minimum average air velocity of 150 ft/min shall be maintained over the entire opening of the enclosure. Swing-frame grinders shall also be exhausted in the same manner as provided for cradles. Baffle to reduce front opening as much as possible.

A METHOD OF APPLYING AN EXHAUST ENCLOSURE TO SWING-FRAME GRINDERS

**Design and Construction of
Spray Booths and Spray Rooms**

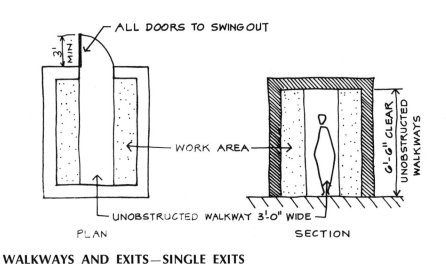

ALL DOORS TO SWING OUT

3' MIN.

WORK AREA

6'-6" CLEAR UNOBSTRUCTED WALKWAYS

UNOBSTRUCTED WALKWAY 3'-0" WIDE

PLAN

SECTION

WALKWAYS AND EXITS—SINGLE EXITS

(c) (3) (i) and (ii)

NOTE:
1. Refer to NFPA 33–1969 and Sec. 1910.107(b).

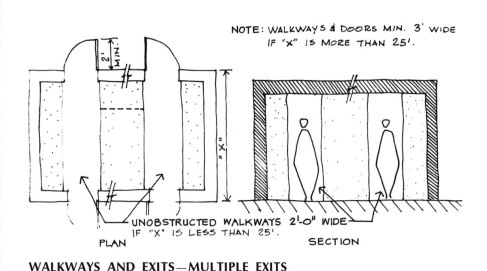

NOTE: WALKWAYS & DOORS MIN. 3' WIDE IF "X" IS MORE THAN 25'.

2' MIN.

"X"

UNOBSTRUCTED WALKWAYS 2'-0" WIDE
IF "X" IS LESS THAN 25'.

PLAN

SECTION

WALKWAYS AND EXITS—MULTIPLE EXITS

(c) (3) (i) and (ii)

NOTE:
1. Refer to NFPA 33–1969 and Sec. 1910.107 (b).

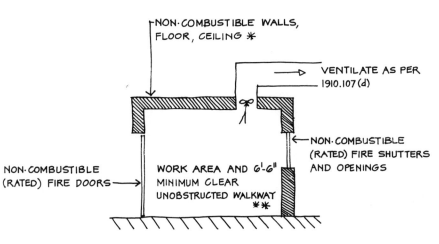

NON-COMBUSTIBLE WALLS, FLOOR, CEILING ✳

VENTILATE AS PER 1910.107 (d)

NON-COMBUSTIBLE (RATED) FIRE SHUTTERS AND OPENINGS

NON-COMBUSTIBLE (RATED) FIRE DOORS

WORK AREA AND 6'-6" MINIMUM CLEAR UNOBSTRUCTED WALKWAY ✳✳

(c) (4) and (c) (5) (i)

NOTE:
✳ Non-combustible to be masonry, concrete, etc.
✳✳ For walkway requirement, conform to Sec. 1910.94(c) (3) (ii).

CONSTRUCTION

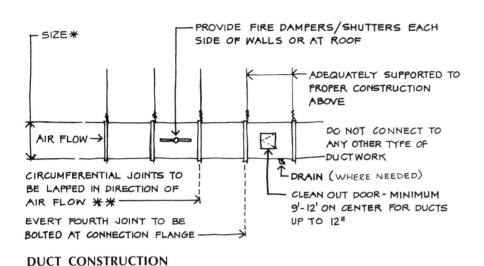

(c) (5) (iii)

SIZE *

PROVIDE FIRE DAMPERS/SHUTTERS EACH SIDE OF WALLS OR AT ROOF

ADEQUATELY SUPPORTED TO PROPER CONSTRUCTION ABOVE

AIR FLOW →

DO NOT CONNECT TO ANY OTHER TYPE OF DUCTWORK

CIRCUMFERENTIAL JOINTS TO BE LAPPED IN DIRECTION OF AIR FLOW **

DRAIN (WHERE NEEDED)

CLEAN OUT DOOR - MINIMUM 9'-12' ON CENTER FOR DUCTS UP TO 12"

EVERY FOURTH JOINT TO BE BOLTED AT CONNECTION FLANGE

DUCT CONSTRUCTION

NOTE:
* Size in accordance with good design practice and American National Standard Z9.2–1960.
** Longitudinal joints to be welded or riveted.
*** See 8.3.21 of ANZ9.1–1951.
Duct gauge sizes:
Up to 8 in.—No. 24
8 in. to 18 in.—No. 22
18 in. to 30 in.—No. 20
Over 30 in.—No. 18

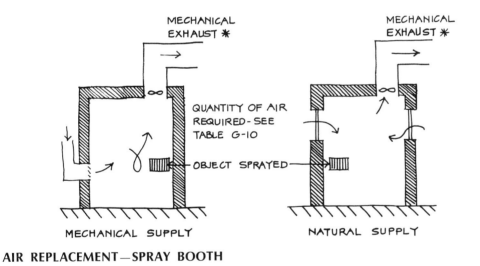

(c) (6) (i), (ii)

MECHANICAL EXHAUST *

MECHANICAL EXHAUST *

QUANTITY OF AIR REQUIRED - SEE TABLE G-10

OBJECT SPRAYED

MECHANICAL SUPPLY

NATURAL SUPPLY

AIR REPLACEMENT—SPRAY BOOTH

NOTE:
*Total air volume exhausted must dilute solvent vapor to 25 percent of lower explosive limit of solvent.

(c) (6) (i)

TABLE G-10 MINIMUM MAINTAINED VELOCITIES INTO SPRAY BOOTHS

Operating conditions for objects completely inside booth	Crossdraft, f.p.m.	Airflow velocities, f.p.m.	
		Design	Range
Electrostatic and automatic airless operation contained in booth without operator.	Negligible	50 large booth	50–75
		100 small booth	75–125
Air-operated guns. manual or automatic	Up to 50	100 large booth	75–125
		150 small booth	125–175
Air-operated guns, manual or automatic	Up to 100	150 large booth	125–175
		200 small booth	150–250

Notes:
   (1) Attention is invited to the fact that the effectiveness of the spray booth is dependent upon the relationship of the depth of the booth to its height and width.
   (2) Crossdrafts can be eliminated through proper design and such design should be sought. Crossdrafts in excess of 100 fpm (feet per minute) should not be permitted.
   (3) Excessive air pressures result in both loss of efficiency and material waste, in addition to creating a backlash that may carry overspray and fumes into adjacent work areas.
   (4) Booths should be designed with velocities shown in the column headed "Design." However, booths operating with velocities shown in the column headed "Range" are in compliance with this standard.

MINIMUM AIR VELOCITY—SPRAY BOOTH

141

TABLE G-12—DETERMINATION OF HAZARD POTENTIAL

Hazard potential	Toxicity group		
	Gas or vapor (p.p.m.)	Mist (m.g./m³)	Flash point (deg. F.)
A	0-10	0-.1	—
B	11-100	.11-1.0	Under 100
C	101-500	1.1-10	100-200
D	Over 500	Over 10	Over 200

TABLE G-13—DETERMINATION OF RATE OF GAS VAPOR OR MIST EVOLUTION

Rate	Liquid temp. °F.	Degrees below boiling point	Relative evaporation	Gassing
1	Over 200	0-20	Fast	High
2	150-200	21-50	Medium	Medium
3	94-149	51-100	Slow	Low
4	Under 94	Over 100	Nil	Nil

DETERMINING HAZARD POTENTIAL AND EVAPORATION

NOTE:

Determine hazard potential and rate of gas, vapor, or mist evolution from Tables G-12 and G-13. (Toxic hazard limits are listed in Sec. 1910.93.) Where ventilation is used to control potential exposures to workers, it shall be adequate to reduce concentration of the air contaminant, so there is no hazard to the worker. (Refer to ANSI Z9.2-1960 for methods on ventilation.)

TABLE G-14—CONTROL VELOCITIES IN FEET PER MINUTE (F.P.M.) FOR UNDISTURBED LOCATIONS

Class (See subparagraph (2) and Table G-12 and G-13)	Enclosing hood (See Subparagraph (4) (ii))		Lateral exhaust [1] (See Subparagraph (4) (iii))	Canopy hood [2] (See Subparagraph (4) (iv))	
	One open side	Two open sides		Three open sides	Four open sides
A-1 and A-2................	100	150	150	Do not use	Do not use
A-3 (Note 2), B-1, B-2, and C-1..	75	100	100	125	175
B-3, C-2, and D-1, (Note 3).....	65	90	75	100	150
A-4 (Note 2), C-3, and D-2..... (Note 3)..................	50	75	50	75	125
B-4, C-4, D-3 (Note 3), and D-4.....................	General room ventilation required.				

[1] See Table G-15 for computation of ventilation rate.
[2] Do not use canopy hood for Hazard Potential A processes.
[3] Where complete control of hot water is desired, design as next highest class.

TABLE G-15—MINIMUM VENTILATION RATE IN CUBIC FEET OF AIR PER MINUTE PER SQUARE FOOT OF TANK AREA FOR LATERAL EXHAUST

Required minimum control velocity, f.p.m. (from Table G-14)	C.f.m. per sq. ft. to maintain required minimum velocities at following ratios (tank width (W)/tank length (L)).[1][2]				
	0.0-0.09	0.1-0.24	0.25-0.49	0.5-0.99	1.0-2.0
Hood along one side of two parallel sides of tank when one hood is against a wall or baffle.[2] Also for a manifold along tank centerline.[3]					
50.............................	50	60	75	90	100
75.............................	75	90	110	130	150
100.............................	100	125	150	175	200
150.............................	150	190	225	260	300
Hood along one side or two parallel sides of free standing tank not against wall or baffle.					
50.............................	75	90	100	110	125
75.............................	110	130	150	170	190
100.............................	150	175	200	225	250
150.............................	225	260	300	340	375

[1] It is not practicable to ventilate across the long dimension of a tank whose ratio $\frac{W}{L}$ exceeds 2.0

It is understandable to do so when $\frac{W}{L}$ exceeds 1.0. For circular tanks with lateral exhaust along up to the circumference, use $W/L = 1.0$; for over one-half the circumference use $W/L = 0.5$.

[2] Baffle is a vertical plate the same length as the tank, and with the top of the plate as high as the tank is wide. If the exhaust hood is on the side of a tank against a building wall or close to it, it is perfectly baffled.

[3] Use $\frac{W}{2}$ as tank width in computing when manifold is along centerline, or when hoods are used on two parallel sides of a tank.

Tank Width (W) means the effective width over which the hood must pull air to operate (for example, where the hood face is set back from the edge of the tank, this set back must be added in measuring tank width). The surface area of tanks can frequently be reduced and better control obtained (particularly on conveyorized systems) by using covers extending from the upper edges of the slots toward the center of the tank.

NOTE:

Control velocities shall conform to Table G-14 in all cases where the flow of air past the breathing or working zone of the operator and into the hoods is undisturbed by local environmental conditions, such as open windows, wall fans, unit heaters, or moving machinery.

All tanks shall be exhausted by means of hood which:

(a) Project over the entire tank;

(b) Are fixed in position in such a location that the head of the workman, in all his normal operating positions while working at the tank, is in front of all hood openings; and

(c) Are completely enclosed on at least two sides, shall be considered to be exhausted through an enclosing hood.

(d) The quantity of air in cubic feet per minute necessary to be exhausted through an enclosing hood shall not be less than the product of the control velocity times the net area of all openings in the enclosure through which air can flow into the hood.

All tanks exhausted by means of hoods which do not project over the entire tank, and in which the direction of air movement into the hood or hoods is substantially horizontal, shall be considered to be laterally exhausted. The quantity of air in cubic feet per minute necessary to be laterally exhausted per square foot of tank area in order to maintain the required control velocity shall be determined from Table G-15 for all variations in ratio of tank width (W) to tank length (L). The total quantity of air in cubic feet per minute required to be exhausted per tank shall be not less than the product of the area of tank surface times the cubic feet per minute per square foot of tank area, determined from Table G-15.

AUTHOR'S NOTE:

Refer to requirements of Sec. 1910.94 for other special conditions. Do not connect two or more operations to same exhaust system where either, or both, may constitute a fire, explosion, or chemical reaction hazard in duct system. Provide traps or other devices so condensate in ducts does not drain back to any tank.

CONTROL REQUIREMENTS

1910.94

Open-Surface Tanks—
Operation and Personal Protection

(d) (8) (iii)

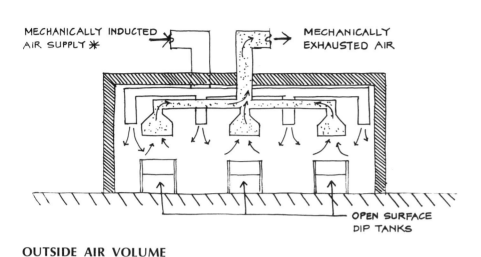

MECHANICALLY INDUCTED
AIR SUPPLY ✱

MECHANICALLY
EXHAUSTED AIR

OPEN SURFACE
DIP TANKS

OUTSIDE AIR VOLUME

NOTE:
 *Minimum quantity of air intake to be equal to 90 percent to 110 percent of total air exhausted. System to be periodically checked.

(d) (9) (vii)

CONTAINER WITH
DANGEROUS LIQUID
OR VAPOR ✱

LOCATE CLOSE TO EACH OTHER

VALVE ✱✱

VACUUM
BREAKER & CHECK

48" OF ¾" MINIMUM
RUBBER HOSE

FLUSHING-WASHING FACILITIES

NOTE:
 * A solution which may burn, irritate, etc.
 **Maximum water pressure, 25 psi of cold water supply.

(d) (9) (x)

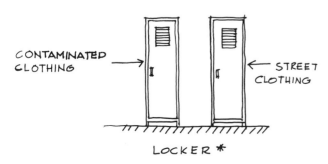

CONTAMINATED
CLOTHING

STREET
CLOTHING

LOCKER ✱

LOCKER FACILITIES

NOTE:
 *Provide locker space or equivalent storage facilities to prevent contamination of street clothing.

(a)

LIMITS FOR PROTECTION

NOTE:
Provide protection against effects of noise when sound levels exceed those in Table G-16 when measured on A scale of a standard sound-level meter at slow response. When noise levels are determined by octave band analysis, the equivalent A-weighted sound level may be determined from the adjacent chart.

(b) (1)

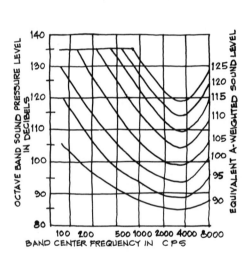

PERMISSIBLE NOISE EXPOSURE

NOTE:
Feasible administrative or engineering controls shall be utilized when employees are subjected to sound levels exceeding those in Table G-16. If such controls fail to reduce sound levels to below those in Table G-16, personal protective equipment shall be provided and used. Exposure to impulsive or impact noise should not exceed 140 dB peak sound pressure level.

(b) (2) and (3)

TABLE G-16:

DURATION PER DAY, HOURS	SOUND LEVEL dBA SLOW RESPONSE
8	90
6	92
4	95
3	97
2	100
1 1/2	102
1	105
1/2	110
1/4 (OR LESS)	115

NOTE:
If the variations in noise level involve maxima at intervals of 1 second or less, it is to be considered continuous.
In all cases where the sound levels exceed the values shown herein, a continuing, effective hearing conservation program shall be administered.

(a) *Definitions applicable to this section.* (1) "Radiation" includes alpha rays, beta rays, gamma rays, X-rays, neutrons, high-speed electrons, high-speed protons, and other atomic particles but such term does not include sound or radio waves, or visible light, or infrared or ultraviolet light.

(2) "Radioactive material" means any material which emits, by spontaneous nuclear disintegration, corpuscular or electromagnetic emanations.

(3) "Restricted area" means any area access to which is controlled by the employer for purposes of protection of individuals from exposure to radiation or radioactive materials.

(4) "Unrestricted area" means any area access to which is not controlled by the employer for purposes of protection of individuals from exposure to radiation or radioactive materials.

(5) "Dose" means the quantity of ionizing radiation absorbed, per unit of mass, by the body or by any portion of the body. When the provisions in this section specify a dose during a period of time, the dose is the total quantity of radiation absorbed, per unit of mass, by the body or by any portion of the body during such period of time. Several different units of dose are in current use. Definitions of units used in this section are set forth in subparagraphs (6) and (7) of this paragraph.

(6) "Rad" means a measure of the dose of any ionizing radiation to body tissues in terms of the energy absorbed per unit of mass of the tissue. One rad is the dose corresponding to the absorption of 100 ergs per gram of tissue (1 millirad (mrad) = 0.001 rad).

(7) "Rem" means a measure of the dose of any ionizing radiation to body tissue in terms of its estimated biological effect relative to a dose of 1 roentgen (r) of X-rays (1 millirem (mrem) = 0.001 rem). The relation of the rem to other dose units depends upon the biological effect under consideration and upon the conditions for irradiation. Each of the following is considered to be equivalent to a dose of 1 rem:

(i) A dose of 1 rad due to X- or gamma radiation;

(ii) A dose of 1 rad due to X-, gamma, or beta radiation;

(iii) A dose of 0.1 rad due to neutrons or high-energy protons;

(iv) A dose of 0.05 rad due to particles heavier than protons and with sufficient energy to reach the lens of the eye.

(b) *Exposure of individuals to radiation in restricted areas.* (1) Except as provided in subparagraph (2) of this paragraph, no employer shall possess, use, or transfer sources of ionizing radiation in such a manner as to cause any individual in a restricted area to receive in any period of one calendar quarter from sources in the employer's possession or control a dose in excess of the limits specified in Table G-18:

TABLE G-18

	Rems per calendar quarter
Whole body: Head and trunk; active blood-forming organs; lens of eyes; or gonads	1¼
Hands and forearms; feet and ankles	18¾
Skin of whole body	7½

NOTE:

Data appearing here are partial and incomplete. Refer to full text of Sec. 1910.96 for details on measuring neutron flux, dosages, exposure, exceptions, etc.

EXPOSURE TO RADIATION IN RESTRICTED AREAS

(c) *Exposure to airborne radioactive material.* (1) No employer shall possess, use, or transport radioactive material in such a manner as to cause any employee, within a restricted area, to be exposed to airborne radioactive material in an average concentration in excess of the limits specified in Table 1 of Appendix B to 10 CFR Part 20. The limits given in Table 1 are for exposure to the concentrations specified for 40 hours in any workweek of 7 consecutive days. In any such period where the number of hours of exposure is less than 40, the limits specified in the table may be increased proportionately. In any such period where the number of hours of exposure is greater than 40, the limits specified in the table shall be decreased proportionately.

(2) No employer shall possess, use, or transfer radioactive material in such a manner as to cause any individual within a restricted area, who is under 18 years of age, to be exposed to airborne radioactive material in an average concentration in excess of the limit specified in Table II of Appendix B to 10 CFR Part 20. For purposes of this subparagraph, concentrations may be averaged over periods not greater than 1 week.

(3) "Exposed" as used in this paragraph means that the individual is present in an airborne concentration. No allowance shall be made for the use of protective clothing or equipment, or particle size.

EXPOSURE TO AIRBORNE RADIOACTIVE MATERIAL

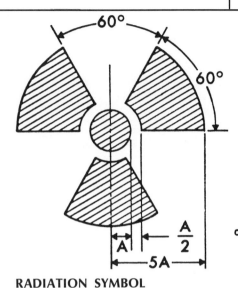

-60°-
60°

$\frac{A}{2}$

A

5A

RADIATION SYMBOL

1. Cross-hatched area is to be magenta or purple.
2. Background is to be yellow.

(e) (1)

NOTE:
Also see Sec. 1910.145 for additional data on radiation warning signs.

(e) (2), (3), (4), and (5)

**CAUTION
RADIATION AREA**

**CAUTION
HIGH RADIATION AREA**

**CAUTION
AIRBORNE RADIOACTIVITY AREA**

**CAUTION
RADIOACTIVE MATERIALS**

NOTE:
Each radioactive area shall be marked with radiation symbol and appropriate words.

"Radiation area" means any area, accessible to personnel, in which there exists radiation at such levels that a major portion of the body could receive in any 1 hour a dose in excess of 5 millirem, or in any 5 consecutive days a dose in excess of 100 millirem; and

"High radiation area" means any area, accessible to personnel, in which there exists radiation at such levels that a major portion of the body could receive in any one hour a dose in excess of 100 millirem.

"Airborne radioactivity area" means:

(a) Any room, enclosure, or operating area in which airborne radioactive materials, composed wholly or partly of radioactive material, exist in concentrations in excess of the amounts specified in column 1 of Table 1 of Appendix B to 10 CFR Part 20 or

(b) Any room, enclosure, or operating area in which airborne radioactive materials exist in concentrations which, averaged over the number of hours in any week during which individuals are in the area, exceed 25 percent of the amounts specified in column 1 of Table 1 of Appendix B to 10 CFR Part 20.

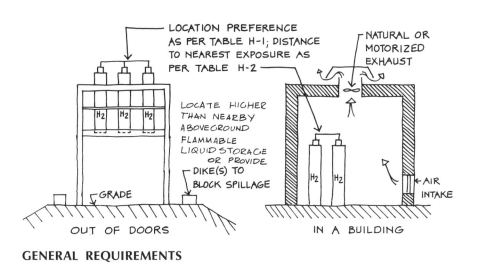

GENERAL REQUIREMENTS

(b) (2) (i), (ii) (a), (b), and (c)

NOTE:
1. Do not locate under electric lines or near flammable-liquid piping or piping of other flammable gases.
2. Distances in Table H-2, items 1, 14, 3 through 10 inclusive, do not apply if fire walls or protective structures are between the system and the exposure.

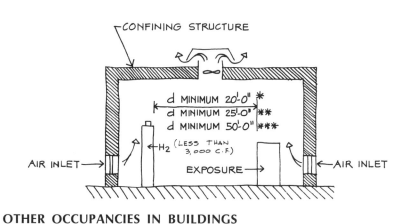

OTHER OCCUPANCIES IN BUILDINGS

(b) (2) (ii) (d) (2) through (6)

NOTE:
* At stored flammable materials or oxidizing liquids.
** At open flames, ordinary electrical equipment or sources of ignition, concentrations of people.
*** At intakes of ventilating or air-conditioning equipment, compressors, flammable gas storage.

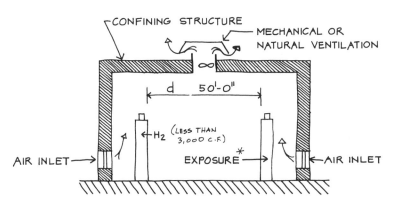

OTHER OCCUPANCIES IN BUILDINGS

(b) (2) (ii) (d) (1), (7), (8)

NOTE:
1. Protect H_2 system against falling objects or work activity.
* More than one system of 3,000 cu ft or less.

147

(b) (2) (ii) (a)

TABLE H-1

Nature of location	Size of hydrogen system		
	Less than 3,000 CF	3,000 CF to 15,000 CF	In excess of 15,000 CF
Outdoors	I	I	I.
In a separate building	II	II	II.
In a special room	III	III	Not permitted.
Inside buildings not in a special room and exposed to other occupancies.	IV	Not permitted.	Not permitted.

LOCATION

NOTE:
Locate in the order of preference indicated by Roman numerals in Table H-1.

(b) (2) (ii) (b)

TABLE H-2

Type of outdoor exposure		Size of hydrogen system		
		Less than 3,000 CF	3,000 CF to 15,000 CF	In excess of 15,000 CF
1. Building or structure	Wood frame construction*	10	25	50
	Heavy timber, noncombustible or ordinary construction*	0	10	**25
	Fire-resistive construction*	0	0	0
2. Wall openings	Not above any part of a system	10	10	10
	Above any part of a system	25	25	25
3. Flammable liquids above ground.	0 to 1,000 gallons	10	25	25
	In excess of 1,000 gallons	25	50	50
4. Flammable liquids below ground— 0 to 1,000 gallons.	Tank	10	10	10
	Vent or fill opening of tank	25	25	25
5. Flammable liquids below ground— in excess of 1,000 gallons.	Tank	20	20	20
	Vent or fill opening of tank	25	25	25
6. Flammable gas storage, either high pressure or low pressure.	0 to 15,000 CF capacity	10	25	25
	In excess of 15,000 CF capacity	25	50	50
7. Oxygen storage	12,000 CF or less	Refer to NFPA No. 51, gas systems for welding and cutting (1969).		
	More than 12,000 CF	Refer to NFPA No. 566, bulk oxygen systems at consumer sites (1969).		
8. Fast burning solids such as ordinary lumber, excelsior or paper		50	50	50
9. Slow burning solids such as heavy timber or coal		25	25	25
10. Open flames and other sources of ignition		25	25	25
11. Air compressor intakes or inlets to ventilating or air-conditioning equipment		50	50	50
12. Concentration of people***		25	50	50
13. Public sidewalks		15	15	15
14. Line of adjoining property which may be built upon		5	5	5

*Refer to NFPA No. 220 Standard Types of Building Construction for definitions of various types of construction. (1969 Ed.)
**But not less than one-half the height of adjacent side wall of the structure.
***In congested areas such as offices, lunchrooms, locker rooms, time-clock areas, and places of public assembly

NOTE:
Table H-2 shows the minimum distance in feet from hydrogen systems located outdoors, in separate buildings, or in special rooms to any outdoor exposure. The distances shown for items 1, 14, and 3 to 10 inclusive do not apply where protective structures such as adequate fire walls are located between the system and the exposure.

LOCATION—DISTANCE TO EXPOSURE

(b) (3) (i)

NON-COMBUSTIBLE PROTECTIVE ROOF *

VENTILATION OPENING

NON-COMBUSTIBLE PROTECTIVE WALL(S)*

HYDROGEN SYSTEM AS PER TABLE H-2

OUTDOOR LOCATIONS

NOTE:
* Where provided,
1. Electrical equipment within 15 ft 0 in. shall conform to Subpart (S) for Class I, Division 2 locations.

(b) (3) (ii)

MECHANICAL OR NATURAL VENTILATION *

EXPLOSION VENTING AT EXTERIOR WALL OR ROOF **

NON-COMBUSTIBLE FLOOR, WALL & ROOF CONSTRUCTION

AIR INLET NEAR FLOOR

H_2

LOCATE DOORS & WINDOWS FOR EASY ACCESS

HEATING (IF PROVIDED) TO BE INDIRECT STEAM OR HOT WATER

SEPARATE BUILDINGS

NOTE:
* Provide 1 sq ft of air inlet opening per 1,000 cu ft of room volume.
** Provide 1 sq ft of venting per 30 cu ft of room volume.
1. No source of ignition flame, electrical equipment, or heating equipment within building/storage area.

(b) (3) (iii)

FLOOR, WALLS & CEILINGS: 2 HOUR RATED CONSTRUCTION MINIMUM

VENTILATE AS PER 1910.103 (b)(3)(ii)

MINIMUM ONE EXTERIOR WALL REQUIRED

CONTINUOUS FLOOR TO CEILING WITH NO OPENINGS

H_2

EXTERIOR BUILDING WALL, WINDOWS AND DOORS AS PER 1910.103 (b)(3)(ii)

VENTILATION INLET NEAR FLOOR ONLY

SPECIAL ROOMS

NOTE:
1. Provide explosion venting as per Sec. 1910.103 (b) (3) (ii).
2. Heating to be as per Sec. 1910.103 (b) (3) (ii).
3. Electrical equipment as per Article 501 of the National Electrical Code, NFPA 70–1971, ANSI C1-1971 (Rev. 1968) for Class I, Division 2 locations.

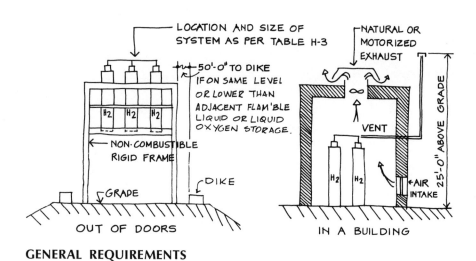

GENERAL REQUIREMENTS

(c) (2) (i)

NOTE:
1. Do not expose to electric power lines, flammable liquid lines, flammable gas lines, or lines carrying oxidizing materials.
2. Locate readily accessible to mobile equipment and authorized personnel.
3. Storage sites to be fenced and have warning signs posted: "Liquefied Hydrogen —Flammable Gas—No Smoking—No Open Flames."

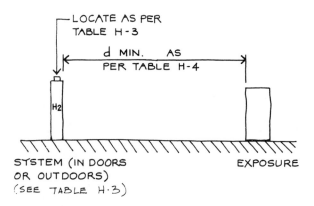

SPECIFIC REQUIREMENTS

(c) (2) (ii)

NOTE:
*Distances in Table H-4 do not apply if fire walls or protecting structures are between the system and the exposure.

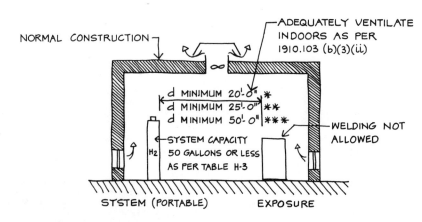

INSIDE MULTI-USE BUILDINGS OR EXPOSED TO OTHER OCCUPANCIES

(c) (2) (iii)

NOTE:
*At flammable liquids and readily combustible materials such as excelsior or paper.
**At ordinary electrical equipment and other sources of ignition (i.e., process equipment), concentrations of people.
***At ventilation and air-conditioning equipment, intake of compressors, flammable gases, oxidizing gases:
1. Protect containers from damage or work activity.

(c) (2) (ii) (a)

TABLE H-3—MAXIMUM TOTAL QUANTITY OF LIQUEFIED HYDROGEN STORAGE PERMITTED

Nature of location	Size of hydrogen storage (capacity in gallons)			
	39.63 (150 liters) to 50	51 to 300	301 to 600	In excess of 600
Outdoors	I	I	I	I.
In a separate building	II	II	II	Not permitted.
In a special room	III	III	Not permitted	Not permitted.
Inside buildings not in a special room and exposed to other occupancies.	IV	Not permitted	Not permitted	Not permitted.

NOTE: This table does not apply to the storage in dewars of the type generally used in laboratories for experimenta purposes.

LOCATION

NOTE:
Locate in the order of preference as indicated by Roman numerals in Table H-3.

(c) (2) (ii) (b)

TABLE H-4—MINIMUM DISTANCE (FEET) FROM LIQUEFIED HYDROGEN SYSTEMS TO EXPOSURE

Type of exposure	Liquefied hydrogen storage (capacity in gallons)		
	39.63 (150 liters) to 3,500	3,501 to 15,000	15,001 to 30,000
1. Fire-resistive building and fire walls*	5	5	5
2. Noncombustible building*	25	50	75
3. Other buildings*	50	75	100
4. Wall openings, air-compressor intakes, inlets for air-conditioning or ventilating equipment	75	75	75
5. Flammable liquids (above ground and vent or fill openings if below ground) (see 513 and 514)	50	75	100
6. Between stationary liquefied hydrogen containers	5	5	5
7. Flammable gas storage	50	75	100
8. Liquid oxygen storage and other oxidizers (see 513 and 514)	100	100	100
9. Combustible solids	50	75	100
10. Open flames, smoking, and welding	50	50	50
11. Concentrations of people†	75	75	75
12. Public ways, railroads, and property lines	25	50	75

*Refer to standard types of building construction, NFPA No. 220-1969 for definitions of various types of construction.
†In congested areas such as offices, lunchrooms, locker rooms, time-clock areas, and places of public assembly.

NOTE 1: The distance in Nos. 2, 3, 5, 7, 9, and 12 in Table H-4 may be reduced where protective structures, such as firewalls equal to height of top of the container, to safeguard the liquefied hydrogen storage system, are located between the liquefied hydrogen storage installation and the exposure.

NOTE 2: Where protective structures are provided, ventilation and confinement of product should be considered. The 5-foot distance in Nos. 1 and 6 facilitates maintenance and enhances ventilation.

NOTE:
Table H-4 shows the minimum distance in feet from liquefied hydrogen systems located outdoors, in a separate building, or in a special room to any specified exposure.

LOCATION—DISTANCE TO EXPOSURE

Liquefied—Design Considerations at Specific Locations

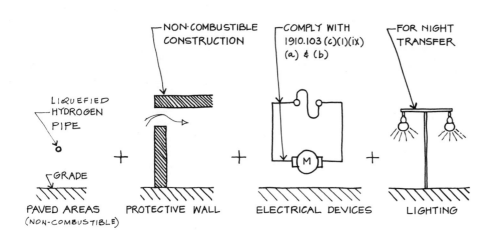

(c) (3) (i)

OUTDOOR LOCATION

NOTE:
1. At outdoor location, maximum number of walls at right angles is to be two.
2. Paved areas to be of non-combustible construction.

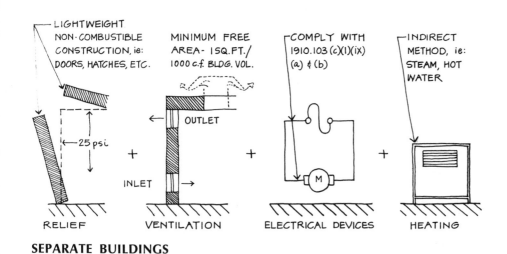

(c) (3) (ii)

SEPARATE BUILDINGS

NOTE:
1. Locate doors and windows so they are easily accessible.
2. Relief elements to be shatterproof and in safe location.

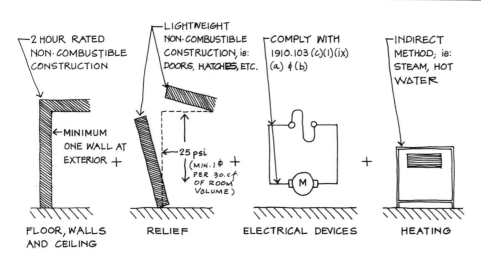

(c) (3) (iii)

SPECIAL ROOMS

NOTE:
1. Ventilate as per Sec. 1910.103 (c) (3) (ii).
2. No sources of ignition allowed.

(a), (b) (1)

NOTE:
This section applies to bulk oxygen systems (storage capacity of more than 13,000 cu ft of oxygen connected or ready for service, or 25,000 cu ft of oxygen including unconnected reserves on hand at site) on industrial and institutional consumer premises. Excluded from section: oxygen manufacturing plants, suppliers' areas for storing or refilling portable containers, trailers, mobile supply trucks, or smaller systems than noted above.

GENERAL

(b) (3) (v through ix)

FROM FLAMMABLE LIQUID STORAGE ABOVEGROUND :

Distance (feet)	Capacity (gallons)
50	0–1000
90	1001 or more

FROM FLAMMABLE LIQUID STORAGE BELOWGROUND :

Distance measured horizontally from oxygen storage container to flammable liquid tank (feet)	Distance from oxygen storage container to filling and vent connections or openings to flammable liquid tank (feet)	Capacity (gallons)
15	50	0–1000
30	50	1001 or more

FROM COMBUSTIBLE LIQUID STORAGE ABOVEGROUND :

Distance (feet)	Capacity (gallons)
25	0–1000
50	1001 or more

FROM COMBUSTIBLE LIQUID STORAGE BELOWGROUND :

Distance measured horizontally from oxygen storage container to combustible liquid tank (feet)	Distance from oxygen storage container to filling and vent connections or openings to combustible liquid tank (feet)
15	40

FROM FLAMMABLE GAS STORAGE :

(Such as compressed flammable gases, liquefied flammable gases and flammable gases in low pressure gas holders):

Distance (feet)	Capacity (cu. ft. NTP)
50	Less than 5000
90	5000 or more

NOTE:
Minimum distances from any bulk oxygen container to exposures listed shall be as indicated.

DISTANCES FROM HAZARDOUS MATERIALS

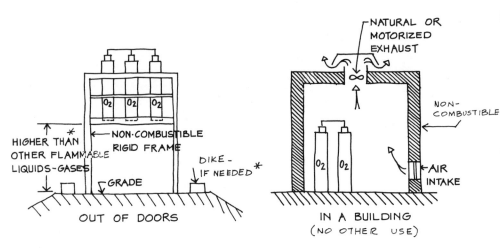

LOCATION

NOTE:
1. Do not expose to power lines, flammable or combustible liquid or gas lines.
2. Locate so the system is easily accessible to mobile equipment and authorized personnel.
3. Paved areas under liquid oxygen containers to be non-combustible.

*At locations near aboveground flammable liquid storage, locate on higher ground or provide dikes.

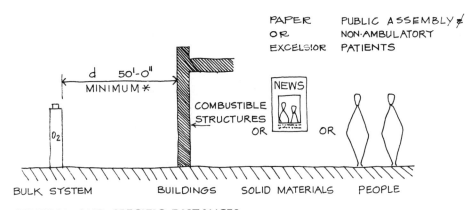

GENERAL AND SPECIFIC DISTANCES

(b) (3) (i), (ii), (x), (xiv), (xv), and (xviii)

NOTE:
1. d minimum is the most direct line except for Sec. 1910.104 (b) (vi) and (viii).
2. d minimum may be reduced to 1 ft 0 in. if a fire-rated structure of adequate height is installed between the system and the exposure.

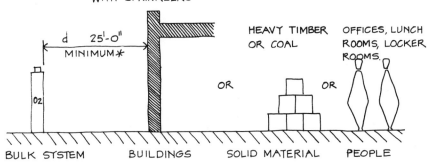

SPECIFIC DISTANCES

(b) (3) (iii), (xi), and (xiii)

NOTE:
* At fire-resistant structures, slow-burning materials, congested areas.
Permitted exception:
See Note 2 under (b) (3) (xviii) above.

154

(b) (3) (iv) and (xvi)

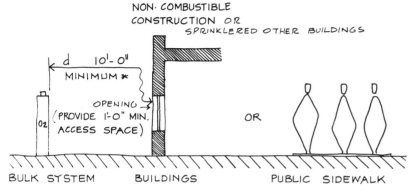

SPECIFIC DISTANCES

NOTE:
* At openings in adjacent buildings or public sidewalks.
  Permitted exception:
  See Note 2 under (b) (3) (xviii).

(b) (3) (xvii)

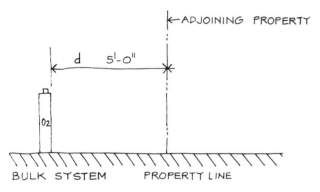

SPECIFIC DISTANCE—ADJACENT PROPERTIES

NOTE:
* At property line of adjoining property, d minimum may be affected by existing construction location on adjacent property.
  Permitted exception:
  See Note 2 under (b) (3) (xviii).

(b) (3) (xvii)

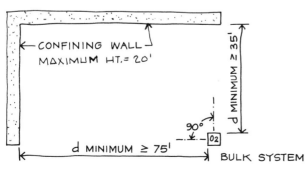

PLAN

SPECIFIC DISTANCE—VENTILATION AT COURTYARDS

(a) *Definitions as used in this section:*

(1) Aerosol shall mean a material which is dispensed from its container as a mist, spray, or foam by a propellant under pressure.

(2) Atmospheric tank shall mean a storage tank which has been designed to operate at pressures from atmospheric through 0.5 psig.

(3) Automotive service station shall mean that portion of property where flammable or combustible liquids used as motor fuels are stored and dispensed from fixed equipment into the fuel tanks of motor vehicles and shall include any facilities available for the sale and service of tires, batteries, and accessories, and for minor automotive maintenance work. Major automotive repairs, painting, body and fender work are excluded.

(4) Basement shall mean a story of a building or structure having one-half or more of its height below ground level and to which access for fire fighting purposes is unduly restricted.

(5) Boiling point shall mean the boiling point of a liquid at a pressure of 14.7 lb per sq in. absolute (psia) (760 mm). Where an accurate boiling point is unavailable for the material in question, or for mixtures which do not have a constant boiling point, for purposes of this section the 10 percent point of a distillation performed in accordance with the Standard Method of Test for Distillation of Petroleum Products, ASTM D-86-62, may be used as the boiling point of the liquid.

(6) Boilover shall mean the expulsion of crude oil (or certain other liquids) from a burning tank. The light fractions of the crude oil burn-off producing a heat wave in the residue, which on reaching a water strata may result in the expulsion of a portion of the contents of the tank in the form of froth.

(7) Bulk plant shall mean that portion of a property where flammable or combustible liquids are received by tank vessel, pipelines, tank car, or tank vehicle, and are stored or blended in bulk for the purpose of distributing such liquids by tank vessel, pipeline, tank car, tank vehicle, or container.

(8) Chemical plant shall mean a large integrated plant or that portion of such a plant other than a refinery or distillery where flammable or combustible liquids are produced by chemical reactions or used in chemical reactions.

(9) Closed container shall mean a container as herein defined, so sealed by means of a lid or other device that neither liquid nor vapor will escape from it at ordinary temperatures.

(10) Crude petroleum shall mean hydrocarbon mixtures that have a flash point below 150°F and which have not been processed in a refinery.

(11) Distillery shall mean a plant or that portion of a plant where flammable or combustible liquids produced by fermentation are concentrated, and where the concentrated products may also be mixed, stored, or packaged.

(12) Fire area shall mean an area of a building separated from the remainder of the building by construction having a fire resistance of at least 1 hour and having all communicating openings properly protected by an assembly having a fire resistance rating of at least 1 hour.

(13) Flammable aerosol shall mean an aerosol which is required to be labeled "Flammable" under the Federal Hazardous Substances Labeling Act (15 U.S.C. 1261). For the purposes of paragraph (d) of this section, such aerosols are considered Class IA liquids.

(14) "Flashpoint" means the minimum temperature at which a liquid gives off vapor within a test vessel in sufficient concentration to form an ignitable mixture with air near the surface of the liquid, and shall be determined as follows:

(i) For a liquid which has a viscosity of less than 45 SUS at 100°F. (37.8°C.), does not contain suspended solids, and does not have a tendency to form a surface film while under test, the procedure specified in the Standard Method of Test for Flashpoint by Tag Closed Tester (ASTM D-56-70) shall be used.

(ii) For a liquid which has a viscosity of 45 SUS or more at 100°F. (37.8°C.), or contains suspended solids, or has a tendency to form a surface film while under test, the Standard Method of Test for Flashpoint by Pensky-Martens Closed Tester (ASTM D-93-71) shall be used, except that the methods specified in Note 1 to section 1.1. of ASTM D-93-71 may be used for the respective materials specified in the Note.

(iii) For a liquid that is a mixture of compounds that have different volatilities and flashpoints, its flashpoint shall be determined by using the procedure specified in paragraph (a) (14) (i) or (ii) of this section on the liquid in the form it is shipped. If the flashpoint, as determined by this test, is 100°F. (37.8°C.) or higher, an additional flashpoint determination shall be run on a sample of the liquid evaporated to 90 percent of its original volume, and the lower value of the two tests shall be considered the flashpoint of the material.

(iv) Organic peroxides, which undergo auto-accelerating thermal decomposition, are excluded from any of the flashpoint determination methods specified in this subparagraph.

(15) Hotel shall mean buildings or groups of buildings under the same management in which there are sleeping accommodations for hire, primarily used by transients who are lodged with or without meals including but not limited to inns, clubs, motels, and apartment hotels.

(16) Institutional occupancy shall mean the occupancy or use of a building or structure or any portion thereof by persons harbored or detained to receive medical, charitable or other care or treatment, or by persons involuntarily detained.

(17) Liquid shall mean, for the purpose of this section, any material which has a fluidity greater than that of 300 penetration asphalt when tested in accordance with ASTM Test for Penetration for Bituminous Materials, D-5-65. When not otherwise identified, the term liquid shall include both flammable and combustible liquids.

(18) "Combustible liquid" means any liquid having a flashpoint at or above 100°F. (37.8°C.). Combustible liquids shall be divided into two classes as follows:

(i) "Class II liquids" shall include those with flashpoints at or above 100°F. (37.8°C.) and below 140°F. (60°C.), except any mixture having components with flashpoints of 200°F. (93.3°C.) or higher, the volume of which make up 99 percent or more of the total volume of the mixture.

(ii) "Class III liquids" shall include those with flashpoints at or above 140°F. (60°C.). Class III liquids are subdivided into two subclasses:

(a) "Class IIIA liquids" shall include those with flashpoints at or above 140°F. (60°C.) and below 200°F. (93.3°C.), except any mixture having components with flashpoints of 200°F. (93.3°C.), or higher, the total volume of which make up 99 percent or more of the total volume of the mixture.

(b) "Class IIIB liquids" shall include those with flashpoints at or above 200°F. (93.3°C.). This section does not cover Class IIIB liquids. Where the term "Class III liquids" is used in this section, it shall mean only Class IIIA liquids.

(iii) When a combustible liquid is heated for use to within 30°F. (16.7°C.) of its flashpoint, it shall be handled in accordance with the requirements for the next lower class of liquids.

(19) "Flammable liquid" means any liquid having a flashpoint below 100°F. (37.8°C.), except any mixture having components with flashpoints of 100°F. (37.8°C.) or higher, the total of which make up 99 percent or more of the total volume of the mixture. Flammable liquids shall be known as Class I liquids. Class I liquids are divided into three classes as follows:

(i) Class IA shall include liquids having flashpoints below 73°F. (22.8°C.) and having a boiling point below 100°F. (37.8°C.).

(ii) Class IB shall include liquids having flashpoints below 73°F. (22.8°C.) and having a boiling point at or above 100°F. (37.8°C.).

(iii) Class IC shall include liquids having flashpoints at or above 73°F. (22.8°C.) and below 100°F. (37.8°C.).

(20) Unstable (reactive) liquid shall mean a liquid which in the pure state or as commercially produced or transported will vigorously polymerize, decompose, condense, or will become self-reactive under conditions of shocks, pressure, or temperature.

(21) Low-pressure tank shall mean a storage tank which has been designed to operate at pressures above 0.5 psig but not more than 15 psig.

(22) Marine service station shall mean that portion of a property where flammable or combustible liquids used as fuels are stored and dispensed from fixed equipment on shore, piers, wharves, or floating docks into the fuel tanks of self-propelled craft, and shall include all facilities used in connection therewith.

(23) Mercantile occupancy shall mean the occupancy or use of a building or structure or any portion thereof for the displaying, selling, or buying of goods, wares, or merchandise.

(24) Office occupancy shall mean the occupancy or use of a building or structure or any portion thereof for the transaction of business, or the rendering or receiving of professional services.

(25) Portable tank shall mean a closed container having a liquid capacity over 60 U.S. gallons not intended for fixed installation.

(26) Pressure vessel shall mean a storage tank or vessel which has been designed to operate at pressures above 15 psig.

(27) Protection for exposure shall mean adequate fire protection for structures on property adjacent to tanks, where there are employees of the establishment.

(28) Refinery shall mean a plant in which flammable or combustible liquids are produced on a commercial scale from crude petroleum, natural gasoline, or other hydrocarbon sources.

(29) Safety can shall mean an approved container, of not more than 5 gallons capacity, having a spring-closing lid and spout cover and so designed that it will safely relieve internal pressure when subjected to fire exposure.

(30) Vapor pressure shall mean the pressure, measured in pounds per square inch (absolute) exerted by a volatile liquid as determined by the "Standard Method of Test for Vapor Pressure of Petroleum Products (Reid Method)," American Society for Testing and Materials ASTM D323-68.

(31) Ventilation as specified in this section is for the prevention of fire and explosion. It is considered adequate if it is sufficient to prevent accumulation of significant quantities of vapor-air mixtures in concentration over one-fourth of the lower flammable limit.

(32) Storage: Flammable or combustible liquids shall be stored in a tank or in a container that complies with paragraph (d)(2) of this section.

(33) Barrel shall mean a volume of 42 U.S. gallons.

(34) Container shall mean any can, barrel, or drum.

(35) Approved unless otherwise indicated, approved, or listed by at least one of the following nationally recognized testing laboratories: Underwriters' Laboratories, Inc.; Factory Mutual Engineering Corp.

(36) Listed: See "approved" in Sec. 1910.106(a) (35).

(j) *Scope:*
This section applies to the handling, storage, and use of flammable and combustible liquids with a flashpoint below 200°F. This section does not apply to:

(1) Bulk transportation of flammable and combustible liquids;

(2) Storage, handling, and use of fuel oil tanks and containers connected with oil burning equipment;

(3) Storage of flammable and combustible liquids on farms;

(4) Liquids without flashpoints that may be flammable under some conditions, such as certain halogenated hydrocarbons and mixtures containing halogenated hydrocarbons;

(5) Mists, sprays, or foams, except flammable aerosols covered in paragraph (d) of this section; or

(6) Installations made in accordance with requirements of the following standards:

(i) National Fire Protection Association Standard for Drycleaning Plants, NFPA No. 32-1970;

(ii) National Fire Protection Association Standard for the Manufacture of Organic Coatings, NFPA No. 35-1970;

(iii) National Fire Protection Association Standard for Solvent Extraction Plants, NFPA No. 36-1967; or

(iv) National Fire Protection Association Standard for the Installation and Use of Stationary Combustion Engines and Gas Turbines, NFPA No. 37-1970.

(b) (2) (i) (a) and (b)

TABLE H-5

Type of tank	Protection	Minimum distance in feet from property line which may be built upon, including the opposite side of a public way	Minimum distance in feet from nearest side of any public way or from nearest important building and shall be not less than 5 feet
Floating roof	Protection for exposures.	½ times diameter of tank but need not exceed 90 ft.	⅙ times diameter of tank but need not exceed 30 ft.
	None	Diameter of tank but need not exceed 175 ft.	⅙ times diameter of tank but need not exceed 30 ft.
Vertical with weak roof to shell seam.	Approved foam or inerting system on the tank.	½ times diameter of tank but need not exceed 90 ft. and shall not be less than 5 ft.	⅙ times diameter of tank but need not exceed 30 ft.
	Protection for exposures.	Diameter of tank but, need not exceed 175 ft.	⅓ times diameter of tank but need not exceed 60 ft.
	None	2 times diameter of tank but need not exceed 350 ft.	⅓ times diameter of tank but need not exceed 60 ft.
Horizontal and vertical, with emergency relief venting to limit pressures to 2.5 p.s.i.g.	Approved inerting system on the tank or approved foam system on vertical tanks.	½ times Table H-9 but shall not be less than 5 ft.	½ times Table H-9.
	Protection for exposures.	Table H-9	Table H-9.
	None	2 times Table H-9	Table H-9.

TABLE H-6

Type of tank	Protection	Minimum distance in feet from property line which may be built upon, including the opposite side of a public way	Minimum distance in feet from nearest side of any public way or from nearest important building
Any type	Protection for exposures.	1½ times Table H-9 but shall not be less than 25 ft.	1½ times Table H-9 but shall not be less than 25 ft.
	None	3 times Table H-9 but shall not be less than 50 ft.	1½ times Table H-9 but shall not be less than 25 ft.

LOCATION OF OUTSIDE ABOVEGROUND TANKS

NOTE:

Every aboveground tank for the storage of flammable or combustible liquids, except those liquids with boilover characteristics and unstable liquids, operating at pressures not in excess of 2.5 psig and equipped with emergency venting which will not permit pressures to exceed 2.5 psig shall be located in accordance with Table H-5.

Every aboveground tank for the storage of flammable or combustible liquids, except those liquids with boilover characteristics and unstable flammable or combustible liquids, operating at pressures exceeding 2.5 psig or equipped with emergency venting which will permit pressures to exceed 2.5 psig shall be located in accordance with Table H-6.

(b) (2) (i) (c)

TABLE H-7

Type of tank	Protection	Minimum distance in feet from property line which may be built upon, including the opposite side of a public way	Minimum distance in feet from nearest side of any public way or from nearest important building
Floating roof	Protection for exposures.	Diameter of tank but need not exceed 175 ft.	⅓ times diameter of tank but need not exceed 60 ft.
	None	2 times diameter of tank but need not exceed 350 ft.	⅓ times diameter of tank but need not exceed 60 ft.
Fixed roof	Approved foam or inerting system.	Diameter of tank but need not exceed 175 ft.	⅓ times diameter of tank but need not exceed 60 ft.
	Protection for exposures.	2 times diameter of tank but need not exceed 350 ft.	⅔ times diameter of tank but need not exceed 120 ft.
	None	4 times diameter of tank but need not exceed 350 ft.	⅔ times diameter of tank but need not exceed 120 ft.

NOTE:

Every aboveground tank for the storage of flammable or combustible liquids with boilover characteristics shall be located in accordance with Table H-7.

LOCATION OF OUTSIDE ABOVEGROUND TANKS

TABLE H-8

Type of tank	Protection	Minimum distance in feet from property line which may be built upon, including the opposite side of a public way	Minimum distance in feet from nearest side of any public way or from nearest important building
Horizontal and vertical tanks with emergency relief venting to permit pressure not in excess of 2.5 p.s.i.g.	Tank protected with any one of the following: Approved water spray, approved inerting, approved insulation and refrigeration, approved barricade.	See table H-9, but the distance may be not less than 25 ft.	Not less than 25 ft.
	Protection for exposures...	2½ times Table H-9 but not less than 50 ft.	Not less than 50 ft.
	None	5 times table H-9 but not less than 100 ft.	Not less than 100 ft.
Horizontal and vertical tanks with emergency relief venting to permit pressure over 2.5 p.s.i.g.	Tank protected with any one of the following: Approved water spray, approved inerting, approved insulation and refrigeration, approved barricade.	2 times table H-9 but not less than 50 ft.	Not less than 50 ft.
	Protection for exposures...	4 times table H-9 but not less than 100 ft.	Not less than 100 ft.
	None	8 times table H-9 but not less than 150 ft.	Not less than 150 ft.

LOCATION OF ABOVEGROUND TANKS

(b) (2) (i) (d)

NOTE:
Every aboveground tank for the storage of unstable liquids shall be located in accordance with Table H-8.

(b) (2) (i) (e)

TABLE H-9

Capacity tank gallons	Minimum distance in feet from property line which may be built upon, including the opposite side of a public way	Minimum distance in feet from nearest side of any public way or from nearest important building
275 or less	5	5
276 to 750	10	5
751 to 12,000	15	5
12,001 to 30,000	20	5
30,001 to 50,000	30	10
50,001 to 100,000	50	15
100,001 to 500,000	80	25
500,001 to 1,000,000	100	35
1,000,001 to 2,000,000	135	45
2,000,001 to 3,000,000	165	55
3,000,001 or more	175	60

MINIMUM DISTANCES FOR TABLES H-5 TO H-8

(b) (2) (ii) (a) and (b)

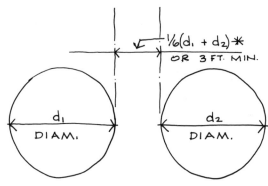

SHELL-TO-SHELL SPACING

NOTE:
 * When the diameter of one tank is less than one-half the diameter of the adjacent tank, the distance between the two tanks shall not be less than one-half the diameter of the smaller tank.

(b) (2) (ii) (c) and (d)

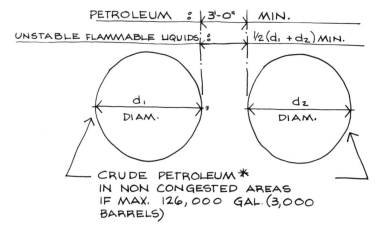

CRUDE PETROLEUM AND UNSTABLE FLAMMABLE LIQUID TANK SPACING

NOTE:
 * This applies to petroleum tanks in conjunction with production facilities.

(b) (2) (ii) (e)

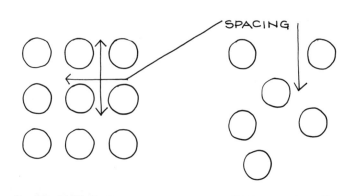

COMPACT ARRANGEMENTS—SPACING

NOTE:
 * Greater spacing than shown above for (b) (ii) (a through d), or other means, shall be provided so that inside tanks are accessible for firefighting purposes.

FLAMMABLE AND COMBUSTIBLE LIQUIDS

(b) (2) (ii) (f)

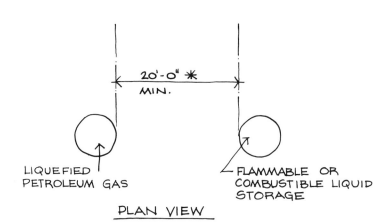

PLAN VIEW

**LP-GAS AND FLAMMABLE OR COMBUSTIBLE
LIQUID STORAGE TANK SPACING**

NOTE:
  * Except in the case of flammable or combustible liquid tanks operating at pressure exceeding 2.5 psig or equipped with emergency venting which will permit pressures to exceed 2.5 psig in which case the provisions of subdivisions (a) and (b) of this subdivision shall apply.

(b) (2) (ii) (f)

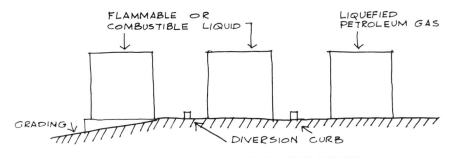

PREVENTING ACCUMULATION OF FLAMMABLE LIQUIDS

NOTE:
  Take suitable means to prevent the accumulation of flammable or combustible liquids under adjacent liquefied petroleum gas containers.

(b) (2) (ii) (f)

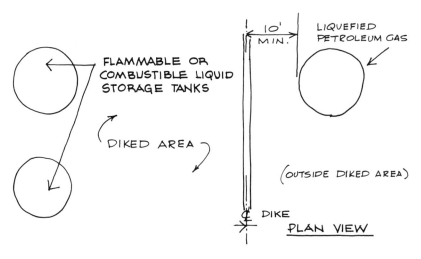

PLAN VIEW

CLEARANCE FROM DIKE

NOTE:
  This does not apply when liquefied petroleum gas containers of 125 gallons or less capacity are installed adjacent to fuel oil supply tanks of 550 gallons or less capacity.

(b) (2) (vii)
(b) (1) and (2)

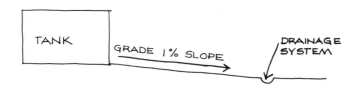

DRAINAGE

NOTE:
Terminate drainage system in vacant land or in an impounding basin with capacity not smaller than largest tank served. Subdivision (vii) here and below is not intended to apply where its requirements do not have a substantial relationship to the safety and health of employees. Consider each case on its own merits.

(b) (2) (vii)
(c) (1) and (2)

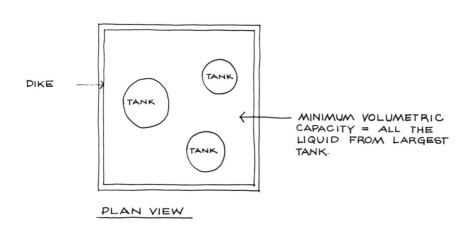

PLAN VIEW

DIKE AREA

NOTE:
Calculate capacity of diked area by deducting the volume of the tanks other than the largest tank below the height of the dike, except for crude petroleum tanks with boil-over characteristics and fixed roofs, then deduct the volume of all tanks below the height of the dike.

(b) (2) (vii)
(c) (3) and (4)

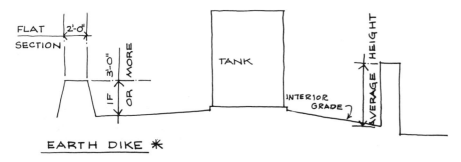

EARTH DIKE ✳

DIKE CONSTRUCTION

NOTE:
*Slope earthen dike walls consistent with angle of repose of material. Design all dikes to be liquid-tight and to withstand a full hydrostatic head. Dikes shall be earth, steel, concrete, or solid masonry.

(b) (3) (i)

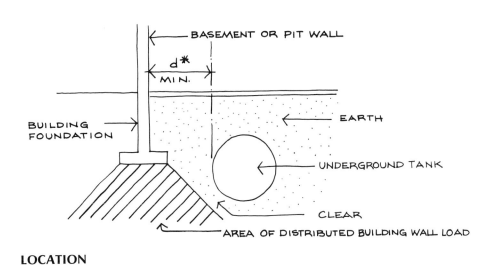

LOCATION

NOTE:
*For Class 1 liquids d = 1 ft to nearest pit or wall of any basement; 3 ft to any property line that may be built upon. For Class II or Class III liquids d = 1 ft to nearest pit, wall of any basement, or property line.

(b) (3) (ii)

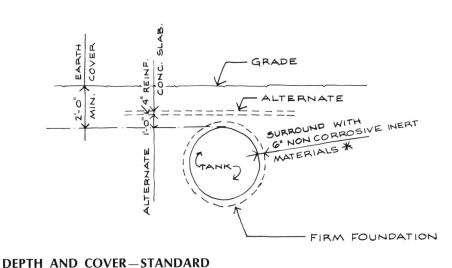

DEPTH AND COVER—STANDARD

NOTE:
* Surround tank with clean sand, earth, or gravel, well tamped in place.
Do not drop or roll tank into hole—place it with care.

(b) (3) (ii)

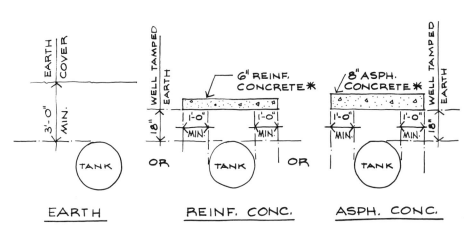

DEPTH AND COVER—SUBJECT TO TRAFFIC

NOTE:
*When asphaltic or reinforced concrete paving is used as part of the protection, it shall extend at least 1 ft horizontally beyond the outline of the tank in all directions.

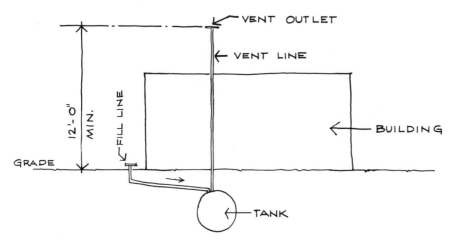

LOCATION—CLASS 1 LIQUIDS

(b) (3) (iv) (a)

NOTE:
   Discharge vent outside of building, higher than fill pipe opening, and only upward to disperse vapors. Locate so that flammable vapors will not enter building openings, or be trapped. If less than 10 ft long, or greater than 2 in. nominal inside diameter, fit outlet with vacuum and pressure relief device or flame arrester.

(b) (3) (iv) (b)

TABLE H-11—VENT LINE DIAMETERS

Maximum flow GPM	Pipe length*		
	50 feet	100 feet	200 feet
	Inches	Inches	Inches
100	1¼	1¼	1¼
200	1¼	1¼	1¼
300	1¼	1¼	1½
400	1¼	1½	2
500	1½	1½	2
600	1½	2	2
700	2	2	2
800	2	2	3
900	2	2	3
1,000	2	2	3

   *Vent lines of 50 ft., 100 ft., and 200 ft. of pipe plus 7 ells.

SIZE OF VENTS

NOTE:
   Vent each tank through piping adequate in size to prevent blowback of vapor or liquid at the fill opening while the tank is being filled. Minimum vent size is 1¼ times nominal inside diameter.

(b) (3) (iv) (c) and (d)

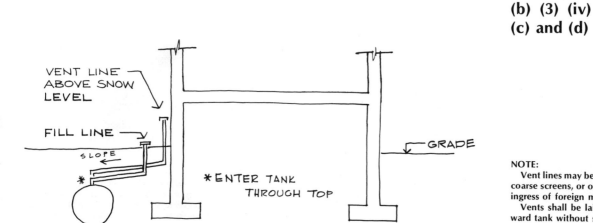

LOCATION—CLASS II OR CLASS III LIQUIDS

NOTE:
   Vent lines may be fitted with return bends, coarse screens, or other devices to minimize ingress of foreign material.
   Vents shall be laid out so as to drain toward tank without sags or traps.

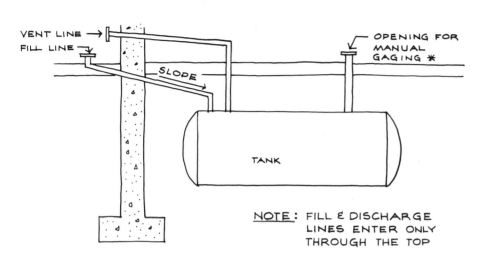

OPENINGS FOR MANUAL GAGING

NOTE: FILL & DISCHARGE LINES ENTER ONLY THROUGH THE TOP

(b) (3) (v) (b) (c)

NOTE:
*If manual gaging is independent of the fill pipe, provide liquid-tight cap or cover.

If inside a building, protect each such opening against liquid overflow and possible vapor release by means of a spring-loaded check valve or other approved device.

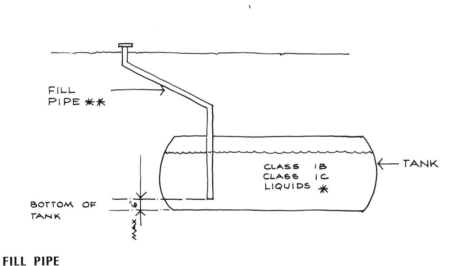

FILL PIPE

(b) (3) (v) (d)

NOTES:
* Other than crude oils, gasolines, and asphalts.
* * Design and install fill pipe to minimize the possibility of generating static electricity.

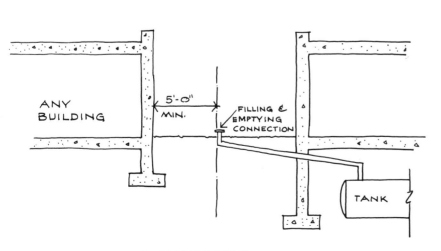

FILLING AND EMPTYING CONNECTIONS

(b) (3) (v) (e)

NOTE:
Filling and emptying connections which are made and broken shall be located outside of buildings at a location free from any source of ignition. Such connections shall be closed and liquid-tight when not in use, and properly identified.

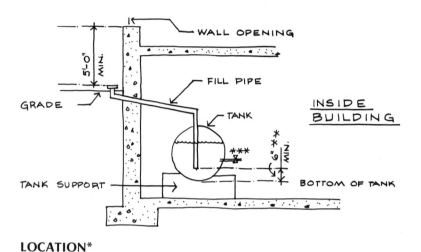

LOCATION*

(b) (4)

NOTE:
Equip tank with a device, or other means, to prevent overflow into building. Inlet of fill pipe shall be closed and liquid-tight when not in use.

*Not permitted except as per paragraph (e), Industrial Plants; (g), Service Stations; (h), Processing Plants; or (i), Refineries, Chemical Plants, and Distilleries.

**For Class IB and Class IC liquids other than crude oil, gasolines, and asphalts.

***Except in one-story buildings, protected for flammable or combustible liquid storage, provide automatic-closing heat-activated valve on each withdrawal connection below the liquid level.

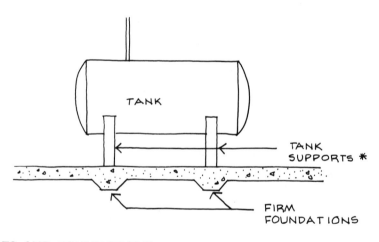

SUPPORTS AND FOUNDATIONS

(b) (5) (i)

NOTE:
* Tank support shall be:
(a) Concrete,
(b) Masonry, or
(c) Protected steel.
Single wood timber supports (not cribbing) laid horizontally may be used for outside aboveground tanks if not more than 12 in. high at their lowest point.

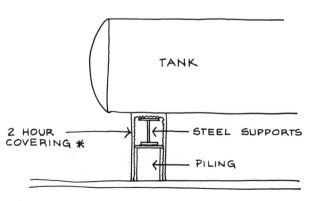

FIRE RESISTANCE

(b) (5) (ii)

NOTE:
* Steel saddles less than 12 in. high at their lowest point need not be protected. Water spray protection, or its equivalent, may be used in lieu of fire-resistive materials to protect supports.

For special precautions in flood areas, refer to full text of Section 1910.106 (b) (5) (vi).

(d) (1) (i) and (ii)

APPLICATION:- FLAMMABLE OR COMBUSTIBLE LIQUIDS
(INCLUDING FLAMMABLE AEROSOLS:

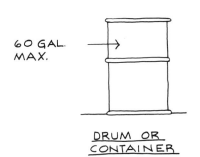

60 GAL.
MAX.

DRUM OR
CONTAINER

660 GAL.
MAX.

PORTABLE TANK

GENERAL

NOTE:
This paragraph (d) does not apply to
(a) Storage of containers in bulk plants, service stations, refineries, chemical plants, and distilleries;
(b) Class I or Class II liquids in the fuel tanks of a motor vehicle, aircraft, boat, or portable or stationary engine;
(c) Flammable or combustible paints, oils, varnishes, and similar mixtures used for painting or maintenance when not kept for a period in excess of 30 days;
(d) Beverages when packaged in individual containers not exceeding 1 gallon in size.

(d) (2) (ii)

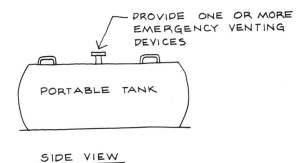

PROVIDE ONE OR MORE
EMERGENCY VENTING
DEVICES

PORTABLE TANK

SIDE VIEW

EMERGENCY VENTING

NOTE:
Vent to limit internal pressure under fire-exposure conditions to 10 psig, or 30 percent of the bursting pressure of the tank, whichever is greater.

(d) (2) (iii)

TABLE H-12—MAXIMUM ALLOWABLE SIZE OF CONTAINERS AND PORTABLE TANKS

Container type	Flammable liquids			Combustible liquids	
	Class IA	Class IB	Class IC	Class II	Class III
Glass or approved plastic	1 pt	1 qt	1 gal	1 gal	1 gal
Metal (other than DOT drums)	1 gal	5 gal	5 gal	5 gal	5 gal
Safety cans	2 gal	5 gal	5 gal	5 gal	5 gal
Metal drums (DOT spec.)	60 gal	60 gal	60 gal	60 gal	60 gal
Approved portable tanks	660 gal	660 gal	660 gal	660 gal	660 gal

Container exemptions: (a) Medicines, beverages, foodstuffs, cosmetics, and other common consumer items, when packaged according to commonly accepted practices, shall be exempt from the requirements of subdivisions (i) and (ii) of this subparagraph.

MAXIMUM ALLOWABLE SIZE

NOTE:
Comply with Table H-12 for flammable and combustible liquids packaged for sale or use.

(d) (3) (i) and (ii)

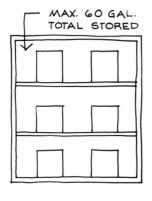

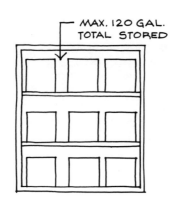

CLASS I OR II LIQUID   CLASS III LIQUID

MAXIMUM CAPACITY—STORAGE CABINETS

NOTE:
Design and contruct storage cabinets to limit internal temperature to not more than 325°F, when subjected to a 10-minute fire test per NFPA 251–1969.

(d) (3) (ii) (a)

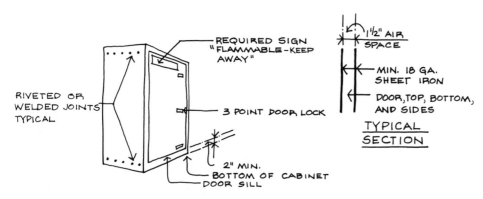

METAL CABINETS

(d) (3) (ii) (b)

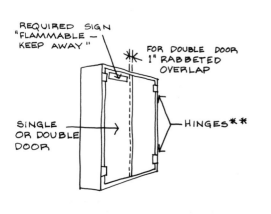

NOTE:
Fasten all joints in two directions with flathead wood screws.
**Mount hinges so as not to lose their holding capacity, due to loosening or burning out of the screws when subjected to the fire test.

WOODEN CABINETS

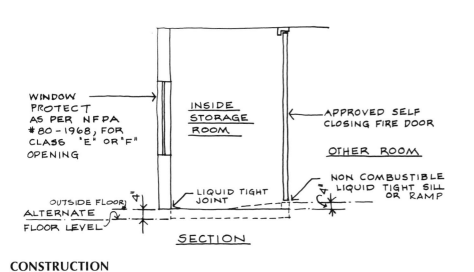

CONSTRUCTION

(d) (4) (i)

NOTE:
 Construct to meet required fire-resistive rating for use of the room, as well as test specifications of NFPA 251–1969.
 * Alternate—an open-grated trench inside of room which drains to a safe location.

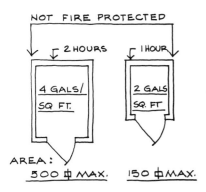

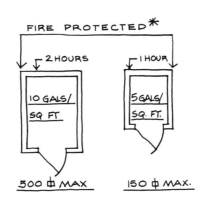

STORAGE CAPACITY AND RATING

(d) (4) (i), (ii), and (v)

NOTE:
 Wood of 1-in. nominal thickness may be used for shelving, racks, dunnage, floor overlay, and similar installations. Maintain one clear aisle—3 ft wide.
 * Fire protection system shall consist of sprinkler, water spray, carbon dioxide, or other systems.

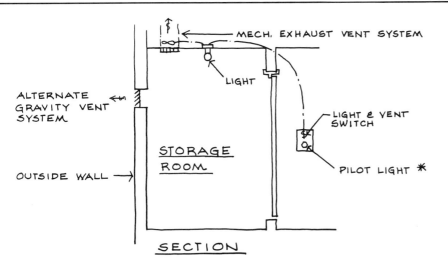

VENTILATION AND WIRING

(d) (4) (iv)

NOTE:
 Ventilation system shall provide one complete air change at least six times per hour.
 * Provide pilot light when Class I flammable liquids are dispensed in room. Electrical wiring and equipment located inside storage rooms used for Class I liquids shall be approved under Subpart I, Division 2, "Hazardous Locations"; for Class II and Class III liquids, shall be approved for general use.

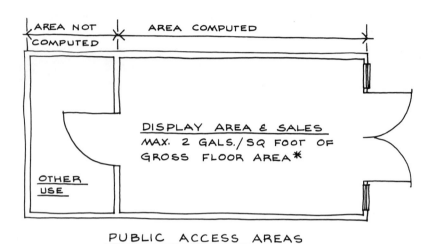

PUBLIC ACCESS AREAS

ALLOWABLE DISPLAY CAPACITY

(d) (5) (iv) (a)

NOTE:
* Storage shall be limited to quantities needed for display and normal merchandising purposes.

MAX.	ALLOWABLE	STOCK *
CLASS I A		60 GALS.
CLASS I B		120 GALS.
CLASS I C		180 GALS.
CLASS II		240 GALS.
CLASS III		500 GALS.
CLASS I + II		240 GALS.

STOCK ALLOWED

(d) (5) (iv) (b)

NOTE:
* If quantities of additional stock exceed those shown, then liquids shall be stored in a room or portion of the building that complies with Section 1910.106 (d) (4), "Inside Storage Rooms." (For water-miscible liquids, these quantities may be doubled.)

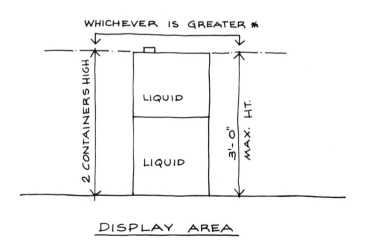

DISPLAY AREA

STACKING LIMITS

(d) (5) (iv) (c)

NOTE:
* Unless the stacking is done on fixed shelving or is otherwise satisfactorily secured.

(d) (5) (v)

TABLE H–14—INDOOR CONTAINER STORAGE

Class liquid	Storage level	Protected storage maximum per pile		Unprotected storage maximum per pile	
		Gallons	Height	Gallons	Height
IA	Ground and upper floors	2,750 (50)	3 ft. (1)	660 (12)	3 ft. (1)
	Basement	Not permitted		Not permitted	
IB	Ground and upper floors	5,500 (100)	6 ft. (2)	1,375 (25)	3 ft. (1)
	Basement	Not permitted		Not permitted	
IC	Ground and upper floors	16,500 (300)	6 ft. (2)	4,125 (75)	3 ft. (1)
	Basement	Not permitted		Not permitted	
II	Ground and upper floors	16,500 (300)	9 ft. (3)	4,125 (75)	9 ft. (3)
	Basement	5,500 (100)	9 ft. (3)	Not permitted	
III	Ground and upper floors	55,000 (1,000)	15 ft. (5)	13,750 (250)	12 ft. (4)
	Basement	8,250 (450)	9 ft. (3)	Not permitted	

NOTE 1: When 2 or more classes of materials are stored in a single pile, the maximum gallonage permitted in that pile shall be the smallest of the 2 or more separate maximum gallonages.
NOTE 2: Aisles shall be provided so that no container is more than 12 ft. from an aisle. Main aisles shall be at least 8 ft. wide and side aisles at least 4 ft. wide.
(Numbers in parentheses indicate corresponding number of 55-gal. drums.)

TABLE H–15—INDOOR PORTABLE TANK STORAGE

Class liquid	Storage level	Protected storage maximum per pile		Unprotected storage maximum per pile	
		Gallons	Height	Gallons	Height
IA	Ground and upper floors	Not permitted		Not permitted	
	Basement	Not permitted		Not permitted	
IB	Ground and upper floors	20,000	7 ft.	2,000	7 ft.
	Basement	Not permitted		Not permitted	
IC	Ground and upper floors	40,000	14 ft.	5,500	7 ft.
	Basement	Not permitted		Not permitted	
II	Ground and upper floors	40,000	14 ft.	5,500	7 ft.
	Basement	20,000	7 ft.	Not permitted	
III	Ground and upper floors	60,000	14 ft.	22,000	7 ft.
	Basement	20,000	7 ft.	Not permitted	

NOTE 1: When 2 or more classes of materials are stored in a single pile, the maximum gallonage permitted in that pile shall be the smallest of the 2 or more separate maximum gallonages.
NOTE 2: Aisles shall be provided so that no portable tank is more than 12 ft. from an aisle. Main aisles shall be at least 8 ft. wide and side aisles at least 4 ft. wide.

STORAGE IN GENERAL-PURPOSE PUBLIC WAREHOUSES

NOTE:
Storage shall be as per Table H-14 or Table H-15 and in buildings or in portions of such buildings cut off by standard fire walls. Material creating no fire-exposure hazard to the flammable, combustible liquids may be stored in the same area.

171

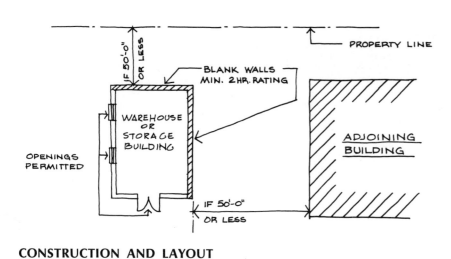

CONSTRUCTION AND LAYOUT

(d) (5) (vi) (a) and (b)

NOTE:
The quantity of liquid within building shall not be restricted, but the arrangement of storage shall comply with Table H-14 or Table H-15 (Section 1910.106 (d) (5) (v)).

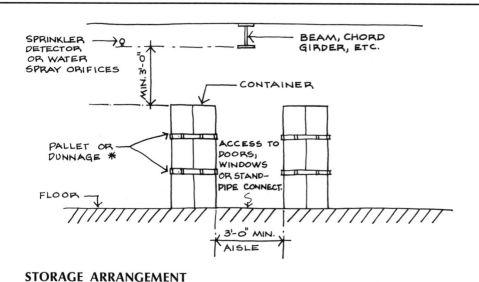

STORAGE ARRANGEMENT

(d) (5) (vi) (c), (d), (e), and (f)

NOTE:
*Pallets or dunnage shall separate containers to prevent excessive stress on container walls.
Portable tanks stored over one tier high shall be designed to nest securely.

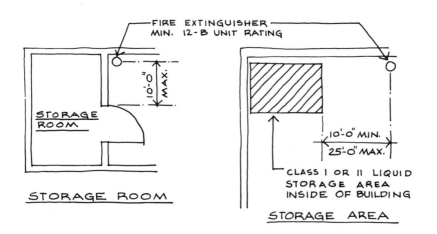

FIRE CONTROL

(d) (7) (a) and (b)

NOTE:
Suitable fire-control devices, such as small hose or portable fire extinguishers, shall be available at locations where flammable or combustible liquids are stored. Do not store materials which will react with water in same room with flammable or combustible liquids.

(d) (6) (i)

STORAGE OUTSIDE BUILDINGS

NOTE:
Comply with Table H-16 or Table H-17
and subdivisions (ii) and (iv) below.

TABLE H-16—OUTDOOR CONTAINER STORAGE

1	2	3	4	5
Class	Maximum per pile gallons (see note 1)	Distance between piles (see note 2)	Distance to property line that can be built upon (see notes 3 and 4)	Distance to street, alley, public way (see note 4)
		ft.	ft.	ft.
IA	1,100	5	20	10
IB	2,200	5	20	10
IC	4,400	5	20	10
II	8,800	5	10	5
III	22,000	5	10	5

NOTE 1: When 2 or more classes of materials are stored in a single pile, the maximum gallonage in that pile shall be the the smallest of the 2 or more separate gallonages.
NOTE 2: Within 200 ft. of each container, there shall be a 12-ft. wide access way to permit approach of fire control apparatus.
NOTE 3: The distances listed apply to properties that have protection for exposures as defined. If there are exposures, and such protection for exposures does not exist, the distances in column 4 shall be doubled.
NOTE 4: When total quantity stored does not exceed 50 percent of maximum per pile, the distances in columns 4 and 5 may be reduced 50 percent, but not less than 3 ft.

(d) (6) (ii), (iii), (iv)

TABLE H-17—OUTDOOR PORTABLE TANK STORAGE

1	2	3	4	5
Class	Maximum per pile gallons	Distance between piles	Distance to property line that can be built upon	Distance to street, alley public way
		ft.	ft.	ft.
IA	2,200	5	20	10
IB	4,400	5	20	10
IC	8,800	5	20	10
II	17,600	5	10	5
III	44,000	5	10	5

NOTE 1: When 2 or more classes of materials are stored in a single pile, the maximum gallonage in that pile shall be the the smallest of the 2 or more separate gallonages.
NOTE 2: Within 200 ft. of each portable tank, there shall be a 12-ft. wide access way to permit approach of fire control apparatus.
NOTE 3: The distances listed apply to properties that have protection for exposures as defined. If there are exposures, and such protection for exposures does not exist, the distances in column 4 shall be doubled.
NOTE 4: When total quantity stored does not exceed 50 percent of maximum per pile, the distances in columns 4 and 5 may be reduced 50 percent, but not less than 3 ft.

STORAGE OUTSIDE BUILDINGS, MAXIMUM STORAGE, SPILL CONTAINMENT, AND SECURITY

NOTE:
(ii) A maximum of 1,100 gallons of flammable or combustible liquids may be located adjacent to buildings located on the same premises and under the same management provided the provisions of subdivisions (a) and (b) of this subdivision are complied with.

(a) The building shall be a one-story building devoted principally to the handling and storing of flammable or combustible liquids or the building shall have 2-hour fire-resistive exterior walls having no opening within 10 ft of such storage.

(b) Where quantity stored exceeds 1,100 gallons, or provisions of subdivision (a) of this subdivision cannot be met, a minimum distance of 10 ft between building and nearest container of flammable or combustible liquid shall be maintained.

(iii) Grade away from building, or provide minimum 6-in.-high curb with drainage).

(iv) Protect storage area against tampering or trespassers where necessary.

(e) (1) (i)

APPLICATION

NOTE:
This paragraph shall apply to those industrial plants where
(a) The use of flammable or combustible liquids is incidental to the principal business, or
(b) Where flammable or combustible liquids are handled or used only in unit physical operations such as mixing, drying, evaporating, filtering, distillation, and similar operations which do not involve chemical reaction. This paragraph shall not apply to chemical plants, refineries, or distilleries.

(e) (2) (i) and (ii) (c)

LARGE QUANTITIES

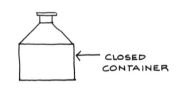

SMALL QUANTITIES

INCIDENTAL STORAGE—CONTAINERS

NOTE:
Applies to those portions of an industrial plant where the use and handling of flammable or combustible liquids are only incidental to the principal business, such as automobile assembly, construction of electronic equipment, furniture manufacturing, or other similar activities.
Where large quantities of flammable or combustible liquids are necessary, storage may be in tanks which shall comply with the applicable requirements of paragraph (b) (below).

(e) (2) (ii) (b)

CONTAINERS

25 GALS. MAX.

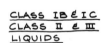

CONTAINERS

120 GALS. MAX.

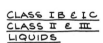

660 GALS. MAX.

LOCATION OUTSIDE OF AN INSIDE STORAGE ROOM OR CABINET*

NOTE:
Except as provided here, comply with paragraph (d) (3) or (4) of this section.
* Or in any one fire area of a building.

174

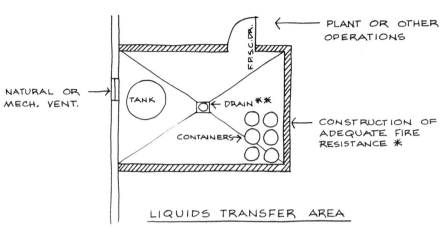

LIQUIDS TRANSFER AREA

SEPARATION AND PROTECTION

(e) (2) (iii)

NOTE:
* Alternate—Adequate distance from other operations.
** Provide drainage or other means to control spills.

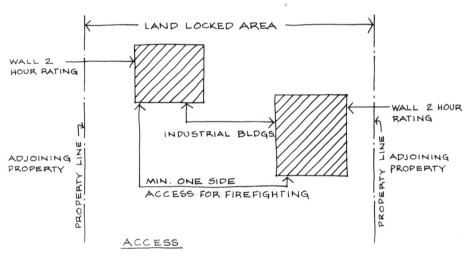

ACCESS

UNIT PHYSICAL OPERATIONS

(e) (3) (i) and (ii)

NOTE:
Applicable in those portions of industrial plants where flammable or combustible liquids are handled or used in unit physical operations such as mixing, drying, evaporating, filtering, distillation, and similar operations which do not involve chemical change. Examples are plants compounding cosmetics, pharmaceuticals, solvents, cleaning fluids, insecticides, and similar types of activities.

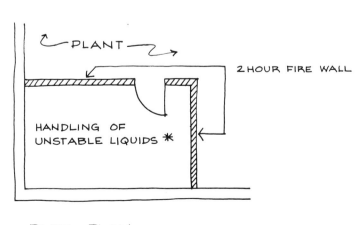

PART PLAN

CHEMICAL PROCESSES

(e) (3) (iii)

NOTE:
* Or areas where small-scale unit chemical processes are carried on.

(e) (3) (iv) (a) and (b)

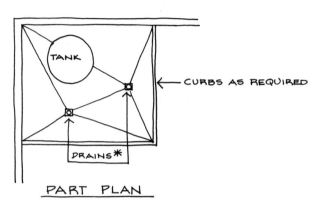

PART PLAN

EMERGENCY DRAINAGE

NOTE:
   Provide emergency drainage systems to direct flammable or combustible liquids leakage to a safe location. If connected to public sewers or waterways, provide traps or separators.
   * May require scuppers or special drainage system to control the spread of fire.

(e) (3) (v) (a)

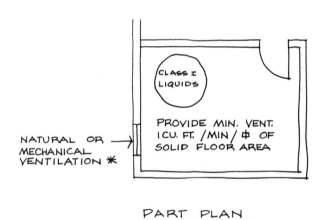

PART PLAN

VENTILATION

NOTE:
   Discharge of exhaust shall be to a safe location outside of the building.
   Makeup air shall be introduced so as not to short-circuit the ventilation.
   *Arrange ventilation to include all floor areas or pits where flammable vapors may collect.

(e) (3) (v) (b)

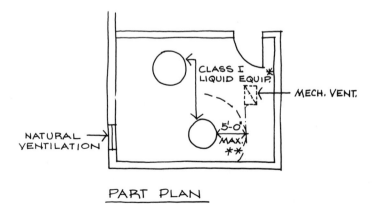

PART PLAN

VENTILATION

NOTE:
   * Equipment such as dispensing stations, open centrifuges, plate and frame filters, and surfaces of open equipment.
   ** Limitation of flammable-vapor–air mixtures under normal operating conditions.

176

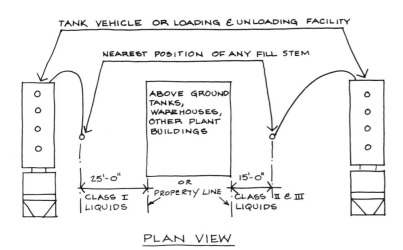

PLAN VIEW

TANK VEHICLE AND TANK CAR LOADING AND UNLOADING

(e) (4) (i)

NOTE:
Buildings for pumps or shelters for personnel may be part of the loading or unloading facility.

(e) (7) (i) (a) and (b)

CLASSIFICATION OF AREAS FOR ELECTRICAL

NOTE:
Install electrical wiring and equipment according to Subpart S of OSHA requirements.
* Applies to equipment installed per Sec. 1910.106 (e) (3) (v) (b). All areas within pits shall be classified Division I, unless the pit is provided with mechanical ventilation.

(e) (7) (i) (c)

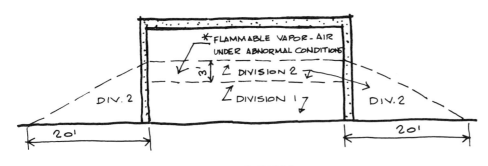

CLASSIFICATION OF AREAS FOR ELECTRICAL

NOTE:
*Division 2 locations from pump, bleeder, withdrawal fitting, meter, or similar device handling Class I liquids measured 3 ft above the floor or grade level:
(a) 25 ft if indoors,
(b) 10 ft outdoors.
Install electrical wiring and equipment according to Subpart S of OSHA requirements. If Class II or Class III liquids only are handled, then ordinary electrical equipment is satisfactory.

(f) (1) (i)

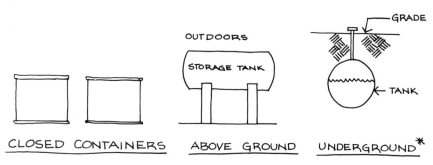

PERMITTED STORAGE—CLASS I LIQUIDS

NOTE:
*In accordance with Section 1910.106 (b).

(f) (1) (iii)

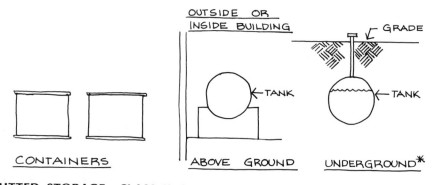

PERMITTED STORAGE—CLASS II AND III LIQUIDS

NOTE:
*In accordance with Section 1910.106 (b).

(f) (i) and (iii)

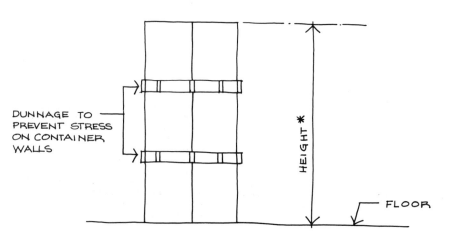

PILING STORAGE CONTAINERS

NOTE:
*The height of the pile shall be consistent with the stability and strength of containers.

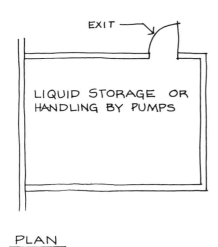

PLAN

BUILDING—EXITS

(f) (2) (i)

NOTE:
Number and locations of exit facilities shall be arranged to prevent occupants from being trapped in the event of fire.

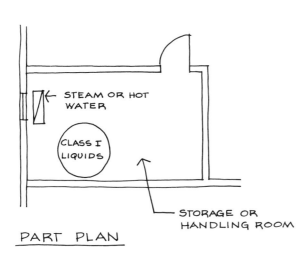

PART PLAN

HEATING

(f) (2) (ii)

NOTE:
Rooms in which Class I liquids are stored or handled shall be heated only by means not constituting a source of ignition, such as steam or hot water. Rooms containing heating appliances involving sources of ignition shall be located and arranged to prevent entry of flammable vapors.

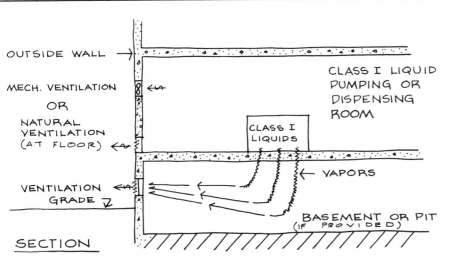

SECTION

VENTILATION

(f) (2) (iii) (a), (b), and (c)

NOTE:
Design of ventilation system shall take into account the relatively high specific gravity of the vapors.

(f) (5)

TABLE H-18—ELECTRICAL EQUIPMENT HAZARDOUS AREAS—BULK PLANTS

Location	NEC Class I Group D division	Extent of classified area
Tank vehicle and tank car:[1]		
Loading through open dome	1	Within 3 feet of edge of dome, extending in all directions.
	2	Area between 3 feet and 5 feet from edge of dome, extending in all directions.
Loading through bottom connections with atmospheric venting.	1	Within 3 feet of point of venting to atmosphere extending in all directions.
	2	Area between 3 feet and 5 feet from point of venting to atmosphere, extending in all directions. Also up to 18 inches above grade within a horizontal radius of 10 feet from point of loading connection.
Loading through closed dome with atmospheric venting.	1	Within 3 feet of open end of vent, extending in all directions.
	2	Area between 3 feet and 5 feet from open end of vent, extending in all directions. Also within 3 feet of edge of dome, extending in all directions.
Loading through closed dome with vapor recovery.	2	Within 3 feet of point of connection of both fill and vapor lines, extending in all directions.
Bottom loading with vapor recovery or any bottom unloading.	2	Within 3 feet of point of connections extending in all directions. Also up to 18 inches above grade within a horizontal radius of 10 feet from point of connection.
Drum and container filling:		
Outdoors, or indoors with adequate ventilation.	1	Within 3 feet of vent and fill opening, extending in all directions.
	2	Area between 3 feet and 5 feet from vent or fill opening, extending in all directions. Also up to 18 inches above floor or grade level within a horizontal radius of 10 feet from vent or fill opening.
Outdoors, or indoors with adequate ventilation.	1	Within 3 feet of vent and fill opening, extending in all directions.
	2	Area between 3 feet and 5 feet from vent or fill opening, extending in all directions. Also up to 18 inches above floor or grade level within a horizontal radius of 10 feet from vent or fill opening.
Tank—Aboveground:		
Shell, ends, or roof and dike area	2	Within 10 feet from shell, ends, or roof of tank, Area inside dikes to level of top of dike.
Vent	1	Within 5 feet of open end of vent, extending in all directions.
	2	Area between 5 feet and 10 feet from open end of vent, extending in all directions.
Floating roof	1	Area above the roof and within the shell.
Pits:		
Without mechanical ventilation	1	Entire area within pit if any part is within a Division 1 or 2 classified area.
With mechanical ventilation	2	Entire area within pit if any part is within a Division 1 or 2 classified area.
Containing valves, fittings or piping, and not within a division 1 or 2 classified area.	2	Entire pit.
Pumps, bleeders, withdrawal fittings, meters and similar devices:		
Indoors	2	Within 5 feet of any edge of such devices, extending in all directions. Also up to 3 feet above floor or grade level within 25 feet horizontally from any edge of such devices.
Outdoors	2	Within 3 feet of any edge of such devices, extending in all directions. Also up to 18 inches above grade level within 10 feet horizontally from any edge of such devices.
Storage and repair garage for tank vehicles	1	All pits or spaces below floor level.
	2	Area up to 18 inches above floor or grade level for entire storage or repair garage.
Drainage ditches, separators, impounding basins.	2	Area up to 18 inches above ditch, separator or basin. Also up to 18 inches above grade within 15 feet horizontally from any edge.
Garages for other than tank vehicles	Ordinary	If there is any opening to these rooms within the extent of an outdoor classified area, the entire room shall be classified the same as the area classification at the point of the opening.
Outdoor drum storage	Ordinary	
Indoor warehousing where there is no flammable liquid transfer.	Ordinary	If there is any opening to these rooms within the extent of an indoor classified area, the room shall be classified the same as if the wall, curb or partition did not exist.
Office and rest rooms	Ordinary	

[1] When classifying the extent of the area, consideration shall be given to the fact that tank cars or tank vehicles may be spotted at varying points. Therefore, the extremities of the loading or unloading positions shall be used.

NOTE:

(i) This subparagraph shall apply to areas where Class I liquids are stored or handled. For areas where Class II or Class III liquids only are stored or handled, the electrical equipment may be installed in accordance with the provisions of Subpart S of this part, for ordinary locations.

(ii) All electrical equipment and wiring shall be of a type specified by and shall be installed in accordance with Subpart S of this part.

(iii) So far as it applies, Table H-18 shall be used to delineate and classify hazardous areas for the purpose of installation of electrical equipment under normal circumstances. In Table H-18 a classified area shall not extend beyond an unpierced wall, roof, or other solid partition. The area classifications listed shall be based on the premise that the installation meets the applicable requirements of this section in all respects.

ELECTRICAL EQUIPMENT

(g) (1) (i) (a) and (iii) (c)

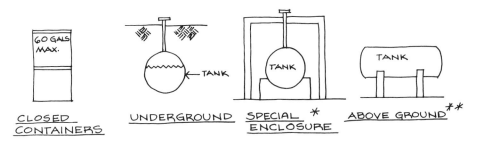

PERMITTED STORAGE AND HANDLING OF LIQUIDS

NOTE:
* In accord with paragraph (g) (1) (ii).
** Marine service stations only. Also permitted: (1) Temporary use of movable tanks for dispensing liquids into motor vehicles or motorized equipment on premises not normally accessible to public. Obtain permit of enforcing authority and subject to definite time limit. (2) Dispensing of flammable liquids in the open from tank vehicle to a motor vehicle. (3) storage and dispensing inside service stations of Class II and Class III liquids from tanks with maximum capacity of 120 gallons each.

(g) (1) (i) (b)

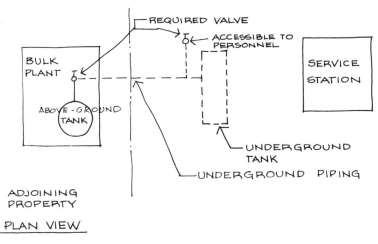
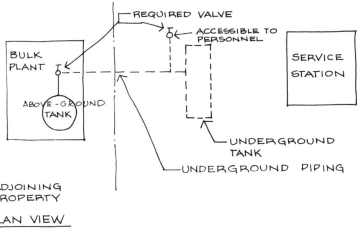

PLAN VIEW

NEAR BULK PLANTS

(g) (1) (i) (c)

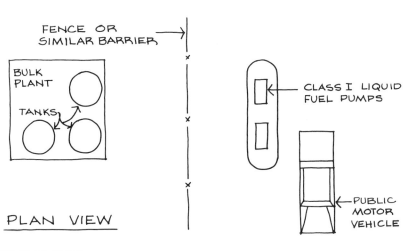

PLAN VIEW

AT BULK PLANTS

181

(g) (1) (ii) (a)

SPECIAL ENCLOSURES—WHEN ALLOWED

NOTE:

When installation of tanks in accordance with Sec. 1910.106 (b) (3) is impractical because of property or building limitation, tanks for flammable or combustible liquids may be installed in buildings if properly enclosed.

(g) (1) (ii) (b)

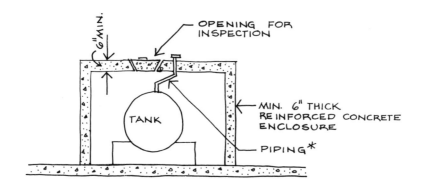

OPENING FOR INSPECTION

6" MIN.

TANK

MIN. 6" THICK REINFORCED CONCRETE ENCLOSURE

PIPING*

SECTION

SPECIAL ENCLOSURES—CONSTRUCTION

NOTE:

Enclosure shall be substantially liquid- and vapor-tight without backfill. Portable equipment shall be able to discharge any leakage to the outside.

* Tank connections shall be so piped or closed that neither vapors nor liquid can escape into the enclosed space.

(g) (1) (ii) (c)

SERVICE STATION

CUSTOMER OR TENANT PARKING

GRADE

EACH TANK 6,000 GAL'S. MAX.

BELOW GRADE

COMMERCIAL, MERCANTILE OR RESIDENTIAL LARGE BUILDINGS

IN CONNECTION WITH PARKING FACILITIES

NOTE:
* 18,000 gallons aggregate capacity.

(g) (1) (iii) (a)

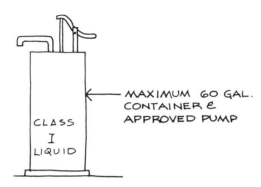

MAXIMUM 60 GAL. CONTAINER & APPROVED PUMP

CLASS I LIQUID

STORAGE AND HANDLING—INSIDE BUILDINGS

NOTE:
No Class I liquid shall be stored within any service station building except if in accord with Section 1910.106 (g) (1) (ii), or as shown in illustration.

(g) (1) (iii) (b)

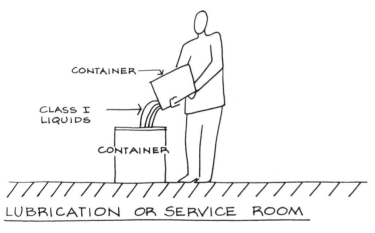

CONTAINER

CLASS I LIQUIDS

CONTAINER

LUBRICATION OR SERVICE ROOM

TRANSFERRING LIQUIDS*

NOTE:
*Transferring is allowed inside buildings provided the electrical installation complies with Table H-19 and that any heating equipment complies with 1910.106 (g) (6).

(g) (1) (iii) (c)

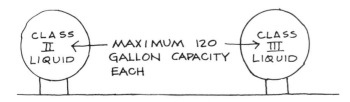

CLASS II LIQUID — MAXIMUM 120 GALLON CAPACITY EACH → CLASS III LIQUID

CLASS II AND CLASS III LIQUIDS

NOTE:
Class II and Class III liquids may be stored and dispensed inside service station buildings from tanks of not more than 120 gallons each.

(g) (3) (i)

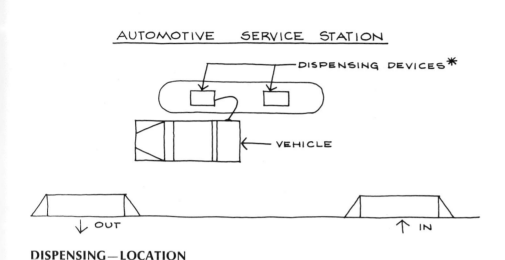

AUTOMOTIVE SERVICE STATION

DISPENSING DEVICES *

VEHICLE

↓ OUT   ↑ IN

DISPENSING—LOCATION

NOTE:
  * Dispensing devices shall be so located that all parts of the vehicle being serviced will be on the premises of the service station.

(g) (3) (ii)

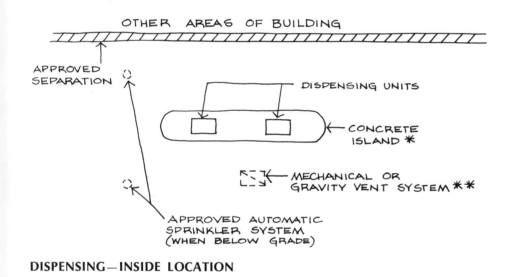

OTHER AREAS OF BUILDING

APPROVED SEPARATION

DISPENSING UNITS

CONCRETE ISLAND *

MECHANICAL OR GRAVITY VENT SYSTEM **

APPROVED AUTOMATIC SPRINKLER SYSTEM (WHEN BELOW GRADE)

DISPENSING—INSIDE LOCATION

NOTE:
  * Dispensing unit and its piping shall be protected against collision damage by concrete island or other suitable means, and located in a position where it cannot be struck by a vehicle descending a ramp or slope.
  ** When below grade, use only mechanical ventilation. Ventilating systems shall be electrically interlocked with gasoline dispensing units to allow units to work only if the ventilating system is on.

(g) (3) (iii)

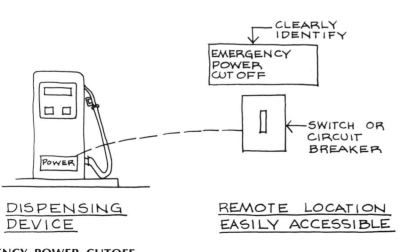

CLEARLY IDENTIFY

EMERGENCY POWER CUT OFF

SWITCH OR CIRCUIT BREAKER

POWER

DISPENSING DEVICE

REMOTE LOCATION EASILY ACCESSIBLE

NOTE:
  Power to all dispensing devices, including remote pumping system, shall be able to be shut off in the event of an emergency.

EMERGENCY POWER CUTOFF

TABLE H-19—ELECTRICAL EQUIPMENT HAZARDOUS AREAS—SERVICE STATIONS

Location	NEC Class I, Group D division	Extent of classified area
Underground tank:		
Fill opening	1	Any pit, box or space below grade level, any part of which is within the Division 1 or 2 classified area.
	2	Up to 18 inches above grade level within a horizontal radius of 10 feet from a loose fill connection and within a horizontal radius of 5 feet from a tight fill connection.
Vent—Discharging upward	1	Within 3 feet of open end of vent, extending in all directions.
	2	Area between 3 feet and 5 feet of open end of vent, extending in all directions.
Dispenser:		
Pits	1	Any pit, box or space below grade level, any part of which is within the Division 1 or 2 classified area.
Dispenser enclosure	1	The area 4 feet vertically above base within the enclosure and 18 inches horizontally in all directions.
Outdoor	2	Up to 18 inches above grade level within 20 feet horizontally of any edge of enclosure.
Indoor:		
With mechanical ventilation	2	Up to 18 inches above grade or floor level within 20 feet horizontally of any edge of enclosure.
With gravity ventilation	2	Up to 18 inches above grade or floor level within 25 feet horizontally of any edge of enclosure.
Remote pump—Outdoor	1	Any pit, box or space below grade level if any part is within a horizontal distance of 10 feet from any edge of pump.
	2	Within 3 feet of any edge of pump, extending in all directions. Also up to 18 inches above grade level within 10 feet horizontally from any edge of pump.
Remote pump—Indoor	1	Entire area within any pit.
	2	Within 5 feet of any edge of pump, extending in all directions. Also up to 3 feet above floor or grade level within 25 feet horizontally from any edge of pump.
Lubrication or service room	1	Entire area within any pit.
	2	Area up to 18 inches above floor or grade level within entire lubrication room.
Dispenser for Class I Liquids	2	Within 3 feet of any fill or dispensing point, extending in all directions.
Special enclosure inside building per section 6020.	1	Entire enclosure.
Sales, storage and rest rooms	Ordinary	If there is any opening to these rooms within the extent of a Division 1 area, the entire room shall be classified as Division 1.

ELECTRICAL EQUIPMENT

NOTE:

(i) This subparagraph shall apply to areas where Class I liquids are stored or handled. For areas where Class II or Class III liquids are stored or handled, the electrical equipment may be installed in accordance with the provisions of Subpart S of this part, for ordinary locations.

(ii) All electrical equipment and wiring shall be of a type specified by and shall be installed in accordance with Subpart S of this part.

(iii) So far as it applies, Table H-19 shall be used to delineate and classify hazardous areas for the purpose of installation of electrical equipment under normal circumstances. A classified area shall not extend beyond an unpierced wall, roof, or other solid partition.

(iv) The area classifications listed shall be used on the assumption that the installation meets the applicable requirements of this section in all respects.

(g) (6) (iii)

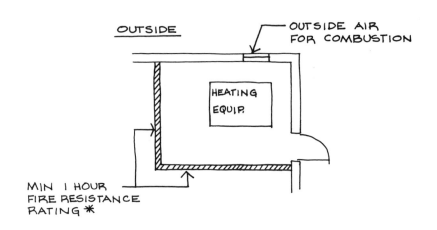

HEATING EQUIPMENT

NOTE:
* No openings allowed in walls within 8 ft of the floor into an area classified in Table H-19.
The heating equipment room may not be used for combustible storage.

(g) (6) (iv)

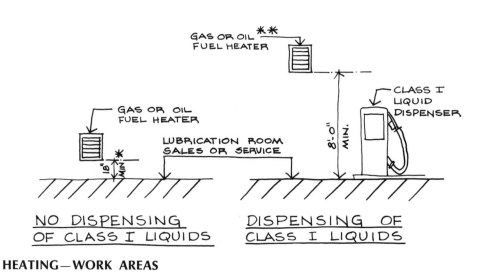

HEATING—WORK AREAS

NOTE:
Protect heater against damage by vehicles.
* Measured from the bottom of the combustion chamber.
** Heating equipment using gas or fuel listed for use in garages.

(g) (9)

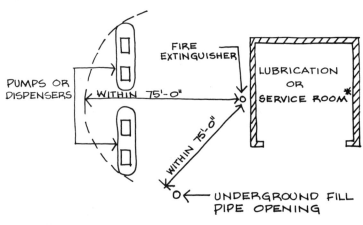

FIRE CONTROL

NOTE:
*Provide fire extinguisher within 75 ft of lubrication or service room.
Fire extinguisher shall have a minimum approved classification of 6 B, C.

(h) (1)

NOTE:
This paragraph shall apply to those plants or buildings which contain chemical operations such as oxidation, reduction, halogenation, hydrogenation, alkylation, polymerization, and other chemical processes but shall not apply to chemical plants, refineries, or distilleries.

APPLICATION

(h) (2) (i)

PROCESSING VESSELS WITH EMERGENCY RELIEF VENTING TO PERMIT PRESSURE	STABLE LIQUIDS	UNSTABLE LIQUIDS
NOT IN EXCESS OF 2.5 P.S.I.G.	OSHA TABLE H-9	2½ TIMES OSHA TABLE H-9
OVER 2.5 P.S.I.G	1½ TIMES OSHA TABLE H-9	4 TIMES OSHA TABLE H-9

NOTE:
Location of each processing vessel shall be based upon the flammable or combustible liquid capacity and with respect to distances to lines of adjoining property which may be built upon, in accordance with data shown, except as shown in (h) (2) (ii) below.

LOCATION

(h) (2) (ii)

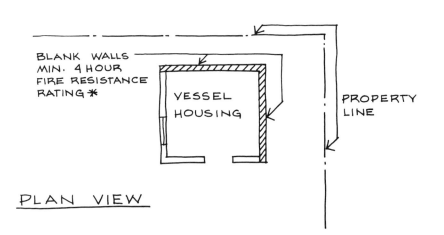

BLANK WALLS
MIN. 4 HOUR
FIRE RESISTANCE
RATING ✳

VESSEL HOUSING

PROPERTY LINE

PLAN VIEW

NOTE:
The distances required in (h) (2) (i) above may be waived when the vessels are housed within buildings meeting the requirements shown.
*When Class IA or unstable liquids are handled, the blank wall shall have explosive resistance in accordance with good engineering practice.
See paragraph (h) (3) (iv).

LOCATION EXCEPTION

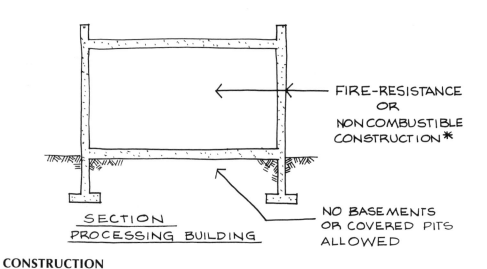

SECTION
PROCESSING BUILDING

FIRE-RESISTANCE
OR
NONCOMBUSTIBLE
CONSTRUCTION *

NO BASEMENTS
OR COVERED PITS
ALLOWED

CONSTRUCTION

(h) (3) (i) (a)

NOTE:
  *Load-bearing walls are prohibited except as provided in (h) (2) (ii) or in the case of explosion-resistant walls used in conjunction with explosion-relieving facilities
  See (h) (3) (iv).
  *Except heavy-timber construction with load-bearing walls may be permitted for plants utilizing only stable Class II or Class III liquids.

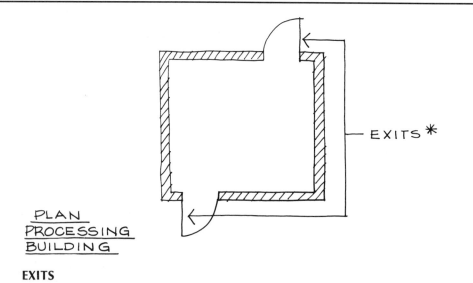

PLAN
PROCESSING
BUILDING

EXITS *

EXITS

(h) (3) (i) (a)

NOTE:
  *Areas shall have adequate exit facilities arranged to prevent occupants from being trapped in the event of fire. Exits shall not be exposed by the drainage facilities described in (h) (3) (ii) below.

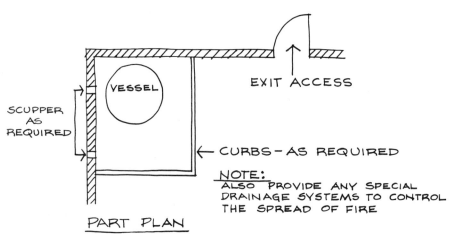

VESSEL

SCUPPER
AS
REQUIRED

EXIT ACCESS

CURBS - AS REQUIRED

NOTE:
ALSO PROVIDE ANY SPECIAL
DRAINAGE SYSTEMS TO CONTROL
THE SPREAD OF FIRE

PART PLAN

DRAINAGE

(h) (3) (ii) (a), (b), and (c)

NOTE:
  Emergency drainage system shall be provided to direct flammable or combustible liquid leakage and fire protection water to a safe location. If system is connected to public sewer or discharged into public waterways, equip with traps or separators.
  Design plant and operate to prevent normal discharge of flammable or combustible liquids to public waterways, sewers, or adjoining property.

(h) (3) (iii) (a) and (b)

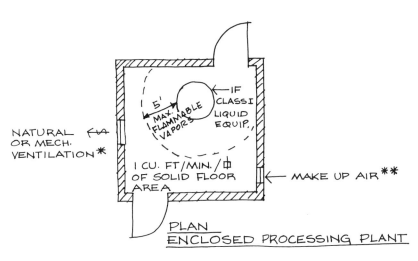

PLAN
ENCLOSED PROCESSING PLANT

VENTILATION

NOTE:
*Discharge or exhaust to a safe location outside of building. Arrange ventilation to include all floor areas or pits where flammable vapors may collect.
**Makeup air shall be introduced in such a manner as not to short-circuit the ventilation.

(h) (3) (iv)

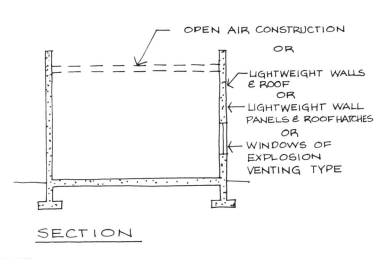

SECTION

EXPLOSION RELIEF

NOTE:
Areas where Class IA or unstable liquids are processed shall have explosive venting through one or more of the methods shown.

(h) (4) (i) (c)

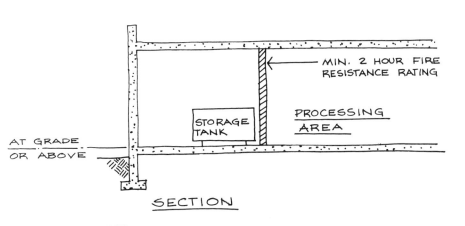

SECTION

LIQUID HANDLING

NOTE:
Storage tanks inside buildings are permitted only in areas at or above grade which have adequate drainage.

(h) (6) (i)

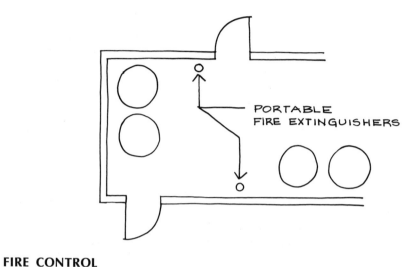

FIRE CONTROL

NOTE:
Approved portable fire extinguishers of appropriate size, type, and number shall be provided.

(h) (6) (ii)

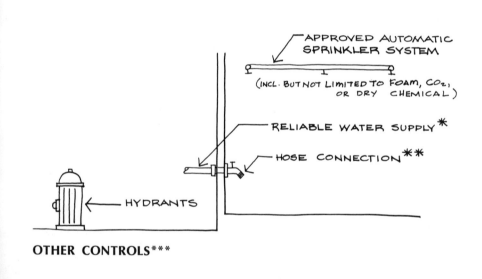

OTHER CONTROLS***

NOTE:
*Pressure and quantity shall be adequate to meet the probable fire demands.
**Installed so that all vessels, pumps, and other equipment containing flammable or combustible liquids can be reached with at least one hose stream.
***Provide when the special hazards of operation indicate a need.

(h) (6) (iii)

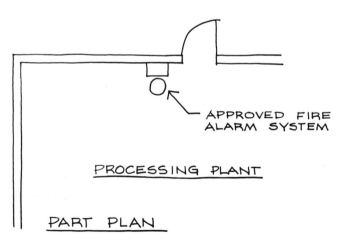

ALARM SYSTEM

NOTE:
Provide an approved means for prompt notification of fire to those within the plant and any public fire department.

(b) (1) through (4)

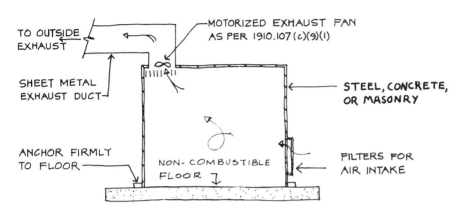

CONSTRUCTION

(c) (2)

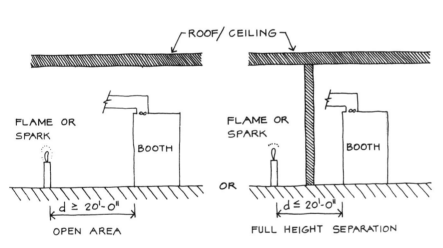

MINIMUM SEPARATION—ELECTRICAL

(c) (6)

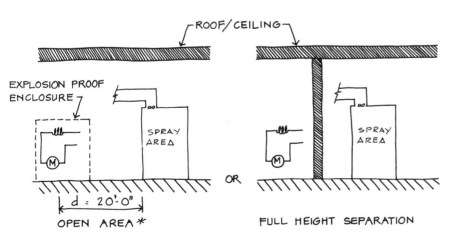

WIRING TYPE APPROVED

NOTE:
*All wiring, and electrical equipment as approved for Class I, Division 2, Hazardous Locations, and no equipment within 20 ft 0 in. of booth may produce sparks.

Wiring and equipment in spray areas: Class I, group D, explosion-proof type; and for Class I, Division I, Hazardous Locations.

(c) (7)

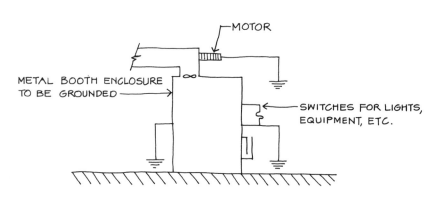

ROOF/CEILING

FULL ENCLOSURE
PROTECTED FROM
MECH. INJURY

SPRAY
AREA

SPRAY
AREA

LESS THAN 20'

OPEN AREA

LESS THAN 20'

FULL HEIGHT SEPARATION

LAMPS

(c) (9) (i)

MOTOR

METAL BOOTH ENCLOSURE
TO BE GROUNDED

SWITCHES FOR LIGHTS,
EQUIPMENT, ETC.

GROUNDING

(d) (3)

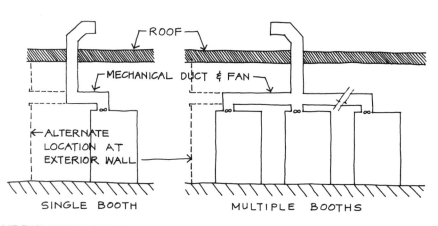

ROOF

MECHANICAL DUCT & FAN

ALTERNATE
LOCATION AT
EXTERIOR WALL

SINGLE BOOTH

MULTIPLE BOOTHS

NOTE:
   1. Multiple-booth exhaust systems may
be connected together only if the same
material is being sprayed with a maximum
frontal area of 28 sq. ft.
   2. Fans to be interconnected so that all
must operate at same time.

INDEPENDENT EXHAUST

(d) (4) and (5)

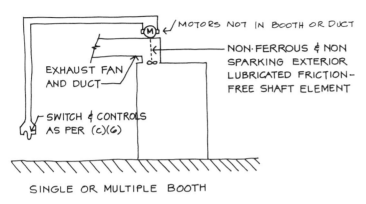

MOTORS NOT IN BOOTH OR DUCT

NON-FERROUS & NON SPARKING EXTERIOR LUBRICATED FRICTION-FREE SHAFT ELEMENT

EXHAUST FAN AND DUCT

SWITCH & CONTROLS AS PER (c)(6)

SINGLE OR MULTIPLE BOOTH

FANS AND MOTORS

NOTE:
1. Electrical wiring and controls to conform to Sec. 1910.107(c).

(d) (7) (i) and (ii)

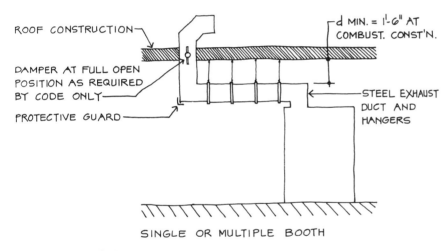

ROOF CONSTRUCTION

d MIN. = 1'-6" AT COMBUST. CONST'N.

DAMPER AT FULL OPEN POSITION AS REQUIRED BY CODE ONLY

PROTECTIVE GUARD

STEEL EXHAUST DUCT AND HANGERS

SINGLE OR MULTIPLE BOOTH

EXHAUST DUCTS

NOTE:
If combustible construction is provided with the following protection applied to all surfaces within 18 in., clearances may be reduced to the distances indicated:
(a) 28-gage sheet metal on ¼-in asbestos mill board—12 in.
(b) 28-gage sheet metal on ⅛-in asbestos mill board spaced out 1 in. on noncombustible spacers—9 in.
(c) 22-gage sheet metal on 1-inch rockwool batts reinforced with wire mesh or the equivalent—3 in.
(d) Where ducts are protected with an approved automatic sprinkler system, properly maintained, the clearance required in Subdivision (i) of this subparagraph may be reduced to 6 in.

(d) (8)

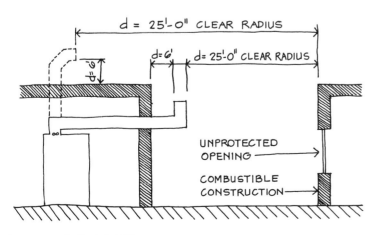

d = 25'-0" CLEAR RADIUS

d = 6'

d = 25'-0" CLEAR RADIUS

UNPROTECTED OPENING

COMBUSTIBLE CONSTRUCTION

DISCHARGE CLEARANCE

(f) (1)

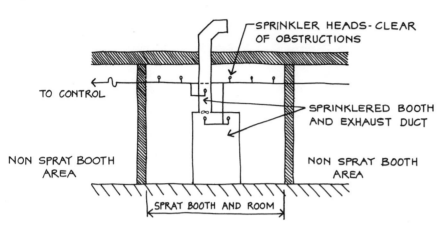

SPRINKLER HEADS - CLEAR OF OBSTRUCTIONS

TO CONTROL

SPRINKLERED BOOTH AND EXHAUST DUCT

NON SPRAY BOOTH AREA

NON SPRAY BOOTH AREA

SPRAT BOOTH AND ROOM

CONFORMANCE

NOTE:
1. Conform to NFPA 13–1969 provisions for extra-hazard occupancy.
2. Sprinkler heads should be cleaned reggularly.

(f) (2)

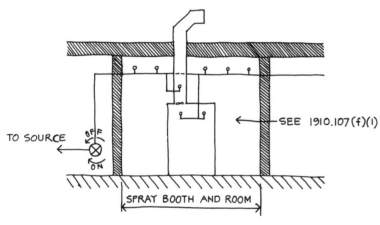

TO SOURCE

SEE 1910.107(f)(1)

SPRAY BOOTH AND ROOM

VALVE ACCESS

NOTE:
Provide accessibly located separate outside stem and yoke (OS&Y) supervised subcontrol valve.

(f) (4)

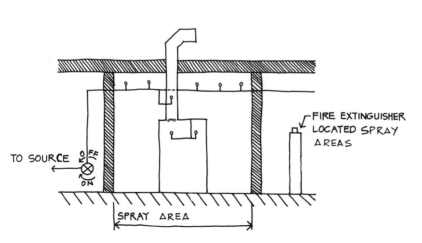

FIRE EXTINGUISHER LOCATED SPRAY AREAS

TO SOURCE

SPRAY AREA

PORTABLE EXTINGUISHERS

(c) (2) (i) through (iv)

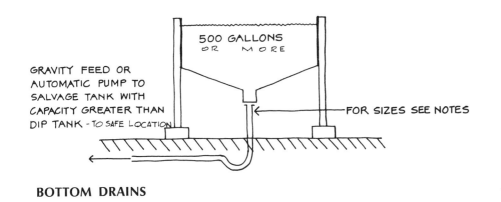

AUTOMATIC SPRINKLERS

6" MINIMUM

3" DIAMETER - MIN.

150 GALLONS OR 10 SQUARE FOOT SURFACE AREA

TO EXTERIOR OF BUILDING

TRAP

DIP TANK

OVERFLOW PIPES

NOTE:
1. Dip tanks less than 150 gallons capacity or 10 sq ft surface area should be similarly equipped where possible.
2. Overflow tank capacity should be adequate to take all anticipated runoff.
3. Connection should be designed for easy inspection.

(c) (3) (iii)

500 GALLONS OR MORE

GRAVITY FEED OR AUTOMATIC PUMP TO SALVAGE TANK WITH CAPACITY GREATER THAN DIP TANK - TO SAFE LOCATION

FOR SIZES SEE NOTES

BOTTOM DRAINS

NOTE:
1. The minimum diameter of the bottom shall be as follows:

Gallons	Inches
500–750	3
750–1,000	4
1,000–2,500	5
2,500–4,000	6
Over 4,000	8

(c) (5)

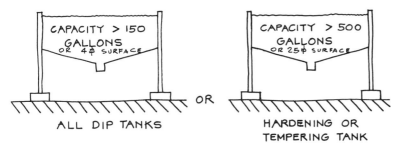

CAPACITY > 150 GALLONS OR 4φ SURFACE

CAPACITY > 500 GALLONS OR 25φ SURFACE

OR

ALL DIP TANKS

HARDENING OR TEMPERING TANK

AUTOMATIC EXTINGUISHING FACILITIES

NOTE:
1. Provide at least one of these automatic extinguishing systems: automatic water spray, automatic foam, automatic carbon dioxide, dry chemical, or automatically closing covers.

(e) (1) (i)

CEILING

VAPOR AREA WITHIN VENTILATION SYSTEM

VAPOR IGNITION

HEATED SURFACE

OR

OR

FLOOR

FLAME   HOT SURFACES   GRINDER   SYSTEM

HEAT NOT ALLOWED WITHIN VAPOR AREA

NOTE:
1. All wiring, electrostatic apparatus, equipment, in vapor area shall be explosion-proof and conform to requirements of Subpart S for Class I, Group D locations.

(e) (1) (ii)

CEILING

LAMPS   SWITCHES, CONTROLS   OPEN WIRING OR ELECTRIC BOX

OR   OR

FLOOR

ELECTRICAL DEVICES   SPLICES

DEVICES NOT ALLOWED WITHIN VAPOR AREA

(e) (2)

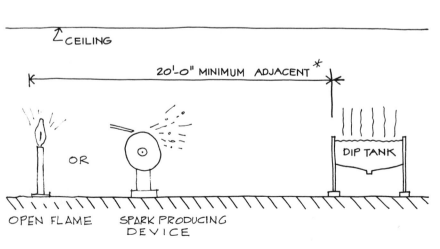

CEILING

20'-0" MINIMUM ADJACENT *

OR

DIP TANK

OPEN FLAME   SPARK PRODUCING DEVICE

DEVICES NOT ALLOWED WITHIN ADJACENT AREAS

NOTE:
* Unless separated by tight partition.

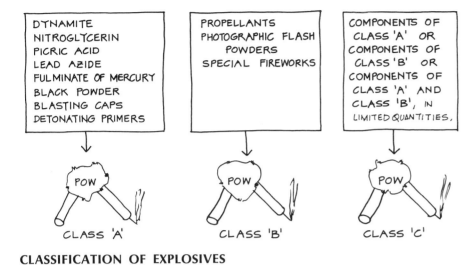

CLASSIFICATION OF EXPLOSIVES

(a) (3) (i), (ii), and (iii)

NOTE:
An explosive is any chemical compound, mixture, or device of which the primary purpose is to instantaneously release gas and heat.

Exceptions are classified as per the U.S. Department of Transportation.

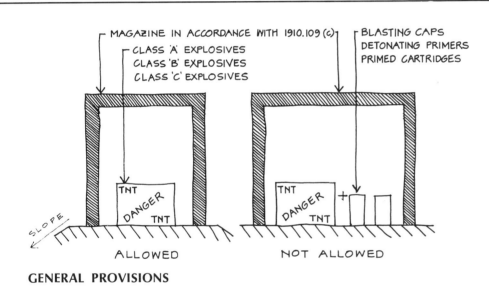

GENERAL PROVISIONS

(c) (1) (i), (ii), and (iii)

NOTE:
Keep ground around magazines clear of debris for a distance of 25 ft 0 in. minimum.

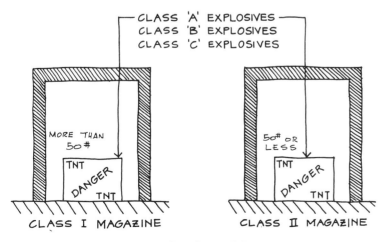

CLASSIFICATION AND LOCATION OF MAGAZINES

(c) (1) (v) and (vi)

NOTE:
Conform to Table H-21 on next page.

(c) (1) (vi), (vii), (viii), and (ix)

TABLE H-21—AMERICAN TABLE OF DISTANCES FOR STORAGE OF EXPLOSIVES

As revised and approved by the Institute of Makers of Explosives, June 5, 1964

Explosives		Distances in feet when storage is barricaded			
Pounds over	Pounds not over	Inhabited buildings	Passenger railways	Public highways	Separation of magazines
2	5	70	30	30	6
5	10	90	35	35	8
10	20	110	45	45	10
20	30	125	50	50	11
30	40	140	55	55	12
40	50	150	60	60	14
50	75	170	70	70	15
75	100	190	75	75	16
100	125	200	80	80	18
125	150	215	85	85	19
150	200	235	95	95	21
200	250	255	105	105	23
250	300	270	110	110	24
300	400	295	120	120	27
400	500	320	130	130	29
500	600	340	135	135	31
600	700	355	145	145	32
700	800	375	150	150	33
800	900	390	155	155	35
900	1,000	400	160	160	36
1,000	1,200	425	170	165	39
1,200	1,400	450	180	170	41
1,400	1,600	470	190	175	43
1,600	1,800	490	195	180	44
1,800	2,000	505	205	185	45
2,000	2,500	545	220	190	49
2,500	3,000	580	235	195	52
3,000	4,000	635	255	210	58
4,000	5,000	685	275	225	61
5,000	6,000	730	295	235	65
6,000	7,000	770	310	245	68
7,000	8,000	800	320	250	72
8,000	9,000	835	335	255	75
9,000	10,000	865	345	260	78
10,000	12,000	875	370	270	82
12,000	14,000	885	390	275	87
14,000	16,000	900	405	280	90
16,000	18,000	940	420	285	94
18,000	20,000	975	435	290	93
20,000	25,000	1,055	470	315	105
25,000	30,000	1,130	500	340	112
30,000	35,000	1,205	525	360	119
35,000	40,000	1,275	550	380	124
40,000	45,000	1,340	570	400	129
45,000	50,000	1,400	580	420	135
50,000	55,000	1,460	610	440	140
55,000	60,000	1,515	630	455	145
60,000	65,000	1,565	645	470	150
65,000	70,000	1,610	660	485	155
70,000	75,000	1,655	675	500	160
75,000	80,000	1,695	690	510	165
80,000	85,000	1,730	705	520	170
85,000	90,000	1,760	720	530	175
90,000	95,000	1,790	730	540	180
95,000	100,000	1,815	745	545	185
100,000	110,000	1,835	770	550	195
110,000	120,000	1,855	790	555	205
120,000	130,000	1,875	810	560	215
130,000	140,000	1,890	835	565	225
140,000	150,000	1,900	850	570	235
150,000	160,000	1,935	870	580	245
160,000	170,000	1,965	890	590	255
170,000	180,000	1,990	905	600	265
180,000	190,000	2,010	920	605	275
190,000	200,000	2,030	935	610	285
200,000	210,000	2,055	955	620	295
210,000	230,000	2,100	980	635	315
230,000	250,000	2,155	1,010	650	335
250,000	275,000	2,215	1,040	670	360
275,000	300,000	2,275	1,075	690	385

NOTE 1. "Natural barricade" means natural features of the ground, such as hills, or timber of sufficient density that the surrounding exposures which require protection cannot be seen from the magazine when the trees are bare of leaves.

NOTE 2. "Artificial barricade" means an artificial mound or revetted wall of earth of a minimum thickness of three feet.

NOTE:

(vii) Except as provided in Subdivision (viii) of this subparagraph, Class II magazines shall be located in conformity with Table H-21, but may be permitted in warehouses and in wholesale and retail establishments when located on a floor which has an entrance at outside grade level and the magazine is located not more than 10 ft from such an entrance. Two Class II magazines may be located in the same building when one is used only for blasting caps in quantities not in excess of 5,000 caps and a distance of 10 ft is maintained between magazines.

(viii) When used for temporary storage at a site for blasting operations, Class II magazines shall be located away from neighboring inhabited buildings, railways, highways, and other magazines. A distance of at least one hundred and fifty (150) ft shall be maintained between Class II magazines and the work in progress when the quantity of explosives kept therein is in excess of 25 lb, and at least 50 ft when the quantity of explosives is 25 lb or less.

(ix) This paragraph (c) does not apply to:

(a) Stocks of small arms ammunition, propellant-activated power cartridges, small arms ammunition primers in quantities of less than 750,000, or smokeless propellants in quantities less than 750 lb;

(b) Explosive-activated power devices when in quantities of less than 50 lb net weight of explosives;

(c) Fuse lighters and fuse igniters;

(d) Safety fuses other than cordeau detonant fuses.

CLASS I AND CLASS II MAGAZINE LOCATIONS

(c) (2) (ii)

RESISTANT TO:

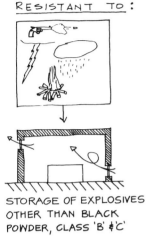

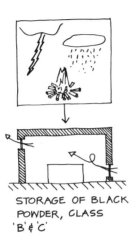

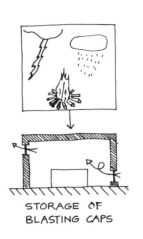

STORAGE OF EXPLOSIVES
OTHER THAN BLACK
POWDER, CLASS 'B' & 'C'

STORAGE OF BLACK
POWDER, CLASS
'B' & 'C'

STORAGE OF
BLASTING CAPS

MAGAZINE CONSTRUCTION

(c) (2) (iv)

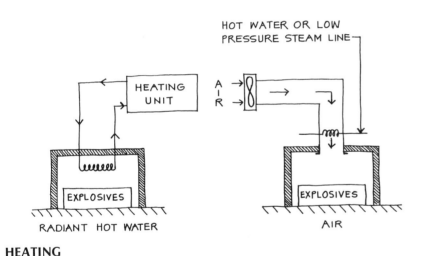

RADIANT HOT WATER

AIR

HEATING

NOTE:
1. Low-pressure steam shall be classifed as less than 15 psi.

(c) (2) (v)

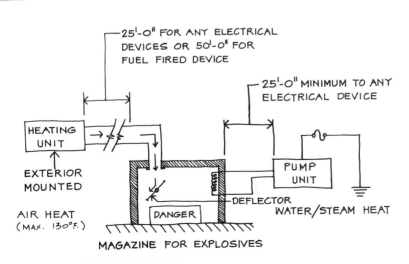

AIR HEAT
(MAX. 130°F.)

MAGAZINE FOR EXPLOSIVES

WATER/STEAM HEAT

NOTE:
Air shall circulate freely between the heating elements and the explosives.
Heating elements or heat direction shall be away from the explosives.
Electrical motors, devices, shall be located a minimum of 25 ft 0 in. from the magazine.

HEATING SYSTEM REQUIREMENTS

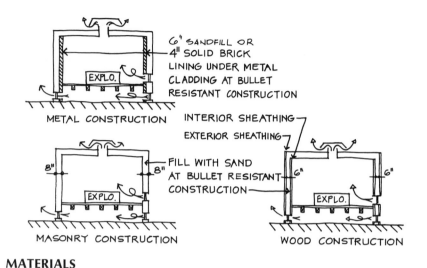

MATERIALS

(c) (3) (i), (ii), (v), and (vi)

NOTE:
1. Sand fill is to be well tamped.
2. Wood floors and roofs are to be of minimum 1-in. nominal tongue and groove.
3. Cover all exterior wood with a minimum of 26-gauge black or galvanized steel or aluminum.

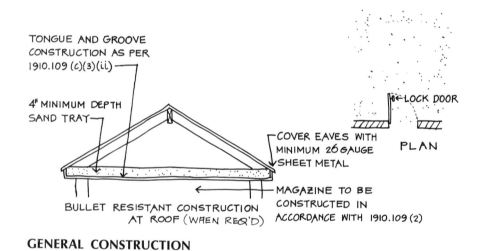

GENERAL CONSTRUCTION

(c) (3) (iii), (iv), (vii), and (viii)

NOTE:
1. Omit sand trays at ventilation openings.
2. Doors are to be locked except at times of loading and unloading. Doors for Class A explosives shall be bullet-resistant.

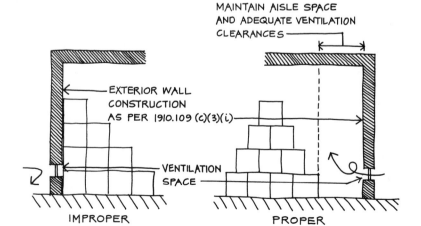

STOCKPILING

(c) (3) (ix)

(c) (4) (i) and (ii)

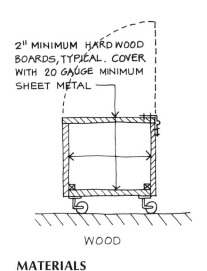

2" MINIMUM HARDWOOD BOARDS, TYPICAL. COVER WITH 20 GAUGE MINIMUM SHEET METAL

WOOD

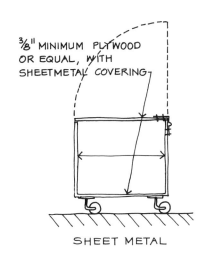

3/8" MINIMUM PLYWOOD OR EQUAL, WITH SHEETMETAL COVERING

SHEET METAL

MATERIALS

NOTE:
1. Countersink all nails at interior of magazines.
2. The magazine is to be locked except during loading and unloading.
3. Magazines to be ventilated as needed by climate.
4. Overlap metal edges by 1 in.

(c) (4) (iii) and (iv)

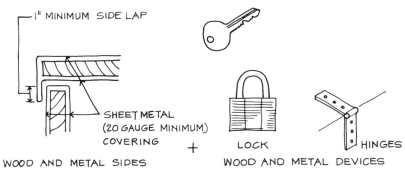

1" MINIMUM SIDE LAP

SHEET METAL (20 GAUGE MINIMUM) COVERING

WOOD AND METAL SIDES

+

LOCK   HINGES
WOOD AND METAL DEVICES

REQUIRED ITEMS

(c) (4) (iv)

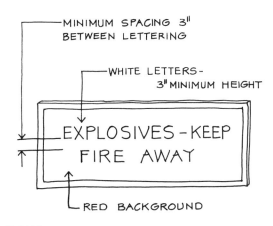

MINIMUM SPACING 3" BETWEEN LETTERING

WHITE LETTERS - 3" MINIMUM HEIGHT

EXPLOSIVES - KEEP FIRE AWAY

RED BACKGROUND

WARNING SIGNS

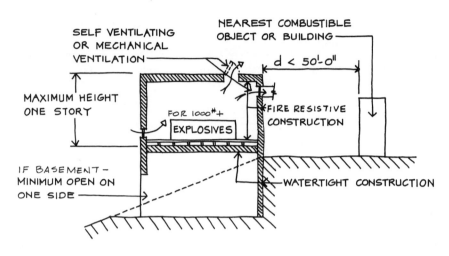

GENERAL PROVISIONS

(i) (2) (i) and (iii)

NOTE:
1. Provide storage areas for all quantities over 1,000 lb.
2. A free-standing wall may be provided in lieu of fire-resistive construction.
3. Roof construction is to be Class "C" or better as per NFPA 203M–1970.
4. Existing building need not comform if ruled not a hazard to life or adjoining property.

STORAGE IN BAGS, DRUMS, OR OTHER CONTAINERS

(i) (3) (ii)

NOTE:
1. Maximum storage temperature, 130 °F.
2. Length of storage units need not be limited at non-combustible or sprinklered construction.

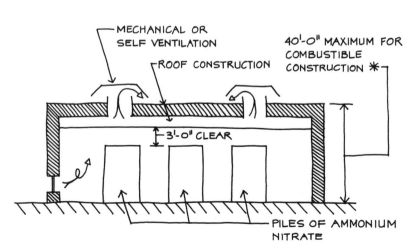

BULK STORAGE

(i) (4) (i) (a and b)
(iii) (b)

NOTE:
* Height may exceed 40 ft 0 in. if adequate facilities provided for fighting roof fire or if building of non-combustible construction.

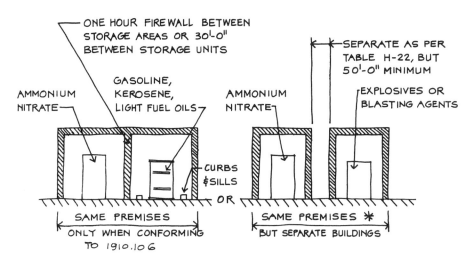

STORAGE OF OTHER FLAMMABLES AND EXPLOSIVES

(i) (5) (i) (c)
(ii) (b) and (c)
(7)

NOTE:
* Except for makers or distributors.
1. Maximum of bagged ammonium nitrate within a single building without automatic sprinklers is 2,500 tons.
2. Sprinklers to be in accord with the Standard for the Installation of Sprinkler Systems NFPA 13–1969.

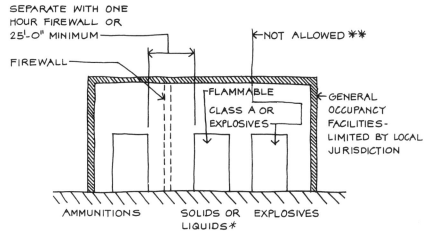

SMALL ARMS AMMUNITION

(j) (2) (i), (ii), and (iii)

NOTE:
* As defined in 49CFR–Part 172.
** Unless facility is adequate for their storage.

(j) (3) (ii), (iv), and (v)

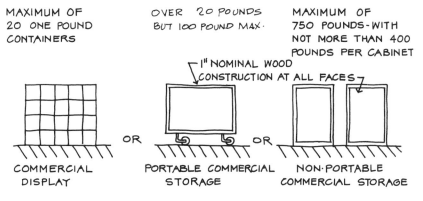

SMOKELESS PROPELLANTS STORAGE

LIQUEFIED PETROLEUM GASES— STORAGE AND HANDLING

(a) (4) and (7)

CONTAINERS—All vessels, such as tanks, cylinders, or drums, used for transportation or storing liquefied petroleum gases.

LIQUEFIED PETROLEUM GASES—"LPG" and "LP-Gas"—Any material which is composed predominantly of any of the following hydrocarbons, or mixtures of them: propane, propylene, butanes (normal butane or iso-butane), and butylenes.

DEFINITIONS

(b) (6) (ii) through (ix)

NOTE:

Install containers per Table H-23.

(iii) Containers installed for use shall not be stacked one above the other.

(iv) In industrial installations involving containers of 180,000 gallons aggregate water capacity or more, where serious mutual exposures between the container and adjacent properties prevail, fire walls or other means of special protection designed and constructed in accordance with good engineering practices are required.

(v) In the case of buildings devoted exclusively to gas manufacturing and distributing operations, the distances required by Table H-23 may be reduced provided that in no case shall containers of water capacity exceeding 500 gallons be located closer than 10 ft to such gas manufacturing and distributing buildings.

(vi) Readily ignitible material such as weeds and long, dry grass shall be removed within 10 ft of any container.

(vii) The minimum separation between liquefied petroleum gas containers and flammable liquid tanks shall be 20 ft, and the minimum separation between a container and the center line of the dike shall be 10 ft. The foregoing provision shall not apply when LP-Gas containers of 125 gallons or less capacity are installed adjacent to Class III flammable liquid tanks of 275 gallons or less capacity.

(viii) Suitable means shall be taken to prevent the accumulation of flammable liquids under adjacent liquefied petroleum gas containers, such as by diking, diversion curbs, or grading.

(ix) When dikes are used with flammable liquid tanks, no liquefied petroleum gas containers shall be located within the diked area.

TABLE H-23

Water capacity per container	Minimum distances		
	Containers		Between above-ground containers
	Under-ground	Above-ground	
Less than 125 gals [1]	10 feet	None	None.
125 to 250 gallons	10 feet	10 feet	None.
251 to 500 gallons	10 feet	10 feet	3 feet.
501 to 2,000 gallons	25 feet [2]	25 feet [2]	3 feet.
2,001 to 30,000 gallons	50 feet	50 feet	5 feet.
30,001 to 70,000 gallons	50 feet	75 feet	¼ of sum of diameters of adjacent containers.
70,001 to 90,000 gallons	50 feet	100 feet	

[1] If the aggregate water capacity of a multi-container installation at a consumer site is 501 gallons or greater, the minimum distance shall comply with the appropriate portion of this table, applying the aggregate capacity rather than the capacity per container. If more than one installation is made, each installation shall be separated from another installation by at least 25 feet. Do not apply the MINIMUM DISTANCES BETWEEN ABOVE-GROUND CONTAINERS to such installations.

[2] NOTE: The above distance requirements may be reduced to not less than 10 feet for a single container of 1,200 gallons water capacity or less, providing such a container is at least 25 feet from any other LP-Gas container of more than 125 gallons water capacity.

CONTAINER LOCATIONS

TABLE H-28

Part	Location	Extent of classified area [1]	Equipment shall be suitable for National Electrical Code, Class 1, Group D [2]
A	Storage containers other than DOT cylinders.	Within 15 feet in all directions from connections, exept connections otherwise covered in Table H-28.	Division 2.
B	Tank vehicle and tank car loading and unloading. [3]	Within 5 feet in all directions from connections regularly made or disconnected for product transfer.	Division 1.
		Beyond 5 feet but within 15 feet in all directions from a point where connections are regularly made or disconnected and within the cylindrical volume between the horizontal equator of the sphere and grade. (See Figure H-1).	Division 2.
C	Gage vent openings other than those on DOT cylinders.	Within 5 feet in all directions from point of discharge.	Division 1.
		Beyond 5 feet but within 15 feet in all directions from point of discharge.	Division 2.
D	Relief valve discharge other than those on DOT cylinders.	Within direct path of discharge.	Divison 1. *Note—* Fixed electrical equipment should preferably not be installed.
		Within 5 feet in all directions from point of discharge.	Division 1.
		Beyond 5 feet but within 15 feet in all directions from point of discharge except within the direct path of discharge.	Division 2.
E	Pumps, compressors, gas-air mixers and vaporizers other than direct fired.	--	
	Indoors without ventilation	Entire room and any adjacent room not separated by a gaslight partition.	Division 1.
		Within 15 feet of the exterior side of any exterior wall or roof that is not vaportight or within 15 feet of any exterior opening.	Division 2.
	Indoors with adequate ventilation. [4]	Entire room and any adjacent room not separated by a gaslight partition.	Division 2.
	Outdoors in open air at or abovegrade.	Within 15 feet in all directions from this equipment and within the cylindrical volume between the horizontal equator of the sphere and grade. See Figure H-1.	Division 2.
F	Service Station Dispensing Units.	Entire space within dispenser enclosure, and 18 inches horizontally from enclosure exterior up to an elevation 4 ft. above dispenser base. Entire pit or open space beneath dispenser.	Division 1.
		Up to 18 inches abovegrade within 20 ft. horizontally from any edge of enclosure. Note: For pits within this area, see Part F of this table.	Division 2.
G	Pits or trenches containing or located beneath LP-Gas valves, pumps, compressors, regulators, and similar equipment.	--	
	Without mechanical ventilation.	Entire pit or trench	Division 1.
		Entire room and any adjacent room not separated by a gaslight partition.	Division 2.
		Within 15 feet in all directions from pit or trench when located outdoors.	Division 2.
	With adequate mechanical ventilation.	Entire pit or trench	Division 2.
		Entire room and any adjacent room not separated by a gastight partition.	Division 2.
		Within 15 feet in all directions from pit or trench when located outdoors.	Division 2.
H	Special buildings or rooms for storage of portable containers.	Entire room	Division 2.
I	Pipelines and connections containing operational bleeds, drips, vents or drains.	Within 5 ft. in all directions from point of discharge.	Division 1.
		Beyond 5 ft. from point of discharge, same as Part E of this table.	
J	Container filling:		
	Indoors without ventilation.	Entire room	Division 1.
	Indoors with adequate ventilation. [4]	Within 5 feet in all directions from connections regularly made or disconnected for product transfer.	Division 1.
		Beyond 5 feet and entire room	Division 2.
	Outdoors in open air	Within 5 feet in all directions from connections regularly made or disconnected for product transfer.	Division 1.
		Beyond 5 feet but within 15 feet in all directions from a point where connections are regularly made or disconnected and within the cylindrical volume between the horizontal equator of the sphere and grade. (See Figure H-1)	Division 2.

[1] The classified area shall not extend beyond an unpierced wall, roof, or solid vaportight partition.
[2] See Subpart S of this part.
[3] When classifying extent of hazardous area, consideration shall be given to possible variations in the spotting of tank cars and tank vehicles at the unloading points and the effect these variations of actual spotting point may have on the point of connection.
[4] Ventilation, either natural or mechanical, is considered adequate when the concentration of the gas in a gas-air mixture does not exceed 25 percent of the lower flammable limit under normal operating conditions.

NOTE:
Electrical equipment and wiring shall be of a type specified by and shall be installed in accordance with Subpart S for ordinary locations except that fixed electrical equipment in classified areas shall comply with Table H-28. LP-gas storage containers do not require lightning protection. LP-gas system need not be electrically conductive or electrically bonded.

Fixed electrical equipment and wiring installed within classified areas specified in Table H-28 shall comply with Table H-28. This provision does not apply to fixed electrical equipment at residential or commercial installations of LP-gas systems or to systems covered by paragraph (e) (LP-gas as a motor fuel, internal combustion engines, etc.) or paragraph (g) (LP-gas systems on commercial vehicles, trailers, mobile libraries, etc.).

LIMIT TO 24 UNITS OF EACH BRAND AND SIZE OR 200 POUNDS OF LIQUID PETROLEUM GAS

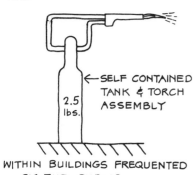

← SELF CONTAINED TANK & TORCH ASSEMBLY

2.5 lbs.

WITHIN BUILDINGS FREQUENTED BY THE PUBLIC

LIMIT TO 300 POUNDS OR 2550 c.f. AT VAPOR FORM✳

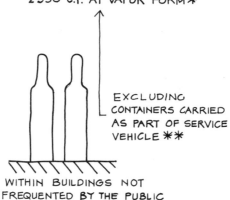

EXCLUDING CONTAINERS CARRIED AS PART OF SERVICE VEHICLE ✳✳

WITHIN BUILDINGS NOT FREQUENTED BY THE PUBLIC

GENERAL STORAGE FACILITIES

(f) (3) (i) and (ii), (4) (i) and (ii)

NOTE:
* See also Sec. 1910.110 (f) (5).
** Limit to 100-lb capacity.

MECHANICAL OR SELF VENTILATION

PRESSURE RELIEVING CONSTRUCTION EQUAL TO 10% OF TOTAL WALL AND ROOF AREA

OTHER AREAS OR SPACES

2 HOUR RATED CONSTRUCTION AT ALL SURFACES

1½ HOUR RATED DOORS AND OTHER OPENINGS →

10,000 lbs. MAXIMUM

NOTE: ALL ELECTRICAL DEVICES IN ACCORDANCE WITH 1910.110 (b) (18)

5'-0" MINIMUM

SEPARATE ROOM OR BUILDING

NO OPEN FLAMES FOR HEATING OR LIGHTING

SPECIAL BUILDING OR ROOM STORAGE

(f) (5)

NOTE:
1. Keep facilities away from property line of schools, churches, hospitals, and other points of public gathering.

(f) (6) (i) and (ii)

AWAITING USE OR RESALE

d REQUIRED MINIMUM AS PER TABLE H-33

← PROTECTED FROM TAMPERING

← L.P. GAS

1. NEAREST IMPORTANT BUILDING (S)
2. ADJOINING PROPERTY LINE OR BUILDABLE SITE.
3. BUSY THOROUGHFARE.
4. ADJOINING SCHOOLS, CHURCHES, HOSPITALS, ETC.

TABLE H-33

Quantity of LP-Gas Stored:	Distance
500 or less	0
501 to 2,500	0*
2,501 to 6,000	10 ft
6,001 to 10,000	20 ft
Over 10,000	25 ft

* Container or containers shall be at least 10 ft from any building on adjoining property, any sidewalk, or any of the exposures described in subparagraph (6) (i) (c) or (d) of this paragraph.

OUTSIDE STORAGE

(b) 5 (ii)

NOTE:
Permanent storage containers shall be located at least 50 ft from a dug well or other sources of potable water supply, unless the container is a part of a water-treatment installation.

CONTAINER LOCATIONS

(b) (5) (iv)

Nominal capacity of container (gallons)	Minimum distances (feet) from container to:		
	Line of adjoining property which may be built upon highways and mainline of railroad	Place of public assembly	Institution occupancy
Over 500 to 2,000	25	150	250
Over 2,000 to 30,000	50	300	500
Over 30,000 to 100,000	50	450	750
Over 100,000	50	600	1,000

CONTAINER LOCATIONS

(c) (5) (iii)

NOTE:
Install so that top of container is below frost line and a minimum of 2 ft below ground surface. Should ground conditions make compliance impracticable, make installation to prevent physical damage. When necessary to prevent floating, securely anchor or weight containers.

UNDERGROUND CONTAINERS

SANITATION

(a) (3) (i)

HOUSEKEEPING

(a) (3) (ii)

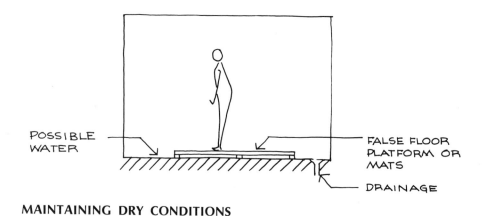

POSSIBLE WATER

FALSE FLOOR PLATFORM OR MATS

DRAINAGE

MAINTAINING DRY CONDITIONS

NOTE:
The floor of every workroom shall be maintained, so far as practicable, in a dry condition. Where wet processes are used, maintain drainage, and, where practicable, provide false floors, platforms, mats, or other dry standing places, or provide waterproof footgear.

(a) (3) (iii)

PREVENT & ELIMINATE :—

FLOOR, WORKING PLACE OR PASSAGEWAY

PROTRUDING NAILS   SPLINTERS   LOOSE BOARDS   HOLES

FACILITATING CLEANING

(a) (4) (i)

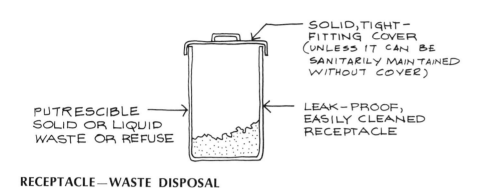

SOLID, TIGHT-FITTING COVER (UNLESS IT CAN BE SANITARILY MAINTAINED WITHOUT COVER)

PUTRESCIBLE SOLID OR LIQUID WASTE OR REFUSE

LEAK-PROOF, EASILY CLEANED RECEPTACLE

RECEPTACLE—WASTE DISPOSAL

NOTE:
This requirement does not prohibit the use of receptacles which are designed to permit the maintenance of a sanitary condition without regard to the requirements indicated.

(a) (4) (ii)

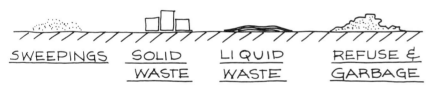

REMOVE OFTEN:

SWEEPINGS   SOLID WASTE   LIQUID WASTE   REFUSE & GARBAGE

WASTE DISPOSAL

NOTE:
Avoid creating a potential health menace by removal as often as necessary.

(a) (5)

NOTE:
Every enclosed workplace shall be so constructed, equipped, and maintained, so far as is reasonably practicable, as to prevent the entrance or harborage of rodents, insects, and other vermin. A continuing and effective extermination program shall be instituted where their presence is detected.

VERMIN CONTROL

(b) (1) (i)

DRINKING   WASHING PERSONS OR UTENSILS   COOKING, FOOD PREP., OR FOOD WASHING

POTABLE WATER

NOTE:
Provide potable water in all places of employment for purposes shown as well as for personal service rooms.

(b) (1) (ii)

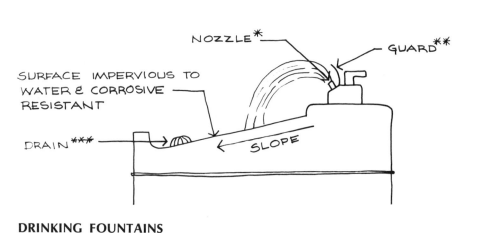

NOZZLE*   GUARD**

SURFACE IMPERVIOUS TO WATER & CORROSIVE RESISTANT

DRAIN***   SLOPE

DRINKING FOUNTAINS

NOTE:
* Nozzle to be at angle and location to prevent return of water in jet or bowl to nozzle orifice.
** Provide guard over nozzle to prevent contact by mouth or nose.
*** Drain shall not have direct physical connection with waste pipe unless trapped.

(b) (1) (iii)

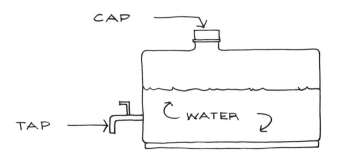

CAP

TAP   WATER

NOTE:
Design portable dispensers so they are constructed and serviced to maintain sanitary conditions.

PORTABLE DRINKING WATER

(b) (1) (v)

OPEN BARREL PAILS TANKS

VESSELS—PROHIBITED

NOTE:
   Open containers such as shown where water must be dipped or poured, whether or not fitted with a cover, are prohibited.

(b) (1) (vi)

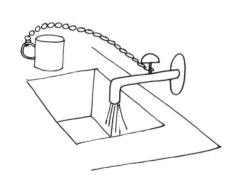

COMMON UTENSILS—PROHIBITED

NOTE:
   Common drinking cup and other utensils are prohibited.

(b) (1) (vii)

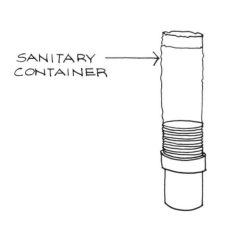

SANITARY CONTAINER

PROVIDE BOTH

RECEPTACLE FOR USED CUPS

NOTE:
   Where single-service cups (to be used only once) are supplied, both dispenser and disposal receptacle shall be provided.

DRINKING CUPS

(b) (2) (i)

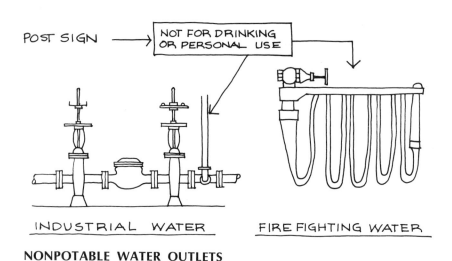

POST SIGN → NOT FOR DRINKING OR PERSONAL USE

INDUSTRIAL WATER   FIRE FIGHTING WATER

NONPOTABLE WATER OUTLETS

NOTE:
 Post or otherwise mark outlets for non-potable water in a manner that will indicate clearly that the water is unsafe and not to be used for drinking, washing, cooking, food preparation, clothes washing, etc.

(b) (2) (ii)

NONPOTABLE WATER SYSTEM—CONSTRUCTION

NOTE:
 Construction of nonpotable water systems shall be such as to prevent back-flow or back-siphonage into a potable water system.

(b) (2) (iii)

CLEANING WORK PREMISES *

NONPOTABLE WATER—USE ALLOWED

NOTE:
 * Usable for cleaning other than food processing if it does not contain concentration of chemicals, fecal coliform, or other substances which could create insanitary conditions or be harmful to employees. Not allowed for washing of persons, cooking or eating utensils, or clothing.

(c) (1) (i)

REQUIRED TOILETS *

GENERAL

NOTE:
  Provide separate toilet rooms for each sex in all places of employment.
  * Where toilet rooms will be occupied by no more than one person at a time, locked from inside, and contain at least one water closet, separate toilet rooms need not be provided.

(c) (1) (i)

NUMBER OF EMPLOYEES	MIN. NUMBER OF WATER CLOSETS
1 TO 15	
16 TO 35	
36 TO 55	
56 TO 80	
81 TO 110	
111 TO 150	
OVER 150	ONE ADDITIONAL FOR EACH ADDITIONAL 40 EMPLOYEES

REQUIRED WATER CLOSETS

NOTE:
  Where toilet facility will not be used by women, urinals may be provided instead of water closets, provided the required number of water closets shall not be reduced to less than ⅔ of the minimum required amount.

(c) (1) (ii)

NOTE:
  The requirements of Subdivision (i) above do not apply to mobile crews or to normally unattended work locations so long as employees have transportation immediately available to nearby toilet facilities which meet the requirements.

EXCEPTIONS

213

(c) (1) (iv)

INCREASE OF TOILET FACILITIES

NOTE:
    Where persons other than employees are permitted the use of toilet facilities, increase same in accord with Section 1910.141 (c) (1) (i) to determine minimum number of toilet facilities required.

(c) (1) (v) and (vi)

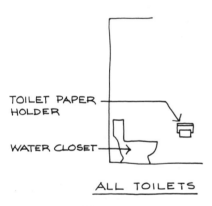

TOILET PAPER AND RECEPTACLE

NOTE:
    Provide each water closet with toilet paper and holder.

(c) (1) (vii)

 TO

REQUIRED LAVATORIES

NOTE:
    Locate lavatories in toilet room or adjacent thereto. Where only one or two water closets (and/or urinals) are provided, install at least one lavatory.

(c) (2) (i)

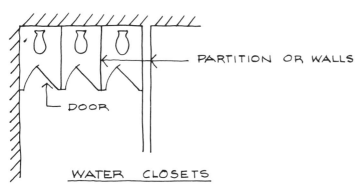

CONSTRUCTION—TOILET ROOMS

NOTE:
Each water closet shall be in separate compartment.

(c) (2) (ii)

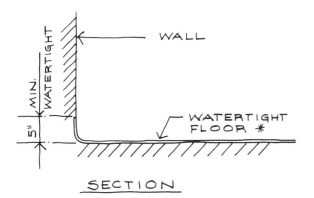

CONSTRUCTION—FLOOR AND WALLS

NOTE:
This applies to all toilet rooms installed after August 31, 1971.
* Excluding doorways and entrances.

(c) (2) (iii)

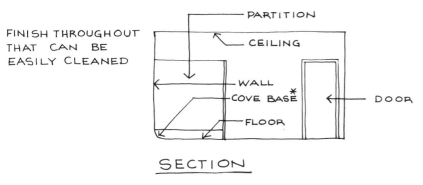

CONSTRUCTION FINISHES

NOTE:
Cove base requirement applies to installations made after August 31, 1971.

(c) (3) (i)

CONSTRUCTION AND INSTALLATION

NOTE:
Water carriage toilet facilities (water closets and urinals connected to a sewer) must be free and open from enclosing structures, with surrounding space easily cleanable. Wall-hung fixtures are permitted.

(c) (3) (ii)

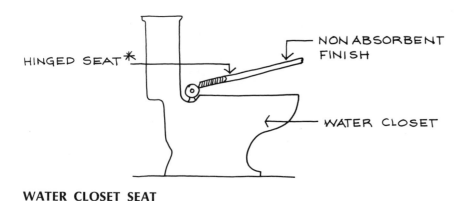

HINGED SEAT *

NON ABSORBENT FINISH

WATER CLOSET

WATER CLOSET SEAT

NOTE:
*Seats installed or replaced after June 4, 1973, shall be of the open-front type.

(c) (3) (iii)

NOTE:
Non-water carriage facilities (water closets and urinals not connected to a sewer) shall be in accord with Section 1910.143.

NON-WATER CARRIAGE TOILET FACILITIES

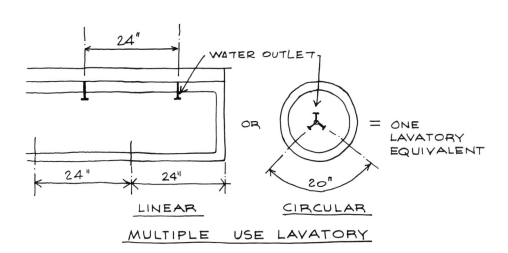

LINEAR OR **CIRCULAR**

= ONE LAVATORY EQUIVALENT

MULTIPLE USE LAVATORY

LAVATORIES

(d) (1) and (2) (i)

NOTE:
Maintain washing facilities in a sanitary condition.

TABLE J–2

Type of employment	Number of employees	Minimum number of lavatories
Nonindustrial—office buildings, public buildings, and similar establishments.	1–15	1.
	16–35	2.
	36–60	3.
	61–90	4.
	91–125	5.
	Over 125	1 additional fixture for each additional 45 employees.
Industrial—factories, warehouses, loft buildings, and similar establishments.	1–100	1 fixture for each 10 employees.
	Over 100	1 fixture for each additional 15 employees.

REQUIRED LAVATORIES

(d) (2) (i)

NOTE:
The requirements of this subdivision do not apply to mobile crews or to normally unattended work locations if employees have transportation readily available to nearby washing facilities which meet the other requirements of paragraph (2).

HAND SOAP OR SIMILAR

HOT* →   ← COLD*

EACH LAVATORY

WATER AND SOAP FOR LAVATORIES

(d) (2) (ii) and (iii)

NOTE:
* Tepid water may be provided.

(d) (2) (iv), (v), and (vi)

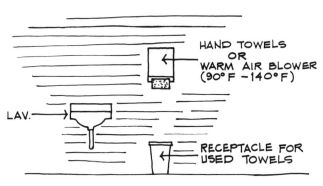

TOWELS AND RECEPTACLES REQUIRED

NOTE:
Provide individual hand towels, or sections thereof, of cloth or paper, warm-air blowers, or clean individual sections of continuous cloth toweling, convenient to lavatories.

(d) (3) (i), (ii), and (iii)

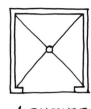

PER 10 PERSONS OF EACH SEX* (OR FRACTION THEREOF)

1 SHOWER

SHOWERS

NOTE:
1. When showers are required by a particular standard, they shall comply with Subdivisions (3) (ii) through (v).
2. Provide body soap or other appropriate cleansing agent convenient to shower.
* For employees required during same shift.

(d) (3) (iv) and (v)

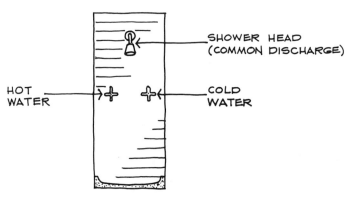

SHOWERS—WATER AND TOWELS

NOTE:
Provide individual clean towels for employees who use showers.

(e)

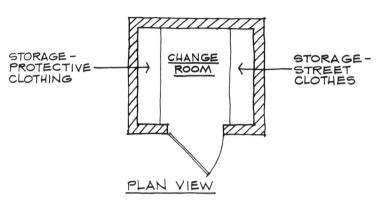

STORAGE – PROTECTIVE CLOTHING → CHANGE ROOM ← STORAGE – STREET CLOTHES

PLAN VIEW

CHANGE ROOMS

NOTE:
Provide change rooms whenever employees are required by a particular standard to wear protective clothing.

(f)

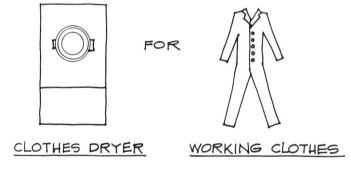

CLOTHES DRYER   FOR   WORKING CLOTHES

CLOTHES-DRYING FACILITIES

NOTE:
Where working clothes are provided by the employer and become wet or are washed between shifts, provision shall be made to ensure that such clothing is dry before re-use. (Clothes dryer is not mandatory, but suggested by author.)

(h)

NOTE:
All employee food service facilities and operations shall be carried out in accordance with sound hygienic principles. In all places of employment where all or part of the food service is provided, the food dispensed shall be wholesome, free from spoilage, and shall be processed, prepared, handled, and stored in such a manner as to be protected against contamination.

FOOD HANDLING

(g) (1) and (2)

FOOD OR DRINK CONSUMPTION NOT ALLOWED

TOILET ROOM

TOXIC MATERIAL

EATING AND DRINKING AREAS

NOTE:
 This section applies only where employees are permitted to consume food and/or beverages on the premises.

(g) (3)

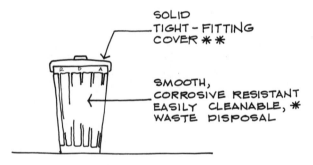

SOLID TIGHT-FITTING COVER **

SMOOTH, CORROSIVE RESISTANT EASILY CLEANABLE, * WASTE DISPOSAL

WASTE DISPOSAL CONTAINERS

NOTE:
 * Disposable material may be used as an alternate.
 ** Unless sanitary conditions can be maintained without use of a cover.
 Containers shall be emptied not less than once each working day, unless unused, and shall be maintained in a clean and sanitary condition.

(g) (4)

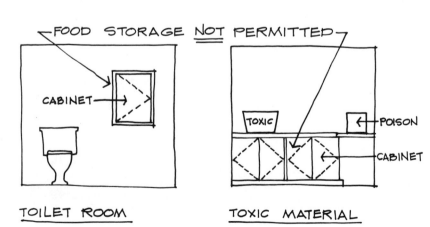

FOOD STORAGE NOT PERMITTED

CABINET

TOILET ROOM

TOXIC

POISON

CABINET

TOXIC MATERIAL

SANITARY STORAGE

NOTE:
 No food or beverages shall be stored in toilet rooms or in an area exposed to a toxic material.

SAFETY COLOR CODE FOR MARKING PHYSICAL HAZARDS

INSTRUCTIONS: Remove backing on strip on reverse side and apply where marked on appropriate page of book — Section 1910.144 "Safety Color Code for Marking Physical Hazards".

This chip represents the approximate sheen of the Semi-Gloss Enamel.

SAFETY RED ENAMEL
Speedhide Gloss 6-301
Lavax Semi-Gloss 23-800

SAFETY BLUE ENAMEL
Speedhide Gloss 6-303
Lavax Semi-Gloss 23-770

SAFETY ORANGE ENAMEL
Speedhide Gloss 6-322
Lavax Semi-Gloss 23-810

SAFETY YELLOW ENAMEL
Speedhiue Gloss 6-302
Lavax Semi-Gloss 23-780

SAFETY PURPLE ENAMEL
Speedhide Gloss 6-305
Lavax Semi-Gloss (not available)

SAFETY GREEN ENAMEL
Speedhide Gloss 6-304
Lavax Semi-Gloss 23-740

Also available — Safety Black Enamel — *Speedhide* Gloss 6-253 and *Lavax* Semi-Gloss 23-840; Safety White Enamel — *Speedhide* Gloss 6-252 and *Lavax* Semi-Gloss 23-830

These color samples have been provided courtesy of PPG Industries and parallel ANSI Z53.1-1967 "Safety Color Code for Marking Physical Hazards" which has been incorporated in OSHA standards 1910.144. Color numbers refer to *Pittsburgh® Paints*. The names *Speedhide* and *Lavax* are registered trade marks of PPG Industries, Inc. (No representation is made herein that other paint manufacturers do not comply with OSHA requirements.)

Printed in U.S.A.

(1) RED used for: Fire protection equipment and apparatus
  Fire alarm boxes (pull boxes)
  Fire blanket boxes
  Fire buckets or pails
  Fire exit signs
  Fire extinguishers (or their housing and/or background)
  Fire hose locations
  Fire hydrants (industrial)
  Fire pumps
  Fire sirens
  Sprinkler piping (see ANSI A13.1—1956)
  Post indicator valves for sprinkler system
  Danger signs
  Red lights at barricades and temporary obstructions (see ANSI A10.2–1944)
  Emergency stop buttons or switches for machinery
  Emergency stop bars on hazardous machinery

(2) ORANGE used for: designating dangerous parts of machines or energized equipment which may cut, crush, shock, or otherwise injure and to emphasize such hazards when enclosure doors are open, or when gear belt or other guards around moving equipment are open or removed, exposing unguarded hazards.

(3) YELLOW used for: designating caution and for marking physical hazards such as: striking against, stumbling, falling, tripping, and "caught in between." Solid yellow, yellow and black checkers (or yellow with suitable contrasting background) should be used interchangeably, using the combination which will attract the most attention in the particular environment.

(4) GREEN used for: designating "Safety" and the location of first aid equipment.

(5) BLUE used for designating caution, limited to warning against the starting, the use of, or the movement of equipment under repair or being worked upon.

(6) PURPLE used for: designating radiation hazards. Use yellow in combination with purple for markers such as tags, labels, signs, and floor markers.

(7) BLACK, WHITE, or a combination of these two, shall be the basic colors for the designation of traffic and housekeeping markings. Solid white, solid black, single-color striping, alternate stripes of black and white, or black and white checkers should be used in accordance with local conditions.

(d) (2)

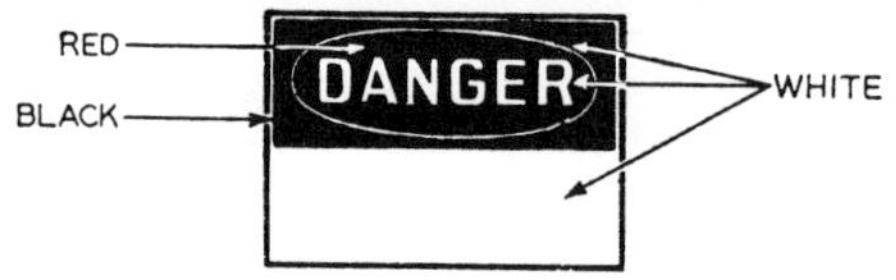
RED
BLACK
DANGER
WHITE

TABLE J-1—STANDARD PROPORTIONS FOR DANGER SIGNS

Sign size, inches Height Width	Black rectangular panel, inches Height Width	Red oval, inches Height Width	Word danger, height inches	Maximum space available for sign wording, inches
		HORIZONTAL PATTERN		
7 x 10	3¼ x 9⅜	2⅞ x 8½	1 7/16	2¾ x 9⅜
10 x 14	4⅝ x 13⅜	4⅛ x 11⅞	2 1/16	4¼ x 13⅜
14 x 20	6½ x 19⅜	5¾ x 17	2⅞	6¼ x 19⅜
20 x 28	9¼ x 27⅜	8¼ x 23⅞	4⅛	9½ x 27⅜
		UPRIGHT PATTERN		
10 x 7	2⅜ x 6⅜	2⅛ x 5⅞	1 1/16	6⅜ x 6⅜
14 x 10	3¼ x 9⅜	2⅞ x 8½	1 7/16	9½ x 9⅜
20 x 14	4⅝ x 13⅜	4⅛ x 11⅞	2 1/16	14 x 13⅜
28 x 20	6½ x 19⅜	5¾ x 17	2⅞	20¼ x 19⅜

DANGER SIGNS

NOTE:
Red, black, and white shall be those of opaque, glossy samples in Table 1 of "Fundamental Specification of Safety Colors for CIE," Standard Source "C", American National Standard Z53.1—1967. Use Standard proportions in Table J-1; when not covered by Table, use ratio of depth of identifying panel to sign width as established by Table.

(e) (3)

Danger—Keep Off, Electric Current.

Danger—No Smoking, Matches, or Open Lights.

Danger—Men Working Above.

Danger—Not Room Enough Here to Clear Men on Cars.

Danger—Keep Away.

Danger—Men in Boiler.

Danger—Insufficient Clearance.

Danger—2,300 Volts.

Danger—Keep Out.

Danger—Crane Overhead.

Danger—Keep Off.

DANGER SIGNS—NATURE OF WORDING

NOTE:
This list is intended to serve as a guide for choosing the correct message, which should be easily read and make a positive, rather than a negative, suggestion.

(d) (3)

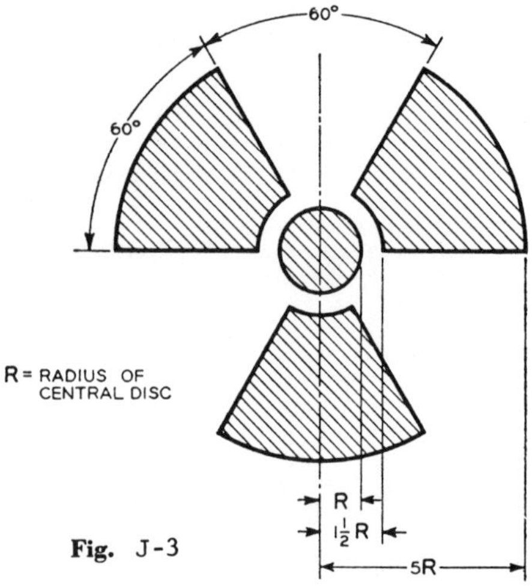
60°
60°
R = RADIUS OF CENTRAL DISC
R
1½R
5R

Fig. J-3

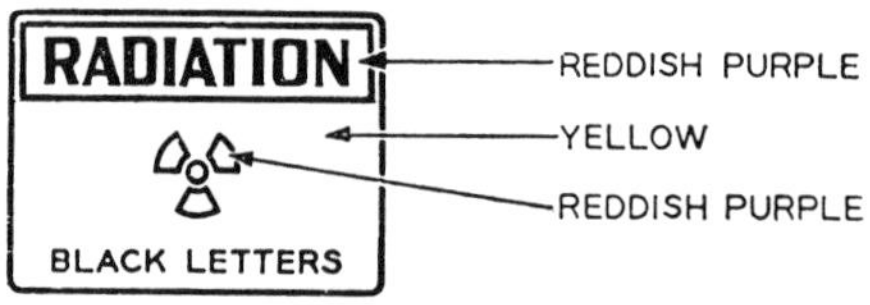
RADIATION
BLACK LETTERS
REDDISH PURPLE
YELLOW
REDDISH PURPLE

Fig.J-2

RADIATION WARNING SIGNS

NOTE:
Use proportions per Table J-1. Background shall be yellow; the panel, reddish purple with yellow letters; the symbol, reddish purple; any letters used against the yellow background shall be black. The colors shall be those of opaque, glossy samples as specified in Table 1 of American National Standard Z53.1—1967.

TABLE J-2—STANDARD PROPORTIONS FOR CAUTION SIGNS

Sign size inches height width	Black rectangular panel, inches height width	Word "Caution" height of letter, inches	Maximum space available for sign wording below panel inches height width
HORIZONTAL PATTERN			
7 x 10	2¼ x 9⅜	1⅝	3¼ x 9⅜
10 x 14	3¼ x 13⅜	2¼	5½ x 13⅜
14 x 20	3¾ x 19⅜	2¾	9 x 19²⅜
20 x 28	4¼ x 27⅜	3¼	14½ x 27⅜
UPRIGHT PATTERN			
10 x 7	1⅝ x 6⅜	1⅛	7 x 6⅜
14 x 10	2¼ x 9⅜	1⅝	10½ x 9⅜
20 x 14	3¼ x 13⅜	2¼	15½ x 13⅜
28 x 20	3¾ x 19⅜	2¾	24 x 19⅜

CAUTION SIGNS

(d) (4)

Fig. J-4

NOTE:
Use proportions indicated in Table J-2. Background shall be yellow, and the panel, black with yellow letters. Letters used against yellow background shall be black. Colors shall be those of opaque, glossy samples as specified in Table 1 of American National Standard Z53.1–1967.

(e) (5)

Caution—Do Not operate, Men Working on Repairs.

Caution—Hands Off Switch, Men Working on Line.

Caution—Working on Machines, Do Not Start.

Caution—Goggles Must Be Worn When Operating This Machine.

Caution—This Door Must Be Kept Closed.

Caution—Electric Trucks, Go Slow.

Caution—This Space Must Be Kept Clear at All Times.

Caution—Stop Machinery to Clean, Oil, or Repair.

Caution—Keep Aisles Clear.

Caution—Operators of This Machine Shall Wear Snug Fitting Clothes—No Gloves.

Caution—Close Clearance.

Caution—Watch Your Step.

Caution—Electric Fence.

CAUTION SIGNS—NATURE OF WORDING

NOTE:
This list is intended to serve as a guide for choosing the correct message, which should be easily read and make a positive, rather than a negative, suggestion.

(d) (5)

NOTE:
Exit signs shall be in accordance with Section 1910.37 (q).

EXIT SIGNS

SPECS FOR ACCIDENT PREVENTION SIGNS AND TAGS

(d) (6)

GREEN
THINK
WHITE
GREEN
BE
CAREFUL
WHITE

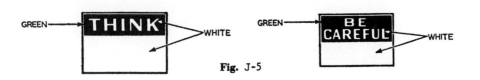

Fig. J-5

TABLE J-3—STANDARD PROPORTIONS FOR SAFETY INSTRUCTION SIGNS

Sign size, inches, height, width	Green rectangular panel, inches, height, width	Word "Think" height of letters, inches	Maximum space available for sign wording below panel, inches height, width	Sign size, inches height, width	Green panel, inches, height, width	Word "Be" height of letters, inches	Word "Careful" height of letters, inches	Maximum space available for sign wording below panel, inches, height, width
7 x 10	2¾ x 9⅜	1⅝	3½ x 9⅜	7 x 10	3⅜ x 9⅜	1¼	1 3/16	2½ x 9⅜
10 x 14	3¼ x 13⅜	2¼	5½ x 13⅜	10 x 14	4¼ x 13⅜	1¾	2 3/16	4 x 13⅜
14 x 20	3¾ x 19⅜	2¾	9 x 19⅜	14 x 20	6¼ x 19⅜	2½	3⅛	6 x 19⅜
20 x 28	4¼ x 27⅜	3¼	14½ x 27⅜	20 x 28	9½ x 27⅜	3½	4⅜	9¼ x 27⅜

SAFETY INSTRUCTION SIGNS

NOTE:

Use proportions as indicated in Table J-3. Background shall be white; and the panel, black with white directional symbol. Any letters used against the white background shall be black. The colors shall be those of opaque, glossy samples as specified in Table 1 of American National Standard Z53.1–1967.

(e) (6)

Report All Injuries to the First-Aid Room at Once.

Walk—Don't Run.

Report All Injuries No Matter How Slight.

Think, If Safe Go Ahead.

Make Your Work Place Safe Before Starting the Job.

Report All Unsafe Conditions to Your Foreman.

Help Keep This Plant Safe and Clean.

SAFETY INSTRUCTION SIGNS—NATURE OF WORDING

NOTE:

This list is intended to serve as a guide for choosing the correct message, which should be easily read and make a positive, rather than a negative, suggestion.

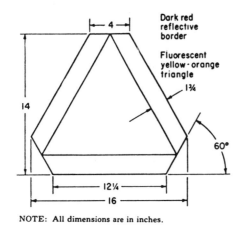

(d) (10)

4
Dark red reflective border
Fluorescent yellow-orange triangle
1¾
14
60°
12¼
16

NOTE: All dimensions are in inches.

Fig. J-7

SLOW-MOVING VEHICLES

NOTE:

Use only for vehicles which, by design, move slowly (25 mph or less). Material, location, and mounting as per American Society of Agricultural Engineers Emblem for Identifying Slow-Moving Vehicles, ASAE R276, 1967, or ASAE S276.2 (ANSI B114.1–1971).

(d) (7)

Fig. J-6

Table J-4—Standard Proportions for Directional Signs

Sign size, inches height width	Black rectangular panel, inches height width	White arrow, inches				Maximum space for sign wording below panel height
		Overall length	Arrow head height width	Arrow shaft height	Arrow tail height width	
6½ x 14	3¼ x 13⅜	12⅝	2¾ x 3	1⅛	2⅜ x 3¼	2¼ x 13⅜
9 x 20	4½ x 19⅜	18⅝	3¾ x 4⅛	1⅝	3¼ x 4½	3⅜ x 19⅜
12 x 28	6 x 27⅜	26⅝	5⅛ x 5⅝	2⅛	4⅜ x 6	4¾ x 27⅜
15 x 36	7½ x 35⅜	34⅝	6⅜ x 6⅞	2⅝	5½ x 7½	6¼ x 35⅜

DIRECTIONAL SIGNS

NOTE:
Use proportions as indicated in Table J-4. Background shall be white, and panel black with white directional symbol. Letters used against white background shall be black. Colors shall be those of opaque, glossy samples as specified in Table 1 of American National Standard Z53.1–1967.

(e) (7)

This Way Out (below arrow panel).

This Way (inside arrow) Out (below arrow panel).

Fire Exit (below arrow panel).

Fire (inside arrow) Extinguisher (below arrow panel).

To the (inside arrow) Fire Escape (below arrow panel).

To the (inside arrow) First Aid (below arrow panel).

Manway (below arrow panel).

This Way to (inside arrow) First-Aid Room (below arrow panel).

DIRECTIONAL SIGNS—NATURE OF WORDING

NOTE:
This list is intended to serve as a guide for choosing the correct message, which should be easily read and make a positive, rather than a negative, suggestion.

(d) (8)

NOTE:
Regulatory and control signs required for the safe movement of vehicles and pedestrians on thoroughfares on plant property shall conform to the standards established in "American National Manual on Uniform Traffic Control. Devices for Streets and Highways," D6.1–1961.

IN-PLANT TRAFFIC SIGNS

(d) (9)

NOTE:

Blue shall be the standard color for informational signs on the public roads. It may be used as the background color for the complete sign or as a panel at the top of such types of "Notice" signs which have a white background. The colors shall be those of opaque, glossy samples as specified in Table 1 of American National Standard Z53.1–1967.

INFORMATIONAL SIGNS

(e) (8)

No Trespassing Under Penalty of the Law.

This Elevator Is for Freight Only, Not for Passengers.

No Admittance Except to Employees on Duty.

No Admittance.

No Admittance, Apply at Office.

No Trespassing.

Men.

Women.

For Employees Only.

Office.

INFORMATIONAL SIGNS—NATURE OF WORDING

(d) (11)

POISON:

ELECTRICITY:

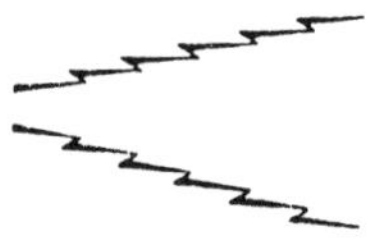

NOTE:

Symbols used on signs shall follow recognized practices, such as in Figure J-8.

Fig. J-8

SYMBOLS USED ON SIGNS

SPECS FOR ACCIDENT PREVENTION
SIGNS AND TAGS

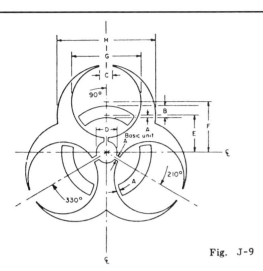

Fig. J-9

BIOLOGICAL HAZARD SYMBOL

Dimension	A	B	C	D	E	F	G	H
Units	1	3½	4	6	11	15	21	30

(e) (4)

NOTE:

Use to signify the actual or potential presence of a biohazard and to identify equipment, containers, rooms, materials, experimental animals, or combinations thereof, which contain, or are contaminated with, viable hazardous agents. For the purpose of this subparagraph the term "biological hazard" or "biohazard" shall include only those infectious agents presenting a risk or potential risk to the well-being of man.

Definitions applicable to Sub-part L (Sections 1910.156 through 1910.165b);

(a) "Class A fires" are fires in ordinary combustible materials, such as wood, cloth, paper, and rubber.

(b) "Class B fires" are fires in flammable liquids, gases, and greases.

(c) "Class C fires" are fires which involve energized electrical equipment where the electrical nonconductivity of the extinguishing media is of importance. (When electrical equipment is de-energized, extinguishers for Class A or B fires may be used safely.)

(d) "Class D fires" are fires in combustible metals, such as magnesium, titanium, zirconium, sodium, and potassium.

(e) Classification of portable fire extinguishers: "Portable fire extinguishers" are classified for use on certain classes of fires and rated for relative extinguishing effectiveness at a temperature of plus 70°F by nationally recognized testing laboratories. This is based upon the preceding classification of fires and the fire extinguishment potentials as determined by fire tests

NOTE: The classification and rating system described in this section is that used by Underwriters' Laboratories, Inc., and Underwriters Laboratories of Canada and is based on extinguishing preplanned fires of determined size and description as follows:
(i) Class A rating—Wood and excelsior fires excluding deep-seated conditions.
(ii) Class B rating—Two-inch depth gasoline fires in square pans.
(iii) Class C rating—No fire test. Agent must be a nonconductor of electricity.
(iv) Class D rating—Special tests on specific combustible metal fires.

(f) A "light hazard" is a situation where the amount of combustibles or flammable liquids present is such that fires of small size may be expected. These may include offices, schoolrooms, churches, assembly halls, telephone exchanges, etc.

(g) An "ordinary hazard" is a situation where the amount of combustibles or flammable liquids present is such that fires of moderate size may be expected. These may include mercantile storage and display, auto showrooms, parking garages, light manufacturing, warehouses not classified as extra hazard, school shop areas, etc.

(h) An "extra hazard" is a situation where the amount of combustibles or flammable liquids present is such that fires of severe magnitude may be expected. These may include woodworking, auto repair, aircraft servicing, warehouses with high-piled (14 ft or higher) combustibles, and processes such as flammable liquid handling, painting, dipping, etc.

(i) Sprinkler system: A "sprinkler system," for fire protection purposes, is an integrated system of underground and overhead piping designed in accordance with fire protection engineering standards. The system includes a suitable water supply, such as a gravity tank, fire pump, reservoir, or pressure tank and/or connection by underground piping to a city main. The portion of the sprinkler system above ground is a network of specially sized or hydraulically designed piping installed in a building, structure or area, generally overhead, and to which sprinklers are connected in a systematic pattern. The system includes a controlling valve and a device for actuating an alarm when the system is in operation. The system is usually activated by heat from a fire and discharges water over the fire area.

NOTE: The design and installation of water supply facilities such as gravity tanks, fire pumps, reservoirs, or pressure tanks, and underground piping are covered by NFPA Standards No. 22–1970, Water Tanks for Private Fire Protection; No. 20–1970, Installation of Centrifugal Fire Pumps; and No. 24–1970, Outside Protection.

(j) Sprinkler alarms: A "sprinkler alarm" unit is an assembly of apparatus approved for the service and so constructed and installed that any flow of water from a sprinkler system equal to or greater than that from a single automatic sprinkler will result in an audible alarm signal on the premises.

(k) Class of service—standpipe systems: "Standpipe systems" are grouped into three general classes of service for the intended use in the extinguishment of fire.

(1) Class I: For use by fire departments and those trained in handling heavy fire streams (2½-inch hose).

(2) Class II: For use primarily by the building occupants until the arrival of the fire department (small hose).

(3) Class III: For use by either fire departments and those trained in handling heavy hose streams or by the building occupants.

(l) Class I service: "Class I service" is a standpipe system capable of furnishing the effective fire streams required during the more advanced stages of fire on the inside of buildings or for exposure fire.

(m) Class II service: "Class II service" is a standpipe system which affords a ready means for the control of incipient fires by the occupants of buildings during working hours and by watchmen and those present during the night time and holidays.

(n) Class III service: "Class III service" is a standpipe system capable of furnishing the effective

fire streams required during the more advanced stages of fire on the inside of buildings as well as providing a ready means for the control of fires by the occupants of the building.

(o) Standpipe systems: "Standpipe systems" are usually of the following types:

(1) A wet standpipe system having a supply valve open and water pressure maintained at all times.

(2) A standpipe system so arranged through the use of approved devices as to admit water to the system automatically by opening a hose valve.

(3) A standpipe system arranged to admit water to the system through manual operation of approved remote control devices located at each hose station.

(4) Dry standpipe having no permanent water supply. See also paragraph (k) of this section.

(p) Type I storage: "Type I storage" is that in which combustible commodities or noncombustible commodities involving combustible packaging or storage aids are stored over 15 ft but not more than 21 ft high in solid piles or over 12 ft but not more than 21 ft high in piles that contain horizontal channels. Minor quantities of commodities of hazard greater than ordinary combustibles may be included without affecting this general classification.

(q) Type II storage: "Type II storage" is that in which combustible commodities or noncombustible commodities involving combustible packaging or storage aids are stored not over 15 ft high in solid piles or not over 12 ft high in piles that contain horizontal channels. Minor quantities of commodities of hazard greater than ordinary combustibles may be included without affecting this general classification.

(r) Type III storage: "Type III storage" is that in which the stored commodities, packaging and storage aids are noncombustible or contain only a small concentration of combustibles which are incapable of producing a fire that would cause appreciable damage to the commodities stored or to noncombustible wall, floor, or roof construction. Ordinary combustible commodities in completely sealed noncombustible containers may qualify in this classification. General commodity storage that is subject to frequent changing and storage of combustible packaging and storage aids is excluded from this category.

(s) "Approved": "Approved" means listed or approved by: (1) At least one of the following nationally recognized testing laboratories: Factory Mutual Engineering Corp.; Underwriters' Laboratories, Inc., or (2) Federal agencies such as Bureau of Mines, Department of the Interior: Department of Transportation; or U.S. Coast Guard, which issue approvals for such equipment.

(a) (6)

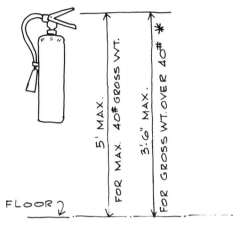

5' MAX.
FOR MAX. 40# GROSS WT.

3'-6" MAX.
FOR GROSS WT. OVER 40#*

FLOOR

MOUNTING HEIGHT

NOTE:
*Except wheeled types.

(b) (2)

NOTE:
Extinguishers shall be selected for the specific class or classes of hazards to be protected in accordance with the following paragraphs.

Extinguishers for protecting Class A hazards shall be selected from among the following: foam, loaded stream, multipurpose dry chemical, and water types. Certain smaller extinguishers which are charged with multipurpose dry chemicals are rated on Class B and Class C fires but have insufficient effectiveness to earn the minimum 1-A rating even though they have value in extinguishing smaller Class A fires.

Such smaller extinguishers shall not be used to meet the requirements of Table L-1.

Extinguishers for protection of Class B hazards shall be selected from the following: bromotrifluoromethane, carbon dioxide, dry chemical. Extinguishers with ratings less than 1-B shall not be considered in determining suitability.

Extinguishers for protection of Class C hazards shall be selected from the following: bromotrifluoromethane, carbon dioxide, dry chemical, and multipurpose dry chemical.

Note: Carbon dioxide extinguishers equipped with metal horns are not considered safe for use on fires in energized electrical equipment and, therefore, are not classified for use on Class C hazards.

Extinguishers and extinguishing agents for the protection of Class D hazards shall be of types approved for use on the specific combustible metal hazard.

SELECTION BY HAZARD

(c) (1) (vi)

NOTE:
Combustible buildings having an occupancy hazard subject to Class B, and/or Class C, fires shall have a standard complement of Class A fire extinguishers as required by Table L-1 for building protection, plus additional Class B and/or Class C extinguishers. Where fire extinguishers have more than one letter classification (such as 2-A: 20-B:C), they may be considered to satisfy the requirements of each letter class.

COMBUSTIBLE BUILDINGS

(c) (2)

TABLE L–1

Basic minimum extinguisher rating for area specified	Maximum travel distances to extinguishers (feet)	Areas to be protected per extinguisher		
		Light hazard occupancy (square feet)	Ordinary hazard occupancy (square feet)	Extra hazard occupancy (square feet)
1A	75	3,000	Note 1	Note 1
2A	75	6,000	3,000	Note 1
3A	75	9,000	4,500	3,000
4A	75	11,250	6,000	4,000
6A	75	11,250	9,000	6,000

NOTE 1: Not permitted except as specified in subdivision (ii) of this subparagraph.

SIZE AND PLACEMENT FOR CLASS A HAZARDS

NOTE:

(ii) The protection requirements specified in Table L-1 may be fulfilled by several extinguishers of lower ratings for ordinary or extra-hazard occupancies.

(iii) Where the floor area of a building is less than that specified in Table L-1, at least one extinguisher of the minimum size recommended shall be provided.

(vi) The protection requirements may be fulfilled with extinguishers of higher rating provided the travel distance to such larger extinguishers shall not exceed 75 ft.

(c) (3)

TABLE L–2

Type of hazard	Basic minimum extinguisher rating	Maximum travel distance to extinguishers (feet)
Light	4B	50
Ordinary	8B	50
Extra	12B	50

SIZE AND PLACEMENT FOR CLASS B FIRES (OTHER THAN FLAMMABLE LIQUID FIRES OF APPRECIABLE DEPTH)

NOTE:

(ii) Two or more extinguishers of lower rating, except for foam extinguishers, shall not be used to fulfill the protection requirements of Table L-2. Up to three foam extinguishers may be used to fulfill these requirements.

(iii) The protection requirements may be fulfilled with extinguishers of higher ratings provided the travel distance to such larger extinguishers shall not exceed 50 ft.

(c) (4) (i) and (ii), and (5)

NOTE:

Class B fires in flammable liquids of appreciable depth:

(i) For flammable liquid hazards of appreciable depth (Class B), such as in dip or quench tanks, Class B fire extinguishers shall be provided on the basis of one numerical unit of Class B extinguishing potential per square foot of flammable liquid surface of the largest tank hazard within the area.

Appreciable depth is defined as a depth of a liquid greater than ¼ in.

(ii) Two or more extinguishers shall not be used in lieu of the extinguishers required for the largest tank. Up to three foam extinguishers may be used to fulfill these requirements.

Class C hazards: (i) Extinguishers with Class C ratings shall be required where energized electrical equipment may be encountered which would require a nonconducting extinguishing medium. This will include fire either directly involving or surrounding electrical equipment. Since the fire itself is a Class A or Class B hazard, the extinguishers are sized and located on the basis of the anticipated Class A or B hazard.

SIZE AND PLACEMENT FOR CLASS B FIRES IN FLAMMABLE LIQUIDS OF APPRECIABLE DEPTH AND FOR CLASS C HAZARDS

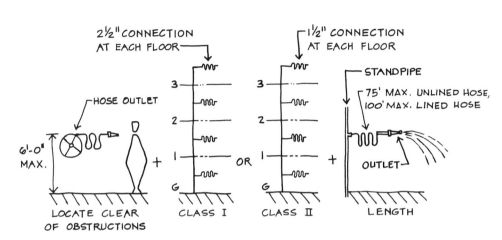

HOSE OUTLETS, CONNECTIONS, LENGTHS

(b) (1) (i) and (ii), (2), (3), and (4)

NOTE:

For Class III service locate in stairway for large hoses and near stairways in corridors for small hoses, and furnish a 2½-in. and a 1½-in. connection on each floor.

Equip each hose outlet for use of building occupants (Class II and III) with approved fire hose.

Equip each small hose station with approved rack or reel.

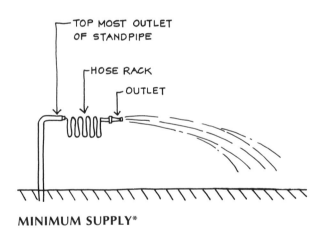

MINIMUM SUPPLY*

(c) (1), (2), and (3)

NOTE:

*Class I, Class III supply:

1. 500 gpm for 30 minutes plus;

2. 250 gpm/additional standpipe (maximum 2,500 gpm) for 30 minutes.

3. Residual pressure equal to 65 psi per standpipe at topmost outlet at 500-gpm flow.

*Class II supply:

1. 100 gpm for 30 minutes.

2. Residual pressure equal to 65 psi per standpipe at topmost outlet at 100-gpm flow.

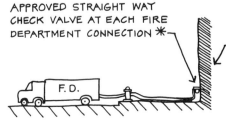

FIRE DEPARTMENT CONNECTIONS

(c) (4) (i), (ii), (v), and (ix)

NOTE:

* Locate connections on the street side free of obstruction from nearby fences, buildings, other fire department connections.

Provide cast sign on plate or fitting with 1-in. letters reading "Standpipe."

**(a) (2) and (3),
and (b) (1)
and (2) (i)**

OPTIONAL FIRE DEPARTMENT
CONNECTION WITH REQUIRED
STRAIGHT-WAY CHECK VALVE

ALTERNATE SUPPLY

PROTECTED BUILDING

OPTIONAL SUPPLY

FIRE DEPARTMENT
PUMP VEHICLE *

RISER

AUTOMATIC VALVE(S)

← TO WATER SUPPLY

GENERAL REQUIREMENTS

NOTE:
* Connection Size:
1. Provide minimum 4-in. pipe for fire
engine connection or 6-in. pipe for fire boat
connection.
2. Provide 3-in. connection at single
3-in. riser.

(c)

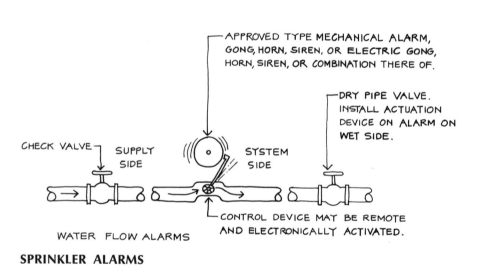

APPROVED TYPE MECHANICAL ALARM,
GONG, HORN, SIREN, OR ELECTRIC GONG,
HORN, SIREN, OR COMBINATION THERE OF.

DRY PIPE VALVE.
INSTALL ACTUATION
DEVICE ON ALARM ON
WET SIDE.

CHECK VALVE

SUPPLY
SIDE

SYSTEM
SIDE

CONTROL DEVICE MAT BE REMOTE
AND ELECTRONICALLY ACTIVATED.

WATER FLOW ALARMS

SPRINKLER ALARMS

NOTE:
1. Locate on outside of building so
that all parts are readily accessible.
2. Locate drains so as to avoid freezing.
3. Arrange drains from alarm device
to avoid overflowing at the alarm apparatus, domestic connections with the drains
full open and under pressure.

(e)

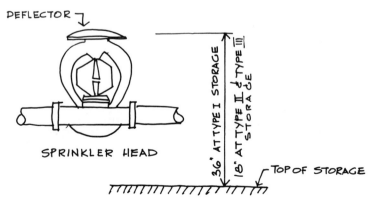

DEFLECTOR

36" AT TYPE I STORAGE

18" AT TYPE II & TYPE III STORAGE

SPRINKLER HEAD

TOP OF STORAGE

"HEAD" CLEARANCE

(a) (1) and (2)

GENERAL REQUIREMENTS

NOTE:
When dry chemical extinguishing systems are provided they shall meet the design requirements of the National Fire Protection Association's "Standard for Dry Chemical Extinguishing Systems," NFPA No. 17–1969, and the requirements of this section.

Where there is a possibility that personnel may be exposed to a dry chemical discharge, suitable safeguards shall be provided to ensure prompt evacuation of such locations, and also to provide means for prompt rescue of any trapped personnel.

(b) (1)

ALARMS AND INDICATORS

NOTE:
Alarms and/or indicators are used to indicate the operation of the system, hazard to personnel, or failure of any supervised device or equipment. The devices may be audible or visual. The type, number, and location of the devices shall be such that their purpose is satisfactorily accomplished.

(b) (2)

OPERATION ALARM

NOTE:
An alarm or indicator shall be provided to show that the system has operated, that personnel response may be needed, and that the system should be charged.

Alarms indicating failure of supervised devices or equipment shall give prompt and positive indication of any failure and shall be distinctive from alarms indicating operation or hazardous conditions.

CARBON DIOXIDE SYSTEMS—GENERAL REQUIREMENTS

(a)

NOTE:

When carbon dioxide extinguishing systems are provided they shall meet the design requirements of the National Fire Protection Association's "Standard on Carbon Dioxide Extinguishing Systems," NFPA No. 12-1968, and the requirements of this section.

In any use of carbon dioxide where there is a possibility that employees may be trapped in, or enter into, atmosphere made hazardous by a carbon dioxide discharge, suitable safeguards shall be provided to ensure prompt evacuation of and to prevent entry into such atmospheres and also to provide means for prompt rescue of any trapped personnel. Such safety items as personnel training, warning signs, discharge alarms, and breathing apparatus shall be considered.

LOCAL FIRE ALARM SYSTEMS—GENERAL REQUIREMENTS

(a)

NOTE:

Where local fire alarm signaling systems are provided they shall meet the design requirements of the National Fire Protection Association's "Standard for the Installation, Maintenance, and Use of Local Protective Signaling Systems for Watchman, Fire Alarm and Supervisory Service," NFPA No. 72A–1967, and the requirements of this section.

FIRE ALARM BOXES

(b)

NOTE:

Manual fire alarm boxes shall be approved for the particular application and shall be used only for fire protective signaling purposes. Combined fire alarm and watchman's signaling boxes are acceptable.

Each box shall be securely mounted.

Manual fire alarm boxes shall be distributed throughout the protected area so that they are unobstructed, readily accessible, and located in the normal path of exit from the area. Additional boxes shall be provided on each floor to obtain a maximum horizontal travel distance of 200 ft to the nearest box.

(a) The requirements contained in the following articles and sections of the National Electrical Code, NFPA 70-1971; ANSI C1-1971 (Rev. of 1968) shall apply to all electrical installations and utilization equipment:

Articles:

500	Hazardous Locations
501	Class I Installations (Hazardous Locations)
502	Class II Installations (Hazardous Locations)
503	Class III Installations (Hazardous Locations)

Sections:

250-58 (a) and (b).	Equipment on Structural Metal
250-59 (a), (b), and (c).	Portable and/or Cord Connected and Plug Connected Equipment, Grounding Method
400-3 (a) and (b).	Flexible Cords and Cable, Uses
400-4	Flexible Cords and Cable Prohibited
400-5	Flexible Cords and Cables, Splices
400-9	Overcurrent Protection and Ampacities of Flexible Cords
410-10	Pull at Joints and Terminals of Flexible Cords and Cables
422-8	Installation of Appliances with Flexible Cords
422-9	Installation of Portable Immersion Heaters
422-10	Installation Appliances Adjacent to Combustible Material
422-11	Stands for Portable Appliances
422-12	Signals for Heated Appliances
422-14	Water Heaters
422-15 (a), (b), and (c).	Installation of Infrared Lamp and Industrial Heating Appliances
110-14 (a) and (b).	Electric Connection
110-17 (a), (b), and (c).	Grounding Live Part
110-18	Arcing Parts
110-21	Marking
110-22	Identification
240-16 (a), (b), (c), and (d)	Location in Premises for Overcurrent Protection Devices

Sections:

240-19 (a) and (b).	Guarding of Arcing or Suddenly Moving Parts of Overcurrent Protection Devices
250-3 (a) and (b).	D.C. System Grounding
250-5 (a), (b) and (c).	A.C. Circuits and Systems to Be Grounded
250-7	Circuits Not to Be Grounded
250-42 (a), (b), (c), and (d).	Fixed Equipment Grounding, General
250-43 (a), (b), (c), (d), (e), (f), (g), (h), and (i).	Fixed Equipment Grounding, Specific
250-44 (a), (b), (c), (d), and (e).	Nonelectrical Equipment, Grounding
250-45 (a), (b), (c), and (d).	Equipment Connected by Cord and Plug, Grounding
430-142 (a), (b), (c), and (d).	Stationary Motor, Grounding
430-143	Portable Motors, Grounding
250-50 (a) and (b).	Equipment Grounding Connections
250-51	Effective Grounding
250-57 (a) and (b).	Fixed Equipment Method of Grounding
422-16	Appliance Grounding
422-17	Installation of Wall-mounted Ovens and Counter-mounted Cooking Units

(b) Every new electrical installation and all new utilization equipment installed after March 15, 1972, and every replacement, modification, or repair or rehabilitation, after March 15, 1972, of any part of any electrical installation or utilization equipment installed before March 15, 1972, shall be installed or made, and maintained, in accordance with the provisions of the 1971 National Electrical Code, NFPA 70-1971; ANSI C1-1971 (Rev. of 1968).

(c) Notwithstanding the provisions of paragraphs (a) and (b) of this section, the effective date of the requirement in section 210-7 of the National Electrical Code, that all 15- and 20-ampere receptacle outlets on single-phase circuits for construction sites shall have approved ground-fault circuit protection for personnel, is postponed pending reconsideration of the requirement.

Appendix A

Location of Regional, Area, and District Offices
U.S. Department of Labor
Occupational Safety and Health Administration

REGIONAL OFFICES

REGION I—Boston
Donald E. Mackenzie
John F. Kennedy Federal Building
Government Center 308 E
Boston, Massachusetts 02203
617-223-6712

REGION II—New York
Alfred Barden
1515 Broadway
Room 3445
New York, New York 10036
212-971-5754

REGION III—Philadelphia
David H. Rhone
Penn Square Building
Room 623
1317 Filbert Street
Philadelphia, Pennsylvania 19107
215-597-4102

REGION IV—Atlanta
Basil Needham
1375 Peachtree Street, NE.
Suite 587
Atlanta, Georgia 30309
404-526-3573

REGION V—Chicago
Edward E. Estkowski
300 South Wacker Drive
Room 1201
Chicago, Illinois 60606
312-353-4716

REGION VI—Dallas
John Barto
Texaco Building, Suite 600
1512 Commerce Street
Dallas, Texas 75201
214-749-2477

REGION VII—Kansas City
Joseph Reidinger
Waltower Building, Room 300
823 Walnut Street
Kansas City, Missouri 64106
816-374-5249

REGION VIII—Denver
Howard J. Schulte
Federal Building, Room 15010
1961 Stout Street
Box 3588
Denver, Colorado 80202
303-837-3883

REGION IX—San Francisco
Warren Fuller
9470 Federal Building
450 Golden Gate Avenue
Box 36017
San Francisco, California 94102
415-556-0584

REGION X—Seattle
James W. Lake
1808 Smith Tower Building
506 Second Avenue
Seattle, Washington 98104
206-442-5930

AREA AND DISTRICT OFFICES

REGION I—Boston
Area Offices
John V. Fiatarone
Custom House Building, Room 703
State Street
Boston, Massachusetts 02109
FTS and commercial phone:
617-223-4511/12

Harold R. Smith
Federal Building, Room 617B
450 Main Street
Hartford, Connecticut 06103
FTS and commercial phone:
203-244-2294

Francis R. Amirault
Federal Building, Room 425
55 Pleasant Street
Concord, New Hampshire 03301
FTS phone:
603-224-7725
Commercial:
603-224-1995/6

District Office
Steven J. Simms
503-A Federal Building
Providence, Rhode Island 02903
FTS and commercial phone:
401-528-4466

REGION II—New York
Area Offices
Nicholas A. DiArchangel
90 Church Street
Room 1405
New York, New York 10007
FTS and commercial phone:
212-264-9840/1/2

William J. Dreeland
Midtown Plaza, Room 203
700 East Water Street
Syracuse, New York 13210
FTS and commercial phone:
315-473-2700/1

James H. Epps
370 Old Country Road
Garden City
Long Island, New York 11530
FTS and commercial phone:
516-294-0400

Thomas W. Fullam, Jr.
Federal Office Building, Room 635
970 Broad Street
Newark, New Jersey 07102
FTS and commercial phone:
201-645-5930/1/2

Louis Jacob
Condominium San Alberto Building
Room 328
605 Condado Avenue
Santurce, Puerto Rico 00907
FTS and commercial phone:
809-724-1059

REGION III—Philadelphia
Area Offices
Harry Sachkar
1317 Filbert Street
Suite 1010
Philadelphia, Pennsylvania 19017
FTS and commercial phone:
215-597-4955

Byron R. Chadwick
Stanwick Building, Room 111
3661 Virginia Beach Boulevard
Norfolk, Virginia 23502
FTS and commercial phone:
703-441-6381/2

Lapsley C. Ewing, Jr.
Federal Building, Room 8015
Post Office Box 10186
400 North 8th Street
Richmond, Virginia 23240
FTS and commercial phone:
703-782-2241/2

Maurice R. Daly
Federal Building, Room 1110A
31 Hopkins Plaza, Charles Center
Baltimore, Maryland 21201
FTS and commercial phone:
301-962-2840

Harry G. Lacey
Federal Building, Room 445 D
1000 Liberty Avenue
Pittsburgh, Pennsylvania 15222
FTS and commercial phone:
412-644-2905/6

REGION IV—Atlanta
Area Offices
William F. Moerlins
1371 Peachtree Street, NE.
Room 723
Atlanta, Georgia 30309
FTS and commercial phone:
404-526-5806/7 or 5883/4

James E. Blount
Bridge Building, Room 204
3200 East Oakland Park Boulevard
Fort Lauderdale, Florida 33308
FTS phone:
305-350-7331
Commercial:
305-525-0611 x 331

William W. Gordon
U.S. Federal Office Building
Box 35062
400 West Bay Street
Jacksonville, Florida 32202
FTS and commercial phone:
904-791-2895

Frank P. Flanagan
600 Federal Place, Room 561
Louisville, Kentucky 40202
FTS and commercial phone:
502-582-6111/12

Harold J. Monegue
Commerce Building, Room 801
11 North Royal Street
Mobile, Alabama 36602
FTS phone:
205-433-4382
Commercial:
205-433-3581 x 482

Quentin F. Haskins
1361 East Morehead Street
Charlotte, North Carolina 28204
FTS phone:
704-372-7495
Commercial:
704-372/0711 x 495

Eugene E. Light
1600 Hayes Street
Suite 302
Nashville, Tennessee 37203
FTS and commercial phone:
615-749-5313

Joseph L. Camp
Todd Mall
2047 Canyon Road
Birmingham, Alabama 35216
FTS phone:
205-325-6081
Commercial:
205-822-7100

Bernard E. Addy
Enterprise Building, Suite 201
6605 Abercorn Street
Savannah, Georgia 31405
FTS phone:
912-232-4393
Commercial:
912-354-0733

REGION V—Chicago
Area Offices
William Funcheon
300 South Wacker Drive
Room 1200
Chicago, Illinois 60606
FTS and commercial phone:
312-353-1390

Peter Schmitt
Bryson Building, Room 224
700 Bryden Road
Columbus, Ohio 43215
FTS and commercial phone:
614-469-5582

Robert B. Hanna
Clark Building, Room 400
633 West Wisconsin Avenue
Milwaukee, Wisconsin 53203
FTS and commercial phone:
414-224-3315/6

J. Fred Keppler
U.S. Post Office and Courthouse
Room 423
46 East Ohio Street
Indianapolis, Indiana 46204
FTS and commercial phone:
317-633-7384

Kenneth Bowman
847 Federal Office Building
1240 East Ninth Street
Cleveland, Ohio 44199
FTS and commercial phone:
216-522-3818

Earl J. Krotzer
Michigan Theatre Building
Room 626
220 Bagley Avenue
Detroit, Michigan 48226
FTS and commercial phone:
313-226-6720

Vernon Fern
110 South Fourth Street
Room 437
Minneapolis, Minnesota 55401
FTS and commercial phone:
612-725-2571

Ronald McCann
Federal Office Building, Room 5522
550 Main Street
Cincinnati, Ohio 45202
FTS and commercial phone:
513-684-2355

Glenn Butler
Federal Office Building, Room 734
234 North Summit Street
Toledo, Ohio 43604
FTS and commercial phone:
419-259-7542

REGION VI—Dallas

Area Offices

Charles J. Adams
Federal Building, Room 6B1
1100 Commerce Street
Dallas, Texas 75202
FTS and commercial phone:
214-749-1786/7/8

Robert B. Simmons
Federal Building, Room 421
1205 Texas Avenue
Lubbock, Texas 79401
FTS phone:
806-747-3681
Commercial:
806-747-3711 x 3681

James T. Knorpp
Petroleum Building, Room 512
420 South Boulder
Tulsa, Oklahoma 74103
FTS and commercial phone:
918-584-7151 x 7676

Thomas T. Curry
Old Federal Office Building
Room 802
201 Fannin Street
Houston, Texas 77002
FTS and commercial phone:
713-226-5431

John K. Parsons
Federal Building, Room 1036
600 South Street
New Orleans, Louisiana 70130
FTS and commercial phone:
504-527-2451/2 or 6166/7

District Office

Burtrand C. Lindquist
U.S. Custom House Building
Room 325
Galveston, Texas 77550
FTS and commercial phone:
713-763-1472/4

REGION VII—Kansas City

Area Offices

Robert J. Borchardt
1627 Main Street
Room 1100
Kansas City, Missouri 64108
FTS and commercial phone:
816-374-2756

A. F. Castranova
210 North 12th Boulevard
Room 554
St. Louis, Missouri 63101
FTS and commercial phone:
314-622-5461/2

Warren P. Wright
City National Bank Building
Room 630
Harney and 16th Streets
Omaha, Nebraska 68102
FTS and commercial phone:
402-221-3276/7

REGION VIII—Denver

Area Offices

Jerome J. Williams
Squire Plaza Building
8527 West Colfax Avenue
Lakewood, Colorado 80125
FTS and commercial phone:
303-234-4471

Charles F. Hines
Executive Building, Suite 309
455 East Fourth South
Salt Lake City, Utah 84111
FTS and commercial phone:
801-524-5080

Vernon A. Strahm
Petroleum Building, Suite 225
2812 First Avenue, North
Billings, Montana 59101
FTS phone:
406-245-6640/6649
Commercial:
406-245-6711, x 6640-6649

REGION IX—San Francisco

Area Offices

Donald T. Pickford
100 McAllister Street
Room 1706
San Francisco, California 94102
FTS and commercial phone:
415-556-0536

Lawrence E. Gromachey
Amerco Towers, Suite 910
2721 North Central Avenue
Phoenix, Arizona 85004
FTS and commercial phone:
602-261-4857/8

Anthony Mignano
Hartwell Building, Room 514
19 Pine Avenue
Long Beach, California 90802
FTS phone: 212-831-9281, then ask
Long Beach FTS operator for
432-3434
Commercial:
213-432-3434

Paul F. Haygood
333 Queen Street
Suite 505
Honolulu, Hawaii 96813
FTS and commercial phone:
808-546-3157/8

REGION X—Seattle

Area Offices

Richard L. Beeston
1906 Smith Tower Building
506 Second Avenue
Seattle, Washington 98104
FTS and commercial phone:
206-442-7520/27

Darrell Miller
Willholth Building, Room 217
610 C Street
Anchorage, Alaska 99501
FTS phone: dial local FTS operator
and ask for 907-272-5661 x 851
Commercial:
907-272-5561 x 851

Eugene Harrower
Pittock Block, Room 526
921 Southwest Washington Street
Portland, Oregon 97205
FTS and commercial phone:
503-221-2251

Appendix B
Standards Incorporated by Reference in Part 1910

I. Abbreviations and Names of Private Standards-Setting Organizations

AAI   Agricultural Ammonia Institute
ACGIH   American Conference of Governmental Industrial Hygienists
AMO   Air Moving and Conditioning Association, Inc.
ANSI   American National Standards Institute, Inc.
API   American Petroleum Institute
ASAE   American Society of Agricultural Engineers
ASHRE   American Society of Heating, Refrigeration and Air Conditioning Engineers,
         Inc.
ASME   American Society of Mechanical Engineers
ASTM   American Society for Testing and Materials
AWS   American Welding Society, Inc.
CGA   Compressed Gas Association, Inc.
CMAA   Crane Manufacturers Association of America (Formerly Electric Overhead
         Crane Institute)
IME   Institute of Makers of Explosives
IPM   International Association of Plumbing and Mechanical Officials
NEMA   National Electrical Manufacturers Association
NFPA   National Fire Protection Association
NPF   National Plant Food Institute
SAE   Society of Automotive Engineers, Inc.
UL   Underwriters' Laboratories, Inc.
USPC   United States Pharmacopeial Convention

II. Abbreviations and Names of Federal Agencies

AEC   Atomic Energy Commission
ESA   Employment Standards Administration, Labor
FAA   Federal Aviation Administration, Transportation
FSS   Federal Supply Service, General Services
HMRB   Hazardous Materials Regulations Board, Transportation

NBS   National Bureau of Standards, Commerce
OSHA   Occupational Safety and Health Administration, Labor
USCG   U.S. Coast Guard, Transportation
USDA   United States Department of Agriculture
USPHS   U.S. Public Health Service, HEW

III. CFR—Code of Federal Regulations
IV. USC—United States Code—Public Law
V. Other

I. PRIVATE STANDARDS-SETTING ORGANIZATIONS
Standards Organization/Title

AAI Agricultural Ammonia Institute
c/o The Fertilizer Institute
1015—18th Street, N.W.
Washington, D.C. 20036 (202-466-2700)

M-5-1963 Hose Specification for Anhydrous Ammonia (Appendix C of the AAI Standards for Storage and Handling of Anhydrous Ammonia)

ACGIH American Conference of Governmental Industrial Hygienists
1014 Broadway
Cincinnati, Ohio 45202 (513-684-3557)

1968 Threshold Limit Values of Airborne Contaminants
1970 Threshold Limit Values of Physical Agents Adopted by ACGIH
1970 Industrial Ventilation, 11th Edition

AMO Air Moving and Conditioning Association, Inc.
30 West University Drive
Arlington Heights, Illinois 60004 (312-394-0150)

Bulletin 210, Standard Test Code for Air Moving Devices, April, 1962

ANSI American National Standards Institute, Inc.
1430 Broadway
New York, New York 10018 (212-868-1220)

A10.2-1944 Building Construction, Safety Code for (Partially revised by A10.4-1963, A10.5-1969, A10.6-1969, A10.7-1970, A10.8-1969 and A10.10-1970)
A10.3-1970 Explosive-Actuated Fastening Tools, Safety Requirements for
A10.5-1969 Material Hoists, Safety Requirements for (Partial Revision of A10.2-1944)
A10.8-1969 Scaffolding, Safety Requirements for (Partial Revision of A10.2-1944)
A11.1-1965 (R1970) Industrial Lighting, Practice for (IES RP 7-1965)
A12.1-1967 Floor and Wall Openings, Railings, and Toe Boards, Safety Requirements for
A13.1-1956 Identification of Piping Systems, Scheme for the
A14.1-1968 Portable Wood Ladders, Safety Code for
A14.2-1956 Portable Metal Ladders, Safety Code for
A14.3-1956 Fixed Ladders, Safety Code for
A17.1-1965 Elevators, Dumbwaiters, and Moving Walks, Safety Code for
A17.1a-1967 Supplement to A17.1-1965
A17.1b-1968 Supplement to A17.1-1965 and A17.1a-1967
A17.1c-1969 Supplement to A17.1-1965, A17.1a-1967, and A17.1b-1968
A17.1d-1970 Supplement to A17.1-1965, A17.1a-1967, A17.1b-1968, and A17.1c-1969
A17.2-1960 Elevators, Practice for the Inspection of (Inspectors' Manual)
A17.2a-1965 Addenda to A17.2-1960
A17.2b-1967 Supplement to A17.2-1960
A40.8-1955 National Plumbing Code
A58.1-1955 Minimum Design Loads in Buildings and Other Structures
A64.1-1968 Fixed Industrial Stairs, Requirements for
A90.1-1969 Manlifts, Safety Standard for
A92.1-1971 Mobile Ladder Stands and Scaffolds
A92.2-1969 Vehicle Mounted Elevating and Rotating Work Platforms
A120.1-1970 Powered Platforms for Exterior Building Maintenance, Safety Code for
B7.1-1970 Use, Care, and Protection of Abrasive Wheels, Safety Code for the
B9.1-1964 Mechanical Refrigeration, Safety Code for (ASHRAE 15-63)
B11.1-1971 Power Presses, Safety Code for
B15.1-1953 (R1958) Mechanical Power-Transmission Apparatus, Safety Code for
B19-1938 Compressed Air Machinery and Equipment, Safety Code for
B20.1-1957 Conveyors, Cableways, and Related Equipment, Safety Code for
B24.1-1971 Forging and Hot Metal Stamping, Safety Code for

B28.1-1967 Mills and Calenders in the Rubber and Plastics Industries, Safety Specifications for

B30.1-1943 (R1952) Jacks, Safety Code for

B30.2-1943 (R1952) Cranes, Derricks, and Hoists, Safety Code for

B30.2.0-1967 Overhead and Gantry Cranes (Partial Revision of B30.2-1943)

B30.5-1968 Crawler, Locomotive, and Truck Cranes (Partial Revision of B30.2-1943)

B30.6-1969 Derricks, Safety Code for (Partial Revision of B30.2-1943)

B31.1-1955 Pressure Piping, Code for

B31.1a-1963 Addenda to B31.1-1955

B31.1.0-1967 Power Piping, with Addenda B31.1.0a-1969

B31.1.0a-1969 Addenda to B31.1.0-1967

B31.2-1968 Fuel Gas Piping

B31.3-1966 Petroleum Refinery Piping

B31.4-1966 Liquid Petroleum Transportation Piping Systems, with Addenda B31.4a-1969

B31.5-1966 Refrigeration Piping, with Addenda B31.5a-1968

B31.5a-1968 Addenda to B31.5-1966

B31.7-1969 Nuclear Power Piping with Addenda B31.7a-1971

B31.8-1968 Gas Transmission and Distribution Piping Systems, including Supplement B31.8b-1969

B31.8b-1969 Supplement to B31.8-1968

B56.1-1969 Powered Industrial Trucks, Safety Standard for (ISO R1074)

B57.1-1965 Compressed Gas Cylinder Valve Outlet and Inlet Connections (CGA V-1-1965) (Agrees with ISO R407)

B71.1-1968 Power Lawn Mowers, Safety Specifications for

B114.1-1971 Slow-Moving Vehicles Identification Emblem (ASAE-S276.2)

B125.1-1970 Welded and Seamless Steel Pipe, Specifications for (ASTM A53-69a) (Revision and Redesignation of B36.1-1966)

C1-1968 National Electrical Code (NFPA 70-1968)

C33.2-1956 Transformer-Type Arc-Welding Machines, Safety Standard for (UL 551-October 1952)

C57.12.00-1968 Distribution, Power, and Regulating Transformers and Shunt Reactors, General Requirements for (IEC 76, 288-2, 289)

C95.1-1966 Electromagnetic Radiation with Respect to Personnel, Safety Level of

C95.2-1966 Radio Frequency Radiation Hazard Warning Symbol

D6.1-1961 Manual on Uniform Traffic Control Devices for Streets and Highways

D8.1-1967 Railroad Highway Grade Crossing Protection, Practices for (AAR Bulletin 6-1967)

G41.5-1970 Structural Steel, Specification for (ASTM A36-69)

H23.1-1970 Seamless Copper Water Tube, Specification for (ASTM B88-69)

H38.7-1969 (2d ed.) Aluminum-Alloy Seamless Pipe and Seamless Extruded Tube, Specification for (ASTM B241-69)

J6.1-1950 (R1962) Rubber Insulating Line Hose (ASTM D1050-59 (1962))

J6.2-1950 (R1962) Rubber Insulator Hoods (ASTM D1049-59 (1965))

J6.4-1970 Rubber Insulating Blankets (ASTM D1048-70)

J6.5-1967 Rubber Insulating Sleeves (ASTM D1051-59 (1965))

J6.6-1967 Rubber Insulating Gloves, Specifications for (ASTM D120-68)

J6.7-1935 (R1962) Rubber Matting for Use around Electric Apparatus (Reaffirmation and Redesignation of C59.4-1935) (ASTM D178-24 (1965))

K13.1-1967 Identification of Gas-Mask Canisters

K61.1-1966 Storage and Handling of Anhydrous Ammonia, Safety Requirements for the (CGA G-2.1-1966)

L1.1-1956 (R1964) Textile Safety Code

N2.3-1967 Immediate Evacuation Signal for Use in Industrial Installations Where Radiation Exposure May Occur

O1.1-1954 (R1961) Woodworking Machinery, Safety Code for

O2.1-1969 Sawmills, Safety Requirements for

O3.1-1971 Pulpwood Logging

P1.1-1969 Pulp, Paper, Paperboard Mills, Safety Standard for

Z4.1-1968 Sanitation in Places of Employment, Requirements for

Z4.2-1942 Drinking Fountains, Specification for

Z4.3-1970 Non-Water Carriage Disposal Systems, Minimum Requirements for

Z4.4-1968 Sanitation in Temporary Labor Camps, Minimum Requirements for

Z8.1-1961 Laundry Machinery and Operations, Safety Code for

Z9.1-1951 Ventilation and Operation of Open-Surface Tanks, Safety Code for

Z9.2-1960 Design and Operation of Local Exhaust Systems, Fundamentals Governing the

Z9.3-1964 (R1971) Design, Construction, and Ventilation of Spray Finishing Operations, Safety Code for the

Z9.4-1968 Ventilation and Safe Practices of Abrasives Blasting Operations

Z11.189-1966 (R1970) Autoignition Temperatures of Liquid Petroleum Products (ASTM D2155-66)

Z12.12-1968 Sulfur Fires and Explosions, Standard for the Prevention of (NFPA No. 655-1968)

Z12.20-1962 (R1969) Woodworking and Wood Flour Manufacturing Plants, Code for the Prevention of Dust Explosions in (NFPA No. 664-May-1962)

Z21.30-1964 Gas Appliances and Gas Piping Installations, Requirements for (NFPA 54-1964)

Z24.22-1957 (R1971) Measurement of Real-Ear Attenuation of Ear Protectors at Threshold, Method of

Z33.1-1961 Installation of Blower and Exhaust Systems for Dust, Stock, and Vapor Removal or Conveying (NFPA 91-1961)

Z35.1-1968 Accident Prevention Signs, Specifications for

Z35.2-1968 Accident Prevention Tags, Specifications for

Z37.2-1966 Hydrogen Sulfide, Acceptable Concentrations of

Z37.3-1968 Carbon Disulfide, Acceptable Concentrations of

Z37.4-1969 Benzene, Acceptable Concentration of

Z37.5-1970 Cadmium Fume and Cadmium Dusts, Acceptable Concentrations of

Z37.7-1943 (R1971) Chromic Acid and Chromates, Allowable Concentration of

Z37.8-1943 (R1971) Mercury, Allowable Concentration of

Z37.11-1969 Lead and Its Inorganic Compounds, Acceptable Concentrations of

Z37.12-1967 Toluene, Acceptable Concentrations of

Z37.15-1969 Styrene, Acceptable Concentrations of

Z37.16-1967 Formaldehyde, Acceptable Concentrations of

Z37.17-1967 Carbon Tetrachloride, Acceptable Concentrations of

Z37.18-1969 Methyl Chloride, Acceptable Concentrations of

Z37.21-1969 Ethylene Dichloride, Acceptable Concentrations of

Z37.22-1967 Tetrachlorethylene, Acceptable Concentrations of

Z37.23-1969 Methylene Chloride (Dichloro Methane), Acceptable Concentrations of

Z37.28-1966 Hydrogen Fluoride and Inorganic Fluoride Dusts, Acceptable Concentrations of

Z37.29-1970 Beryllium and Beryllium Compounds, Acceptable Concentration of

Z37.30-1969 Organo (Alkyl) Mercury, Acceptable Concentrations of

Z37.31-1970 Ethylene Dibromide, Acceptable Concentrations of

Z41.1-1967 Men's Safety-Toe Footwear

Z43.1-1966 Ventilation Control of Grinding, Polishing, and Buffing Operations

Z48.1-1954 (R1971) Marking Portable Compressed Gas Containers to Identify the Material Contained, Method for (CGA C-4-1954) (ISO R443 and R448)

Z49.1-1967 Welding and Cutting, Safety in

Z50.1-1947 Bakery Equipment, Safety Code for

Z53.1-1967 Marking Physical Hazards and the Identification of Certain Equipment, Safety Color Code for (ISO R408)

Z54.1-1963 Non-Medical X-Ray and Sealed Gamma-Ray Sources, Safety Standard for, Part 1—General (NBS Handbook H93)

Z87.1-1968 Occupational and Educational Eye and Face Protection, Practice for (Partial Revision of Z2.1-1959)

Z88.2-1969 Practices for Respiratory Protection

Z89.1-1969 Industrial Head Protection, Safety Requirements for

API American Petroleum Institute

1801 K Street, N.W.
Washington, D.C. 20006 (202-833-5600)

Std 12A, Specification for Oil Storage Tanks with Riveted Shells, Seventh Edition, 1941 (reissued 1951)

Std 12B, Specification for Bolted Production Tanks, Eleventh Edition, May 1958, and supplement made 1962

Std 12D, Specification for Large Welded Production Tanks, Seventh Edition, August 1957

Std 12F, Specification for Small Welded Production Tanks, Fifth Edition, March 1961

Std 620, Recommended Rules for Design and Construction of Large, Welded, Low-Pressure Storage Tanks, Second Edition, 1963, and Appendix R-1965; Third Edition, 1966; Fourth Edition, 1970

Std 650, Welded Steel Tanks for Oil Storage, Fourth Edition, 1970; Third Edition, 1966

Std 1104, Standard for Welding Pipelines and Related Facilities, Eleventh Edition, 1968

Std 2000, Venting Atmospheric and Low-Pressure Storage Tanks, 1968

PSD 2201, Welding or Hot Tapping on Equipment Containing Flammables, 1963

1951 Edition, API-ASME Code, 1954 Attachment

(All Editions, API-ASME Code)

ASAE American Society of Agricultural Engineers

P.O. Box 229
St. Joseph, Michigan 49085 (616-983-6521)

ASAE S276.2, ASAE Standard: Slow-Moving Vehicle Identification Emblem (ANSI B114.1-1971)

ASAE R276 ASAE Proposed Standard: Emblem for Identifying Slow-Moving Vehicles

ASHRE American Society of Heating, Refrigeration and Air Conditioning Engineers, Inc.

United Engineering Center
345 East 47th Street
New York, New York 10017 (212-PL2-6800)

ASHRE 15-63 Safety Code for Mechanical Refrigeration (ANSI B9.1-1964)

ASME American Society of Mechanical Engineers

United Engineering Center
345 East 47th Street
New York, New York 10017 (212-PL2-6800)

(ASME Boiler and Pressure Vessel Code, All Editions)

ASTM American Society for Testing and Materials

1916 Race Street
Philadelphia, Pennsylvania 19103 (215-LO9-4200)

A47-68 Malleable Iron Castings, Standard Specifications for

A53-69 Welded and Seamless Steel Pipe, Standard Specification for

A126-66 Gray Iron Casting for Valves, Flanges, and Pipe Fitting, Standard Specification for

A395-68 Ductile Iron for Pressure Containing Castings for Use at Elevated Temperatures, Standard Specifications for

B88-66a Seamless Copper Water Tube, Standard Specification for

B210-68 Aluminum-Alloy Drawn Seamless Tubes, Standard Specification for

B241-69 Aluminum-Alloy Seamless Pipe and Seamless Extruded Tube, Standard Specification for

D5-65 Penetration of Bituminous Materials, Standard Method of Test for

D56-68 Flash Point by Tag Closed Tester, Standard Method of Test for

D86-62 Distillation of Petroleum Products, Standard Method of Test for

D93-69 Flash Point by Pensky-Martens Closed Tester, Standard Method of Test for

D323-58 (R68) Vapor Pressure of Petroleum Products (Reid Method), Standard Method of Test for

D1692-68 Flammability of Plastic Sheeting and Cellular Plastics, Standard Method of Test for

AWS American Welding Society, Inc.
2501-7th Street, N.W.
Miami, Florida 33125 (305-642-7090)

A3.0-1969 Terms and Definitions
A6.1-1966 Recommended Safe Practices for Gas Shielded Arc Welding
D1.0-1966 Code for Welding in Building Construction

CGA Compressed Gas Association, Inc.
500 Fifth Avenue
New York, New York 10036 (212-LA4-4796)

C-6-1968 Standards for Visual Inspection of Compressed Gas Cylinders
C-8-1962 Standard for Requalification of ICC-3HT Cylinders
G-1-1966 Acetylene
G-1.3-1959 Acetylene Transmission for Chemical Synthesis
G-1.4-1966 Standard for Acetylene Cylinder Charging Plants
G-4-1962 Oxygen
G-5.1-1961 Standard for Gaseous Hydrogen at Consumer Sites
G-5.2-1966 Standard for Liquefied Hydrogen Systems at Consumer Sites
G-7.1-1966 Commodity Specification for Air
G-8.1-1964 Standard for the Installation of Nitrous Oxide Systems at Consumer Sites
P-1-1965 Safe Handling of Compressed Gases
P-3-1963 Standards for Solid Ammonium Nitrate (Nitrous Oxide Grade)
S-1.1-1963, 1965 Attachment, Safety Relief Device Standards—Cylinders for Compressed Gases
S-1.2-1963 Safety Relief Device Standards—Cargo and Portable Tanks for Compressed Gases
S-1.3-1959 Safety Relief Device Standards—Compressed Gas Storage Containers
1957 Standard Hose Connection Specification
1958 Regulator Connection Standard
Specification for Rubber Welding Hose, 1958

CMAA Crane Manufacturers Association of America, Inc.
(formerly Electric Overhead Crane Institute)
1326 Freeport Road
Pittsburgh, Pennsylvania 15238 (412-782-1624)

EOCI Specification No. 61—Specifications for Electric Overhead Traveling Cranes

IME Institute of Makers of Explosives
420 Lexington Avenue
New York, New York 10017 (212-689-3237)

Pamphlet No. 17, 1960—Safety in the Handling and Use of Explosives

IPM International Association of Plumbing and Mechanical Officials
5032 Alhambra Avenue
Los Angeles, California 90032 (213-223-1471)

TSC-12-65 Self-Contained, Electrically Operated, Recirculating, Chemically Controlled Toilet, Trailer Standard

NEMA National Electrical Manufacturers Association
155 East 44th Street
New York, New York 10017 (212-682-1500)

NEMA EW-1-1962 Requirements for Electric Arc Welding Apparatus

NFPA National Fire Protection Association
  470 Atlantic Avenue
  Boston, Massachusetts 02210 (617-482-8755)

NFPA10-1970 Standard for the Installation of Portable Fire Extinguishers

NFPA10A-1970 Recommended Good Practice for the Maintenance and Use of Portable Fire Extinguishers

NFPA11-1970 Standard for Foam Extinguishing Systems

NFPA12-1968 Standard on Carbon Dioxide Extinguishing Systems (ANSI A54.1-1968)

NFPA13-1969 Standard for the Installation of Sprinkler Systems

NFPA14-1970 Standard for the Installation of Standpipe and Hose Systems

NFPA15-1969 Standard for Water Spray Fixed Systems for Fire Protection

NFPA17-1969 Standard for Dry Chemical Extinguishing Systems

NFPA20-1970 Standard for the Installation of Centrifugal Fire Pumps

NFPA22-1970 Standard for Water Tanks for Private Fire Protection

NFPA24-1970 Standard for Outside Protection

NFPA30-1969 Flammable and Combustible Liquids Code

NFPA31-1968 Standard for the Installation of Oil Burning Equipment (ANSI Z95.1-1968)

NFPA32-1970 Standard for Drycleaning Plants

NFPA33-1969 Standard for Spray Finishing Using Flammable and Combustible Materials

NFPA34-1966 Standard for Dip Tanks Containing Flammable or Combustible Liquids

NFPA35-1970 Standard for the Manufacture of Organic Coatings

NFPA36-1967 Standard for Solvent Extraction Plants

NFPA37-1970 Standard for the Installation and Use of Stationary Combustion Engines and Gas Turbines

NFPA50A-1969 Standard for Gaseous Hydrogen Systems at Consumer Sites (Not Listed in *Federal Register*)

NFPA50B-1968 Standard for Liquefied Hydrogen Systems at Consumer Sites

NFPA51-1969 Standard for the Installation and Operation of Oxygen-Fuel Gas Systems for Welding and Cutting

NFPA51B-1962 Standard for Fire Protection in Use of Cutting and Welding Processes

NFPA54-1969 Standard for the Installation of Gas Appliances and Gas Piping

NFPA54A-1969 Standard for the Installation of Gas Piping and Gas Equipment on Industrial Premises and Certain Other Premises (ANSI Z83.1-1968, Z83.1a-1969)

NFPA58-1969 Standard for the Storage and Handling of Liquefied Petroleum Gases (ANSI Z106.1-1970)

NFPA59-1968 Standard for the Storage and Handling of Liquefied Petroleum Gases at Utility Gas Plants

NFPA62-1967 Standard for the Prevention of Dust Explosions in the Production, Packaging, and Handling of Pulverized Sugar and Cocoa

NFPA68-1954 Guide for Explosion Venting

NFPA70-1971 National Electrical Code (ANSI C1-1971)

NFPA72A-1967 Standard for the Installation, Maintenance, and Use of Local Protective Signaling Systems for Watchman, Fire Alarm, and Supervisory Service

NFPA78-1968 Lightning Protection Code

NFPA80-1970 Standard for Fire Doors and Windows

NFPA86A-1969 Standard for Ovens and Furnaces Design, Location, and Equipment

NFPA91-1961 Standard for the Installation of Blower and Exhaust Systems for Dust, Stock, and Vapor Removal or Conveying (ANSI Z33.1-1961)

NFPA96-1970 Standard for the Installation of Equipment for the Removal of Smoke and Grease-Laden Vapors from Commercial Cooking Equipment

NFPA101-1970 Code for Life Safety from Fire in Buildings and Structures

NFPA194-1968 Standard for Screw Threads and Gaskets for Fire Hose Couplings

NFPA198-1969 Standard for Care of Fire Hose (Including Couplings and Nozzles)

NFPA203M-1970 Manual on Roof Coverings

NFPA220-1961 Standard Types of Building Construction

NFPA231-1970 Standard for Indoor General Storage

NFPA251-1969 Standard Methods of Fire Tests of Building Construction and Materials

NFPA302-1968 Fire Protection Standard for Motor-craft (Pleasure & Commercial)

NFPA385-1966 Recommended Regulatory Standard for Tank Vehicles for Flammable & Combustible Liquids

NFPA490-1970 Code for the Storage of Ammonium Nitrate

NFPA492-1968 Recommended Separation Distances of Ammonium Nitrate and Blasting Agents from Explosives or Blasting Agents (Not Listed in Federal Register)

NFPA495-1970 Code for the Manufacture, Transportation, Storage, and Use of Explosives and Blasting Agents

NFPA496-1967 Standard for Purged Enclosures for Electrical Equipment in Hazardous Locations

NFPA505-1969 Standard for Type Designations, Areas of Use, Maintenance and Operation of Powered Industrial Trucks

NFPA566-1965 Standard for the Installation of Bulk Oxygen Systems at Consumer Sites

NFPA655-1968 Standard for Prevention of Sulfur Fires and Explosions (ANSI Z12.12-1968)

NFPA656-1959 Code for the Prevention of Dust Ignition in Spice Grinding Plants

NFPA664-1962 Code for the Prevention of Dust Explosions in Woodworking and Wood Flour Manufacturing Plants (ANSI Z12.20-1962)

NPF National Plant Food Institute
    c/o The Fertilizer Institute
    1015-18th Street, N.W.
    Washington, D.C. 20036 (202-466-2700)

1964 Definitions and Test Procedures for Ammonium Nitrate Fertilizer

SAE Society of Automotive Engineers, Inc.
    Two Pennsylvania Plaza
    New York, New York 10001 (212-594-5700)

SAE J765-SAE Recommended Practice: Crane Load Stability Test Code, 1961

UL Underwriters' Laboratories, Inc.
    207 East Ohio Street
    Chicago, Illinois 60611 (312-M12-6969)

UL 58-1961 Underground Tanks for Flammable Liquids, December, 1961

UL 80-1963 Steel Inside Tanks for Oil-Burner Fuel, September, 1963

UL 142-1968 Standard for Steel Aboveground Tanks for Flammable and Combustible Liquids, May, 1968

USPC United States Pharmacopeial Convention
    46 Park Avenue
    New York, New York 10016 (N.A.)

1970, US Pharmacopeia, 18th Revision

II. FEDERAL AGENCIES

AEC Atomic Energy Commission

42 USC 2011 et seq Atomic Energy Act of 1954 as amended
42 USC 2021 Atomic Energy Act of 1954 as amended
10 CFR 20

ESA Employment, Labor

29 CFR 505

FAA Federal Aviation Administration, Transportation

14 CFR 103

FSS Federal Supply Services, General Services

Federal Specification BB-A-1034a, June 21, 1968
Interim Federal Specification GG-B-00675b, April 27, 1965

HMRB Hazardous Materials Regulations Board, Transportation

49 CFR Chapter I

NBS National Bureau of Standards, Commerce

Commercial Standard CS202-56, Industrial Lifts and Hinged Ramps, 1961

OSHA Occupational Safety and Health Administration, Labor

29 CFR 1915-1918
29 CFR 1925
29 CFR 1926
41 CFR 50-204

USCG United States Coast Guard, Transportation

46 CFR 146-149
46 CFR 160.009
46 CFR 160.050

USDA United States Department of Agriculture

Handbook No. 72, Wood Handbook
Technical Bulletin, No. 479

USPHS United States Public Health Service, HEW

Pub. No. 546 The Vending of Food and Beverages, 1965
Pub. No. 934 Food Service Sanitation Manual, 1962

III. CFR—CODE OF FEDERAL REGULATIONS

10 CFR 20—Atomic Energy Commission
14 CFR 103—Federal Aviation Administration, Transportation
29 CFR 505—Employment Standards Administration, Labor
29 CFR 1915-1918—Occupational Safety and Health Administration, Labor
29 CFR 1925—Occupational Safety and Health Administration, Labor
29 CFR 1926—Occupational Safety and Health Administration, Labor
41 CFR 50-204—Occupational Safety and Health Administration, Labor
46 CFR 146-149—U.S. Coast Guard, Transportation
46 CFR 160—U.S. Coast Guard, Transportation
49 CFR Chapter I—Hazardous Materials Regulations Board, Transportation

IV. USC—UNITED STATES CODE—PUBLIC LAW

PL 86-613, 15 USC 1261 Hazardous Substances Labeling Act
PL 91-596, 29 USC 655 Williams-Steiger Occupational Safety and Health Act of 1970
PL 91-596, 29 USC 657 Williams-Steiger Occupational Safety and Health Act of 1970
PL 74-846, 41 USC 35-45 Walsh-Healey Public Contracts Act
PL 83-703, 42 USC 2011 et seq—Atomic Energy Act of 1954 as amended
PL 83-703, 42 USC 2021 Atomic Energy Act of 1954 as amended

V. OTHER

Doolittle, Arthur K. 1935. "Solvents in Commercial Use", *Industrial and Engineering Chemistry.* 27:1169-1179

NBBPVI National Board of Boiler and Pressure Vessel Inspectors

National Board Inspection Code

NBS National Bureau of Standards

Product Standard PS 1-66, Softwood Plywood, Construction and Industrial, and Amendments 1-5

USDA United States Department of Agriculture

USDA Handbook No. 41 Checklist of Native and Naturalized Trees of the United States (including Alaska) by Elbert L. Little, pp. 440-443.

Appendix C

Text of the Occupational Safety and Health Act

 Public Law 91-596
91st Congress, S. 2193
December 29, 1970

An Act

84 STAT. 1590

To assure safe and healthful working conditions for working men and women; by authorizing enforcement of the standards developed under the Act; by assisting and encouraging the States in their efforts to assure safe and healthful working conditions; by providing for research, information, education, and training in the field of occupational safety and health; and for other purposes.

Be it enacted by the Senate and House of Representatives of the United States of America in Congress assembled, That this Act may be cited as the "Occupational Safety and Health Act of 1970".

Occupational Safety and Health Act of 1970.

CONGRESSIONAL FINDINGS AND PURPOSE

SEC. (2) The Congress finds that personal injuries and illnesses arising out of work situations impose a substantial burden upon, and are a hindrance to, interstate commerce in terms of lost production, wage loss, medical expenses, and disability compensation payments.

(b) The Congress declares it to be its purpose and policy, through the exercise of its powers to regulate commerce among the several States and with foreign nations and to provide for the general welfare, to assure so far as possible every working man and woman in the Nation safe and healthful working conditions and to preserve our human resources—

(1) by encouraging employers and employees in their efforts to reduce the number of occupational safety and health hazards at their places of employment, and to stimulate employers and employees to institute new and to perfect existing programs for providing safe and healthful working conditions;

(2) by providing that employers and employees have separate but dependent responsibilities and rights with respect to achieving safe and healthful working conditions;

(3) by authorizing the Secretary of Labor to set mandatory occupational safety and health standards applicable to businesses affecting interstate commerce, and by creating an Occupational Safety and Health Review Commission for carrying out adjudicatory functions under the Act;

(4) by building upon advances already made through employer and employee initiative for providing safe and healthful working conditions;

(5) by providing for research in the field of occupational safety and health, including the psychological factors involved, and by developing innovative methods, techniques, and approaches for dealing with occupational safety and health problems;

(6) by exploring ways to discover latent diseases, establishing causal connections between diseases and work in environmental conditions, and conducting other research relating to health problems, in recognition of the fact that occupational health standards present problems often different from those involved in occupational safety;

(7) by providing medical criteria which will assure insofar as practicable that no employee will suffer diminished health, functional capacity, or life expectancy as a result of his work experience;

(8) by providing for training programs to increase the number and competence of personnel engaged in the field of occupational safety and health;

(9) by providing for the development and promulgation of occupational safety and health standards;

(10) by providing an effective enforcement program which shall include a prohibition against giving advance notice of any inspection and sanctions for any individual violating this prohibition;

(11) by encouraging the States to assume the fullest responsibility for the administration and enforcement of their occupational safety and health laws by providing grants to the States to assist in identifying their needs and responsibilities in the area of occupational safety and health, to develop plans in accordance with the provisions of this Act, to improve the administration and enforcement of State occupational safety and health laws, and to conduct experimental and demonstration projects in connection therewith;

(12) by providing for appropriate reporting procedures with respect to occupational safety and health which procedures will help achieve the objectives of this Act and accurately describe the nature of the occupational safety and health problem;

(13) by encouraging joint labor-management efforts to reduce injuries and disease arising out of employment.

DEFINITIONS

SEC. 3. For the purposes of this Act—

(1) The term "Secretary" mean the Secretary of Labor.

(2) The term "Commission" means the Occupational Safety and Health Review Commission established under this Act.

(3) The term "commerce" means trade, traffic, commerce, transportation, or communication among the several States, or between a State and any place outside thereof, or within the District of Columbia, or a possession of the United States (other than the Trust Territory of the Pacific Islands), or between points in the same State but through a point outside thereof.

(4) The term "person" means one or more individuals, partnerships, associations, corporations, business trusts, legal representatives, or any organized group of persons.

(5) The term "employer" means a person engaged in a business affecting commerce who has employees, but does not include the United States or any State or political subdivision of a State.

(6) The term "employee" means an employee of an employer who is employed in a business of his employer which affects commerce.

(7) The term "State" includes a State of the United States, the District of Columbia, Puerto Rico, the Virgin Islands, American Samoa, Guam, and the Trust Territory of the Pacific Islands.

(8) The term "occupational safety and health standard" means a standard which requires conditions, or the adoption or use of one or more practices, means, methods, operations, or processes, reasonably necessary or appropriate to provide safe or healthful employment and places of employment.

(9) The term "national consensus standard" means any occupational safety and health standard or modification thereof which (1), has been adopted and promulgated by a nationally recognized standards-producing organization under procedures whereby it can be determined by the Secretary that persons interested

and affected by the scope or provisions of the standard have reached substantial agreement on its adoption, (2) was formulated in a manner which afforded an opportunity for diverse views to be considered and (3) has been designated as such a standard by the Secretary, after consultation with other appropriate Federal agencies.

(10) The term "established Federal standard" means any operative occupational safety and health standard established by any agency of the United States and presently in effect, or contained in any Act of Congress in force on the date of enactment of this Act.

(11) The term "Committee" means the National Advisory Committee on Occupational Safety and Health established under this Act.

(12) The term "Director" means the Director of the National Institute for Occupational Safety and Health.

(13) The term "Institute" means the National Institute for Occupational Safety and Health established under this Act.

(14) The term "Workmen's Compensation Commission" means the National Commission on State Workmen's Compensation Laws established under this Act.

APPLICABILITY OF THIS ACT

SEC. 4. (a) This Act shall apply with respect to employment performed in a workplace in a State, the District of Columbia, the Commonwealth of Puerto Rico, the Virgin Islands, American Samoa, Guam, the Trust Territory of the Pacific Islands, Wake Island, Outer Continental Shelf lands defined in the Outer Continental Shelf Lands Act, Johnston Island, and the Canal Zone. The Secretary of the Interior shall, by regulation, provide for judicial enforcement of this Act by the courts established for areas in which there are no United States district courts having jurisdiction.

67 Stat. 462.
43 USC 1331
note.

(b)(1) Nothing in this Act shall apply to working conditions of employees with respect to which other Federal agencies, and State agencies acting under section 274 of the Atomic Energy Act of 1954, as amended (42 U.S.C. 2021), exercise statutory authority to prescribe or enforce standards or regulations affecting occupational safety or health.

73 Stat. 688.

(2) The safety and health standards promulgated under the Act of June 30, 1936, commonly known as the Walsh-Healey Act (41 U.S.C. 35 et seq.), the Service Contract Act of 1965 (41 U.S.C. 351 et seq.), Public Law 91-54, Act of August 9, 1969 (40 U.S.C. 333), Public Law 85-742, Act of August 23, 1958 (33 U.S.C. 941), and the National Foundation on Arts and Humanities Act (20 U.S.C. 951 et seq.) are superseded on the effective date of corresponding standards, promulgated under this Act, which are determined by the Secretary to be more effective. Standards issued under the laws listed in this paragraph and in effect on or after the effective date of this Act shall be deemed to be occupational safety and health standards issued under this Act, as well as under such other Acts.

49 Stat. 2036.
79 Stat. 1034.
83 Stat. 96.
72 Stat. 835.
79 Stat. 845;
Ante, p. 443.

(3) The Secretary shall, within three years after the effective date of this Act, report to the Congress his recommendations for legislation to avoid unnecessary duplication and to achieve coordination between this Act and other Federal laws.

Report to
Congress.

(4) Nothing in this Act shall be construed to supersede or in any manner affect any workmen's compensation law or to enlarge or diminish or affect in any other manner the common law or statutory rights, duties, or liabilities of employers and employees under any law with respect to injuries, diseases, or death of employees arising out of, or in the course of, employment.

DUTIES

SEC. 5. (a) Each employer—
(1) shall furnish to each of his employees employment and a place of employment which are free from recognized hazards that are causing or are likely to cause death or serious physical harm to his employees;
(2) shall comply with occupational safety and health standards promulgated under this Act.
(b) Each employee shall comply with occupational safety and health standards and all rules, regulations, and orders issued pursuant to this Act which are applicable to his own actions and conduct.

OCCUPATIONAL SAFETY AND HEALTH STANDARDS

80 Stat. 381; 81 Stat. 195. 5 USC 500.

SEC. 6. (a) Without regard to chapter 5 of title 5, United States Code, or to the other subsections of this section, the Secretary shall, as soon as practicable during the period beginning with the effective date of this Act and ending two years after such date, by rule promulgate as an occupational safety or health standard any national consensus standard, and any established Federal standard, unless he determines that the promulgation of such a standard would not result in improved safety or health for specifically designated employees. In the event of conflict among any such standards, the Secretary shall promulgate the standard which assures the greatest protection of the safety or health of the affected employees.

(b) The Secretary may by rule promulgate, modify, or revoke any occupational safety or health standard in the following manner:

Advisory committee, recommendations.

(1) Whenever the Secretary, upon the basis of information submitted to him in writing by an interested person, a representative of any organization of employers or employees, a nationally recognized standards-producing organization, the Secretary of Health, Education, and Welfare, the National Institute for Occupational Safety and Health, or a State or political subdivision, or on the basis of information developed by the Secretary or otherwise available to him, determines that a rule should be promulgated in order to serve the objectives of this Act, the Secretary may request the recommendations of an advisory committee appointed under section 7 of this Act. The Secretary shall provide such an advisory committee with any proposals of his own or of the Secretary of Health, Education, and Welfare, together with all pertinent factual information developed by the Secretary or the Secretary of Health, Education, and Welfare, or otherwise available, including the results of research, demonstrations, and experiments. An advisory committee shall submit to the Secretary its recommendations regarding the rule to be promulgated within ninety days from the date of its appointment or within such longer or shorter period as may be prescribed by the Secretary, but in no event for a period which is longer than two hundred and seventy days.

(2) The Secretary shall publish a proposed rule promulgating, modifying, or revoking an occupational safety or health standard in the Federal Register and shall afford interested persons a period of thirty days after publication to submit written data or comments. Where an advisory committee is appointed and the Secretary determines that a rule should be issued, he shall publish the proposed rule within sixty days after the submission of the advisory committee's recommendations or the expiration of the period prescribed by the Secretary for such submission.

(3) On or before the last day of the period provided for the submission of written data or comments under paragraph (2), any interested person may file with the Secretary written objections to the proposed rule, stating the grounds therefor and requesting a public hearing on such objections. Within thirty days after the last day for filing such objections, the Secretary shall publish in the Federal Register a notice specifying the occupational safety or health standard to which objections have been filed and a hearing requested, and specifying a time and place for such hearing.

(4) Within sixty days after the expiration of the period provided for the submission of written data or comments under paragraph (2), or within sixty days after the completion of any hearing held under paragraph (3), the Secretary shall issue a rule promulgating, modifying, or revoking an occupational safety or health standard or make a determination that a rule should not be issued. Such a rule may contain a provision delaying its effective date for such period (not in excess of ninety days) as the Secretary determines may be necessary to insure that affected employers and employees will be informed of the existence of the standard and of its terms and that employers affected are given an opportunity to familiarize themselves and their employees with the existence of the requirements of the standard.

(5) The Secretary, in promulgating standards dealing with toxic materials or harmful physical agents under this subsection, shall set the standard which most adequately assures, to the extent feasible, on the basis of the best available evidence, that no employee will suffer material impairment of health or functional capacity even if such employee has regular exposure to the hazard dealt with by such standard for the period of his working life. Development of standards under this subsection shall be based upon research, demonstrations, experiments, and such other information as may be appropriate. In addition to the attainment of the highest degree of health and safety protection for the employee, other considerations shall be the latest available scientific data in the field, the feasibility of the standards, and experience gained under this and other health and safety laws. Whenever practicable, the standard promulgated shall be expressed in terms of objective criteria and of the performance desired.

(6) (A) Any employer may apply to the Secretary for a temporary order granting a variance from a standard or any provision thereof promulgated under this section. Such temporary order shall be granted only if the employer files an application which meets the requirements of clause (B) and establishes that (i) he is unable to comply with a standard by its effective date because of unavailability of professional or technical personnel or of materials and equipment needed to come into compliance with the standard or because necessary construction or alteration of facilities cannot be completed by the effective date, (ii) he is taking all available steps to safeguard his employees against the hazards covered by the standard, and (iii) he has an effective program for coming into compliance with the standard as quickly as

Publication in Federal Register.

Hearing, notice.

Publication in Federal Register.

Toxic materials.

Temporary variance order.

Notice,
hearing.

Renewal.

Time limita-
tion.

practicable. Any temporary order issued under this paragraph shall prescribe the practices, means, methods, operations, and processes which the employer must adopt and use while the order is in effect and state in detail his program for coming into compliance with the standard. Such a temporary order may be granted only after notice to employees and an opportunity for a hearing: *Provided*, That the Secretary may issue one interim order to be effective until a decision is made on the basis of the hearing. No temporary order may be in effect for longer than the period needed by the employer to achieve compliance with the standard or one year, whichever is shorter, except that such an order may be renewed not more than twice (I) so long as the requirements of this paragraph are met and (II) if an application for renewal is filed at least 90 days prior to the expiration date of the order. No interim renewal of an order may remain in effect for longer than 180 days.

(B) An application for a temporary order under this paragraph (6) shall contain:

(i) a specification of the standard or portion thereof from which the employer seeks a variance,

(ii) a representation by the employer, supported by representations from qualified persons having firsthand knowledge of the facts represented, that he is unable to comply with the standard or portion thereof and a detailed statement of the reasons therefor,

(iii) a statement of the steps he has taken and will take (with specific dates) to protect employees against the hazard covered by the standard,

(iv) a statement of when he expects to be able to comply with the standard and what steps he has taken and what steps he will take (with dates specified) to come into compliance with the standard, and

(v) a certification that he has informed his employees of the application by giving a copy thereof to their authorized representative, posting a statement giving a summary of the application and specifying where a copy may be examined at the place or places where notices to employees are normally posted, and by other appropriate means.

A description of how employees have been informed shall be contained in the certification. The information to employees shall also inform them of their right to petition the Secretary for a hearing.

(C) The Secretary is authorized to grant a variance from any standard or portion thereof whenever he determines, or the Secretary of Health, Education, and Welfare certifies, that such variance is necessary to permit an employer to participate in an experiment approved by him or the Secretary of Health, Education, and Welfare designed to demonstrate or validate new and improved techniques to safeguard the health or safety of workers.

Labels, etc.

(7) Any standard promulgated under this subsection shall prescribe the use of labels or other appropriate forms of warning as are necessary to insure that employees are apprised of all hazards to which they are exposed, relevant symptoms and appropriate emergency treatment, and proper conditions and precautions of safe use or exposure.

Protective
equipment,
etc.

Where appropriate, such standard shall also prescribe suitable protective equipment and control or technological procedures to be used in connection with such hazards and shall provide for monitoring or measuring employee exposure at such locations and intervals, and in such manner as may be necessary for the protection of employees. In addition, where appropriate, any such standard shall prescribe the type and frequency of medical examinations or other tests which shall be made available, by the employer or at his cost, to employees exposed to such hazards in order to most effectively determine whether the health of such employees is adversely affected by such exposure. In the event such medical examinations are in the nature of research, as determined by the Secretary of Health, Education, and Welfare, such examinations may be furnished at the expense of the Secretary of Health, Education, and Welfare. The results of such examinations or tests shall be furnished only to the Secretary or the Secretary of Health, Education, and Welfare, and, at the request of the employee, to his physician. The Secretary, in consultation with the Secretary of Health, Education, and Welfare, may by rule promulgated pursuant to section 553 of title 5, United States Code, make appropriate modifications in the foregoing requirements relating to the use of labels or other forms of warning, monitoring or measuring, and medical examinations, as may be warranted by experience, information, or medical or technological developments acquired subsequent to the promulgation of the relevant standard.

Medical examinations.

80 Stat. 383.

(8) Whenever a rule promulgated by the Secretary differs substantially from an existing national consensus standard, the Secretary shall, at the same time, publish in the Federal Register a statement of the reasons why the rule as adopted will better effectuate the purposes of this Act than the national consensus standard.

Publication in Federal Register.

(c)(1) The Secretary shall provide, without regard to the requirements of chapter 5, title 5, United States Code, for an emergency temporary standard to take immediate effect upon publication in the Federal Register if he determines (A) that employees are exposed to grave danger from exposure to substances or agents determined to be toxic or physically harmful or from new hazards, and (B) that such emergency standard is necessary to protect employees from such danger.

Temporary standard. Publication in Federal Register. 80 Stat. 381; 81 Stat. 195. 5 USC 500.

(2) Such standard shall be effective until superseded by a standard promulgated in accordance with the procedures prescribed in paragraph (3) of this subsection.

Time limitation.

(3) Upon publication of such standard in the Federal Register the Secretary shall commence a proceeding in accordance with section 6(b) of this Act, and the standard as published shall also serve as a proposed rule for the proceeding. The Secretary shall promulgate a standard under this paragraph no later than six months after publication of the emergency standard as provided in paragraph (2) of this subsection.

(d) Any affected employer may apply to the Secretary for a rule or order for a variance from a standard promulgated under this section. Affected employees shall be given notice of each such application and an opportunity to participate in a hearing. The Secretary shall issue such rule or order if he determines on the record, after opportunity for an inspection where appropriate and a hearing, that the proponent of the variance has demonstrated by a preponderance of the evidence that the conditions, practices, means, methods, operations, or processes used or proposed to be used by an employer will provide employment and places of employment to his employees which are as safe and healthful as those which would prevail if he complied with the standard. The rule or order so issued shall prescribe the conditions the employer must maintain, and the practices, means, methods, operations, and processes which he must adopt and utilize to the extent they

Variance rule.

differ from the standard in question. Such a rule or order may be modified or revoked upon application by an employer, employees, or by the Secretary on his own motion, in the manner prescribed for its issuance under this subsection at any time after six months from its issuance.

(e) Whenever the Secretary promulgates any standard, makes any rule, order, or decision, grants any exemption or extension of time, or compromises, mitigates, or settles any penalty assessed under this Act, he shall include a statement of the reasons for such action, which shall be published in the Federal Register.

(f) Any person who may be adversely affected by a standard issued under this section may at any time prior to the sixtieth day after such standard is promulgated file a petition challenging the validity of such standard with the United States court of appeals for the circuit wherein such person resides or has his principal place of business, for a judicial review of such standard. A copy of the petition shall be forthwith transmitted by the clerk of the court to the Secretary. The filing of such petition shall not, unless otherwise ordered by the court, operate as a stay of the standard. The determinations of the Secretary shall be conclusive if supported by substantial evidence in the record considered as a whole.

(g) In determining the priority for establishing standards under this section, the Secretary shall give due regard to the urgency of the need for mandatory safety and health standards for particular industries, trades, crafts, occupations, businesses, workplaces or work environments. The Secretary shall also give due regard to the recommendations of the Secretary of Health, Education, and Welfare regarding the need for mandatory standards in determining the priority for establishing such standards.

ADVISORY COMMITTEES; ADMINISTRATION

SEC. 7. (a)(1) There is hereby established a National Advisory Committee on Occupational Safety and Health consisting of twelve members appointed by the Secretary, four of whom are to be designated by the Secretary of Health, Education, and Welfare, without

regard to the provisions of title 5, United States Code, governing appointments in the competitive service, and composed of representatives of management, labor, occupational safety and occupational health professions, and of the public. The Secretary shall designate one of the public members as Chairman. The members shall be selected upon the basis of their experience and competence in the field of occupational safety and health.

(2) The Committee shall advise, consult with, and make recommendations to the Secretary and the Secretary of Health, Education, and Welfare on matters relating to the administration of the Act. The Committee shall hold no fewer than two meetings during each calendar year. All meetings of the Committee shall be open to the public

and a transcript shall be kept and made available for public inspection.

(3) The members of the Committee shall be compensated in accordance with the provisions of section 3109 of title 5, United States

Code.

(4) The Secretary shall furnish to the Committee an executive secretary and such secretarial, clerical, and other services as are deemed necessary to the conduct of its business.

(b) An advisory committee may be appointed by the Secretary to assist him in his standard-setting functions under section 6 of this Act. Each such committee shall consist of not more than fifteen members

84 STAT. 1598

and shall include as a member one or more designees of the Secretary of Health, Education, and Welfare, and shall include among its members an equal number of persons qualified by experience and affiliation to present the viewpoint of the employers involved, and of persons similarly qualified to present the viewpoint of the workers involved, as well as one or more representatives of health and safety agencies of the States. An advisory committee may also include such other persons as the Secretary may appoint who are qualified by knowledge and experience to make a useful contribution to the work of such committee, including one or more representatives of professional organizations of technicians or professionals specializing in occupational safety or health, and one or more representatives of nationally recognized standards-producing organizations, but the number of persons so appointed to any such advisory committee shall not exceed the number appointed to such committee as representatives of Federal and State agencies. Persons appointed to advisory committees from private life shall be compensated in the same manner as consultants or experts under section 3109 of title 5, United States Code. The Secretary shall pay to any State which is the employer of a member of such a committee who is a representative of the health or safety agency of that State, reimbursement sufficient to cover the actual cost to the State resulting from such representative's membership on such committee. Any meeting of such committee shall be open to the public and an accurate record shall be kept and made available to the public. No member of such committee (other than representatives of employers and employees) shall have an economic interest in any proposed rule.

80 Stat. 416.

Recordkeeping.

(c) In carrying out his responsibilities under this Act, the Secretary is authorized to—

(1) use, with the consent of any Federal agency, the services, facilities, and personnel of such agency, with or without reimbursement, and with the consent of any State or political subdivision thereof, accept and use the services, facilities, and personnel of any agency of such State or subdivision with reimbursement; and

(2) employ experts and consultants or organizations thereof as authorized by section 3109 of title 5, United States Code, except that contracts for such employment may be renewed annually; compensate individuals so employed at rates not in excess of the rate specified at the time of service for grade GS-18 under section 5332 of title 5, United States Code, including traveltime, and allow them while away from their homes or regular places of business, travel expenses (including per diem in lieu of subsistence) as authorized by section 5703 of title 5, United States Code, for persons in the Government service employed intermittently, while so employed.

Ante, p. 198-1.

80 Stat. 499;
83 Stat. 190.

INSPECTIONS, INVESTIGATIONS, AND RECORDKEEPING

SEC. 8. (a) In order to carry out the purposes of this Act, the Secretary, upon presenting appropriate credentials to the owner, operator, or agent in charge, is authorized—

(1) to enter without delay and at reasonable times any factory, plant, establishment, construction site, or other area, workplace or environment where work is performed by an employee of an employer; and

84 STAT. 1599

(2) to inspect and investigate during regular working hours and at other reasonable times, and within reasonable limits and in a reasonable manner, any such place of employment and all pertinent conditions, structures, machines, apparatus, devices, equipment, and materials therein, and to question privately any such employer, owner, operator, agent or employee.

Subpoena power.

(b) In making his inspections and investigations under this Act the Secretary may require the attendance and testimony of witnesses and the production of evidence under oath. Witnesses shall be paid the same fees and mileage that are paid witnesses in the courts of the United States. In case of a contumacy, failure, or refusal of any person to obey such an order, any district court of the United States or the United States courts of any territory or possession, within the jurisdiction of which such person is found, or resides or transacts business, upon the application by the Secretary, shall have jurisdiction to issue to such person an order requiring such person to appear to produce evidence if, as, and when so ordered, and to give testimony relating to the matter under investigation or in question, and any failure to obey such order of the court may be punished by said court as a contempt thereof.

Recordkeeping.

(c) (1) Each employer shall make, keep and preserve, and make available to the Secretary or the Secretary of Health, Education, and Welfare, such records regarding his activities relating to this Act as the Secretary, in cooperation with the Secretary of Health, Education, and Welfare, may prescribe by regulation as necessary or appropriate for the enforcement of this Act or for developing information regarding the causes and prevention of occupational accidents and illnesses. In order to carry out the provisions of this paragraph such regulations may include provisions requiring employers to conduct periodic inspections. The Secretary shall also issue regulations requiring that employers, through posting of notices or other appropriate means, keep their employees informed of their protections and obligations under this Act, including the provisions of applicable standards.

Work-related deaths, etc.; reports.

(2) The Secretary, in cooperation with the Secretary of Health, Education, and Welfare, shall prescribe regulations requiring employers to maintain accurate records of, and to make periodic reports on, work-related deaths, injuries and illnesses other than minor injuries requiring only first aid treatment and which do not involve medical treatment, loss of consciousness, restriction of work or motion, or transfer to another job.

(3) The Secretary, in cooperation with the Secretary of Health, Education, and Welfare, shall issue regulations requiring employers to maintain accurate records of employee exposures to potentially toxic materials or harmful physical agents which are required to be monitored or measured under section 6. Such regulations shall provide employees or their representatives with an opportunity to observe such monitoring or measuring, and to have access to the records thereof. Such regulations shall also make appropriate provision for each employee or former employee to have access to such records as will indicate his own exposure to toxic materials or harmful physical agents. Each employer shall promptly notify any employee who has been or is being exposed to toxic materials or harmful physical agents in concentrations or at levels which exceed those prescribed by an applicable occupational safety and health standard promulgated under section 6, and shall inform any employee who is being thus exposed of the corrective action being taken.

(d) Any information obtained by the Secretary, the Secretary of Health, Education, and Welfare, or a State agency under this Act shall be obtained with a minimum burden upon employers, especially those operating small businesses. Unnecessary duplication of efforts in obtaining information shall be reduced to the maximum extent feasible.

(e) Subject to regulations issued by the Secretary, a representative of the employer and a representative authorized by his employees shall be given an opportunity to accompany the Secretary or his authorized representative during the physical inspection of any workplace under subsection (a) for the purpose of aiding such inspection. Where there is no authorized employee representative, the Secretary or his authorized representative shall consult with a reasonable number of employees concerning matters of health and safety in the workplace.

(f)(1) Any employees or representative of employees who believe that a violation of a safety or health standard exists that threatens physical harm, or that an imminent danger exists, may request an inspection by giving notice to the Secretary or his authorized representative of such violation or danger. Any such notice shall be reduced to writing, shall set forth with reasonable particularity the grounds for the notice, and shall be signed by the employees or representative of employees, and a copy shall be provided the employer or his agent no later than at the time of inspection, except that, upon the request of the person giving such notice, his name and the names of individual employees referred to therein shall not appear in such copy or on any record published, released, or made available pursuant to subsection (g) of this section. If upon receipt of such notification the Secretary determines there are reasonable grounds to believe that such violation or danger exists, he shall make a special inspection in accordance with the provisions of this section as soon as practicable, to determine if such violation or danger exists. If the Secretary determines there are no reasonable grounds to believe that a violation or danger exists he shall notify the employees or representative of the employees in writing of such determination.

(2) Prior to or during any inspection of a workplace, any employees or representative of employees employed in such workplace may notify the Secretary or any representative of the Secretary responsible for conducting the inspection, in writing, of any violation of this Act which they have reason to believe exists in such workplace. The Secretary shall, by regulation, establish procedures for informal review of any refusal by a representative of the Secretary to issue a citation with respect to any such alleged violation and shall furnish the employees or representative of employees requesting such review a written statement of the reasons for the Secretary's final disposition of the case.

(g)(1) The Secretary and Secretary of Health, Education, and Welfare are authorized to compile, analyze, and publish, either in summary or detailed form, all reports or information obtained under this section. *Reports, publication.*

(2) The Secretary and the Secretary of Health, Education, and Welfare shall each prescribe such rules and regulations as he may deem necessary to carry out their responsibilities under this Act, including rules and regulations dealing with the inspection of an employer's establishment. *Rules and regulations.*

84 STAT. 1601

CITATIONS

SEC. 9. (a) If, upon inspection or investigation, the Secretary or his authorized representative believes that an employer has violated a requirement of section 5 of this Act, of any standard, rule or order promulgated pursuant to section 6 of this Act, or of any regulations prescribed pursuant to this Act, he shall with reasonable promptness issue a citation to the employer. Each citation shall be in writing and shall describe with particularity the nature of the violation, including a reference to the provision of the Act, standard, rule, regulation, or order alleged to have been violated. In addition, the citation shall fix a reasonable time for the abatement of the violation. The Secretary may prescribe procedures for the issuance of a notice in lieu of a citation with respect to de minimis violations which have no direct or immediate relationship to safety or health.

(b) Each citation issued under this section, or a copy or copies thereof, shall be prominently posted, as prescribed in regulations issued by the Secretary, at or near each place a violation referred to in the citation occurred.

Limitation.

(c) No citation may be issued under this section after the expiration of six months following the occurrence of any violation.

PROCEDURE FOR ENFORCEMENT

SEC. 10. (a) If, after an inspection or investigation, the Secretary issues a citation under section 9(a), he shall, within a reasonable time after the termination of such inspection or investigation, notify the employer by certified mail of the penalty, if any, proposed to be assessed under section 17 and that the employer has fifteen working days within which to notify the Secretary that he wishes to contest the citation or proposed assessment of penalty. If, within fifteen working days from the receipt of the notice issued by the Secretary the employer fails to notify the Secretary that he intends to contest the citation or proposed assessment of penalty, and no notice is filed by any employee or representative of employees under subsection (c) within such time, the citation and the assessment, as proposed, shall be deemed a final order of the Commission and not subject to review by any court or agency.

(b) If the Secretary has reason to believe that an employer has failed to correct a violation for which a citation has been issued within the period permitted for its correction (which period shall not begin to run until the entry of a final order by the Commission in the case of any review proceedings under this section initiated by the employer in good faith and not solely for delay or avoidance of penalties), the Secretary shall notify the employer by certified mail of such failure and of the penalty proposed to be assessed under section 17 by reason of such failure, and that the employer has fifteen working days within which to notify the Secretary that he wishes to contest the Secretary's notification or the proposed assessment of penalty. If, within fifteen working days from the receipt of notification issued by the Secretary, the employer fails to notify the Secretary that he intends to contest the notification or proposed assessment of penalty, the notification and assessment, as proposed, shall be deemed a final order of the Commission and not subject to review by any court or agency.

(c) If an employer notifies the Secretary that he intends to contest a citation issued under section 9(a) or notification issued under subsection (a) or (b) of this section, or if, within fifteen working days

84 STAT. 1602

of the issuance of a citation under section 9(a), any employee or representative of employees files a notice with the Secretary alleging that the period of time fixed in the citation for the abatement of the violation is unreasonable, the Secretary shall immediately advise the Commission of such notification, and the Commission shall afford an opportunity for a hearing (in accordance with section 554 of title 5, United States Code, but without regard to subsection (a)(3) of such section). The Commission shall thereafter issue an order, based on findings of fact, affirming, modifying, or vacating the Secretary's citation or proposed penalty, or directing other appropriate relief, and such order shall become final thirty days after its issuance. Upon a showing by an employer of a good faith effort to comply with the abatement requirements of a citation, and that abatement has not been completed because of factors beyond his reasonable control, the Secretary, after an opportunity for a hearing as provided in this subsection, shall issue an order affirming or modifying the abatement requirements in such citation. The rules of procedure prescribed by the Commission shall provide affected employees or representatives of affected employees an opportunity to participate as parties to hearings under this subsection.

80 Stat. 384.

JUDICIAL REVIEW

SEC. 11. (a) Any person adversely affected or aggrieved by an order of the Commission issued under subsection (c) of section 10 may obtain a review of such order in any United States court of appeals for the circuit in which the violation is alleged to have occurred or where the employer has its principal office, or in the Court of Appeals for the District of Columbia Circuit, by filing in such court within sixty days following the issuance of such order a written petition praying that the order be modified or set aside. A copy of such petition shall be forthwith transmitted by the clerk of the court to the Commission and to the other parties, and thereupon the Commission shall file in the court the record in the proceeding as provided in section 2112 of title 28, United States Code. Upon such filing, the court shall have jurisdiction of the proceeding and of the question determined therein, and shall have power to grant such temporary relief or restraining order as it deems just and proper, and to make and enter upon the pleadings, testimony, and proceedings set forth in such record a decree affirming, modifying, or setting aside in whole or in part, the order of the Commission and enforcing the same to the extent that such order is affirmed or modified. The commencement of proceedings under this subsection shall not, unless ordered by the court, operate as a stay of the order of the Commission. No objection that has not been urged before the Commission shall be considered by the court, unless the failure or neglect to urge such objection shall be excused because of extraordinary circumstances. The findings of the Commission with respect to questions of fact, if supported by substantial evidence on the record considered as a whole, shall be conclusive. If any party shall apply to the court for leave to adduce additional evidence and shall show to the satisfaction of the court that such additional evidence is material and that there were reasonable grounds for the failure to adduce such evidence in the hearing before the Commission, the court may order such additional evidence to be taken before the Commission and to be made a part of the record. The Commission may modify its findings as to the facts, or make new findings, by reason of additional evidence so taken and filed, and it shall file such modified or new findings, which findings with respect to questions of fact, if supported by substantial evi-

72 Stat. 941;
80 Stat. 1323.

dence on the record considered as a whole, shall be conclusive, and its recommendations, if any, for the modification or setting aside of its original order. Upon the filing of the record with it, the jurisdiction of the court shall be exclusive and its judgment and decree shall be final, except that the same shall be subject to review by the Supreme Court of the United States, as provided in section 1254 of title 28, United States Code. Petitions filed under this subsection shall be heard expeditiously.

62 Stat. 928.

(b) The Secretary may also obtain review or enforcement of any final order of the Commission by filing a petition for such relief in the United States court of appeals for the circuit in which the alleged violation occurred or in which the employer has its principal office, and the provisions of subsection (a) shall govern such proceedings to the extent applicable. If no petition for review, as provided in subsection (a), is filed within sixty days after service of the Commission's order, the Commission's findings of fact and order shall be conclusive in connection with any petition for enforcement which is filed by the Secretary after the expiration of such sixty-day period. In any such case, as well as in the case of a noncontested citation or notification by the Secretary which has become a final order of the Commission under subsection (a) or (b) of section 10, the clerk of the court, unless otherwise ordered by the court, shall forthwith enter a decree enforcing the order and shall transmit a copy of such decree to the Secretary and the employer named in the petition. In any contempt proceeding brought to enforce a decree of a court of appeals entered pursuant to this subsection or subsection (a), the court of appeals may assess the penalties provided in section 17, in addition to invoking any other available remedies.

(c) (1) No person shall discharge or in any manner discriminate against any employee because such employee has filed any complaint or instituted or caused to be instituted any proceeding under or related to this Act or has testified or is about to testify in any such proceeding or because of the exercise by such employee on behalf of himself or others of any right afforded by this Act.

(2) Any employee who believes that he has been discharged or otherwise discriminated against by any person in violation of this subsection may, within thirty days after such violation occurs, file a complaint with the Secretary alleging such discrimination. Upon receipt of such complaint, the Secretary shall cause such investigation to be made as he deems appropriate. If upon such investigation, the Secretary determines that the provisions of this subsection have been violated, he shall bring an action in any appropriate United States district court against such person. In any such action the United States district courts shall have jurisdiction, for cause shown to restrain violations of paragraph (1) of this subsection and order all appropriate relief including rehiring or reinstatement of the employee to his former position with back pay.

(3) Within 90 days of the receipt of a complaint filed under this subsection the Secretary shall notify the complainant of his determination under paragraph 2 of this subsection.

THE OCCUPATIONAL SAFETY AND HEALTH REVIEW COMMISSION

Establishment; membership.

SEC. 12. (a) The Occupational Safety and Health Review Commission is hereby established. The Commission shall be composed of three members who shall be appointed by the President, by and with the advice and consent of the Senate, from among persons who by reason

84 STAT. 1604

of training, education, or experience are qualified to carry out the functions of the Commission under this Act. The President shall designate one of the members of the Commission to serve as Chairman.

(b) The terms of members of the Commission shall be six years Terms.
except that (1) the members of the Commission first taking office shall serve, as designated by the President at the time of appointment, one for a term of two years, one for a term of four years, and one for a term of six years, and (2) a vacancy caused by the death, resignation, or removal of a member prior to the expiration of the term for which he was appointed shall be filled only for the remainder of such unexpired term. A member of the Commission may be removed by the President for inefficiency, neglect of duty, or malfeasance in office.

(c)(1) Section 5314 of title 5, United States Code, is amended by 80 Stat. 460.
adding at the end thereof the following new paragraph:

"(57) Chairman, Occupational Safety and Health Review
Commission."

(2) Section 5315 of title 5, United States Code, is amended by add- Ante, p. 776.
ing at the end thereof the following new paragraph:

"(94) Members, Occupational Safety and Health Review
Commission."

(d) The principal office of the Commission shall be in the District Location.
of Columbia. Whenever the Commission deems that the convenience of the public or of the parties may be promoted, or delay or expense may be minimized, it may hold hearings or conduct other proceedings at any other place.

(e) The Chairman shall be responsible on behalf of the Commission for the administrative operations of the Commission and shall appoint such hearing examiners and other employees as he deems necessary to assist in the performance of the Commission's functions and to fix their compensation in accordance with the provisions of chapter 51 and subchapter III of chapter 53 of title 5, United States Code, 5 USC 5101,
relating to classification and General Schedule pay rates: *Provided*, 5331.
That assignment, removal and compensation of hearing examiners Ante, p. 198-1.
shall be in accordance with sections 3105, 3344, 5362, and 7521 of title 5, United States Code.

(f) For the purpose of carrying out its functions under this Act, two Quorum.
members of the Commission shall constitute a quorum and official action can be taken only on the affirmative vote of at least two members.

(g) Every official act of the Commission shall be entered of record, Public records.
and its hearings and records shall be open to the public. The Commission is authorized to make such rules as are necessary for the orderly transaction of its proceedings. Unless the Commission has adopted a different rule, its proceedings shall be in accordance with the Federal Rules of Civil Procedure. 28 USC app.

(h) The Commission may order testimony to be taken by deposition in any proceedings pending before it at any state of such proceeding. Any person may be compelled to appear and depose, and to produce books, papers, or documents, in the same manner as witnesses may be compelled to appear and testify and produce like documentary evidence before the Commission. Witnesses whose depositions are taken under this subsection, and the persons taking such depositions, shall be entitled to the same fees as are paid for like services in the courts of the United States.

(i) For the purpose of any proceeding before the Commission, the provisions of section 11 of the National Labor Relations Act (29 U.S.C. 161) are hereby made applicable to the jurisdiction and powers 61 Stat. 150;
of the Commission. Ante, p. 930.

84 STAT. 1605

Report.

(j) A hearing examiner appointed by the Commission shall hear, and make a determination upon, any proceeding instituted before the Commission and any motion in connection therewith, assigned to such hearing examiner by the Chairman of the Commission, and shall make a report of any such determination which constitutes his final disposition of the proceedings. The report of the hearing examiner shall become the final order of the Commission within thirty days after such report by the hearing examiner, unless within such period any Commission member has directed that such report shall be reviewed by the Commission.

(k) Except as otherwise provided in this Act, the hearing examiners shall be subject to the laws governing employees in the classified civil service, except that appointments shall be made without regard to section 5108 of title 5, United States Code. Each hearing examiner shall receive compensation at a rate not less than that prescribed for GS-16 under section 5332 of title 5, United States Code.

80 Stat. 453.

Ante, p. 198-1.

PROCEDURES TO COUNTERACT IMMINENT DANGERS

SEC. 13. (a) The United States district courts shall have jurisdiction, upon petition of the Secretary, to restrain any conditions or practices in any place of employment which are such that a danger exists which could reasonably be expected to cause death or serious physical harm immediately or before the imminence of such danger can be eliminated through the enforcement procedures otherwise provided by this Act. Any order issued under this section may require such steps to be taken as may be necessary to avoid, correct, or remove such imminent danger and prohibit the employment or presence of any individual in locations or under conditions where such imminent danger exists, except individuals whose presence is necessary to avoid, correct, or remove such imminent danger or to maintain the capacity of a continuous process operation to resume normal operations without a complete cessation of operations, or where a cessation of operations is necessary, to permit such to be accomplished in a safe and orderly manner.

(b) Upon the filing of any such petition the district court shall have jurisdiction to grant such injunctive relief or temporary restraining order pending the outcome of an enforcement proceeding pursuant to this Act. The proceeding shall be as provided by Rule 65 of the Federal Rules, Civil Procedure, except that no temporary restraining order issued without notice shall be effective for a period longer than five days.

28 USC app.

(c) Whenever and as soon as an inspector concludes that conditions or practices described in subsection (a) exist in any place of employment, he shall inform the affected employees and employers of the danger and that he is recommending to the Secretary that relief be sought.

(d) If the Secretary arbitrarily or capriciously fails to seek relief under this section, any employee who may be injured by reason of such failure, or the representative of such employees, might bring an action against the Secretary in the United States district court for the district in which the imminent danger is alleged to exist or the employer has its principal office, or for the District of Columbia, for a writ of mandamus to compel the Secretary to seek such an order and for such further relief as may be appropriate.

84 STAT. 1606

REPRESENTATION IN CIVIL LITIGATION

SEC. 14. Except as provided in section 518(a) of title 28, United States Code, relating to litigation before the Supreme Court, the Solicitor of Labor may appear for and represent the Secretary in any civil litigation brought under this Act but all such litigation shall be subject to the direction and control of the Attorney General.

80 Stat. 613.

CONFIDENTIALITY OF TRADE SECRETS

SEC. 15. All information reported to or otherwise obtained by the Secretary or his representative in connection with any inspection or proceeding under this Act which contains or which might reveal a trade secret referred to in section 1905 of title 18 of the United States Code shall be considered confidential for the purpose of that section, except that such information may be disclosed to other officers or employees concerned with carrying out this Act or when relevant in any proceeding under this Act. In any such proceeding the Secretary, the Commission, or the court shall issue such orders as may be appropriate to protect the confidentiality of trade secrets.

62 Stat. 791.

VARIATIONS, TOLERANCES, AND EXEMPTIONS

SEC. 16. The Secretary, on the record, after notice and opportunity for a hearing may provide such reasonable limitations and may make such rules and regulations allowing reasonable variations, tolerances, and exemptions to and from any or all provisions of this Act as he may find necessary and proper to avoid serious impairment of the national defense. Such action shall not be in effect for more than six months without notification to affected employees and an opportunity being afforded for a hearing.

PENALTIES

SEC. 17. (a) Any employer who willfully or repeatedly violates the requirements of section 5 of this Act, any standard, rule, or order promulgated pursuant to section 6 of this Act, or regulations prescribed pursuant to this Act, may be assessed a civil penalty of not more than $10,000 for each violation.

(b) Any employer who has received a citation for a serious violation of the requirements of section 5 of this Act, of any standard, rule, or order promulgated pursuant to section 6 of this Act, or of any regulations prescribed pursuant to this Act, shall be assessed a civil penalty of up to $1,000 for each such violation.

(c) Any employer who has received a citation for a violation of the requirements of section 5 of this Act, of any standard, rule, or order promulgated pursuant to section 6 of this Act, or of regulations prescribed pursuant to this Act, and such violation is specifically determined not to be of a serious nature, may be assessed a civil penalty of up to $1,000 for each such violation.

(d) Any employer who fails to correct a violation for which a citation has been issued under section 9(a) within the period permitted for its correction (which period shall not begin to run until the date of the final order of the Commission in the case of any review proceeding under section 10 initiated by the employer in good faith and not solely for delay or avoidance of penalties), may be assessed a civil penalty of not more than $1,000 for each day during which such failure or violation continues.

84 STAT. 1607

(e) Any employer who willfully violates any standard, rule, or order promulgated pursuant to section 6 of this Act, or of any regulations prescribed pursuant to this Act, and that violation caused death to any employee, shall, upon conviction, be punished by a fine of not more than $10,000 or by imprisonment for not more than six months, or by both; except that if the conviction is for a violation committed after a first conviction of such person, punishment shall be by a fine of not more than $20,000 or by imprisonment for not more than one year, or by both.

(f) Any person who gives advance notice of any inspection to be conducted under this Act, without authority from the Secretary or his designees, shall, upon conviction, be punished by a fine of not more than $1,000 or by imprisonment for not more than six months, or by both.

(g) Whoever knowingly makes any false statement, representation, or certification in any application, record, report, plan, or other document filed or required to be maintained pursuant to this Act shall, upon conviction, be punished by a fine of not more than $10,000, or by imprisonment for not more than six months, or by both.

65 Stat. 721;
79 Stat. 234.

(h)(1) Section 1114 of title 18, United States Code, is hereby amended by striking out "designated by the Secretary of Health, Education, and Welfare to conduct investigations, or inspections under the Federal Food, Drug, and Cosmetic Act" and inserting in lieu thereof "or of the Department of Labor assigned to perform investigative, inspection, or law enforcement functions".

62 Stat. 756.

(2) Notwithstanding the provisions of sections 1111 and 1114 of title 18, United States Code, whoever, in violation of the provisions of section 1114 of such title, kills a person while engaged in or on account of the performance of investigative, inspection, or law enforcement functions added to such section 1114 by paragraph (1) of this subsection, and who would otherwise be subject to the penalty provisions of such section 1111, shall be punished by imprisonment for any term of years or for life.

(i) Any employer who violates any of the posting requirements, as prescribed under the provisions of this Act, shall be assessed a civil penalty of up to $1,000 for each violation.

(j) The Commission shall have authority to assess all civil penalties provided in this section, giving due consideration to the appropriateness of the penalty with respect to the size of the business of the employer being charged, the gravity of the violation, the good faith of the employer, and the history of previous violations.

(k) For purposes of this section, a serious violation shall be deemed to exist in a place of employment if there is a substantial probability that death or serious physical harm could result from a condition which exists, or from one or more practices, means, methods, operations, or processes which have been adopted or are in use, in such place of employment unless the employer did not, and could not with the exercise of reasonable diligence, know of the presence of the violation.

(l) Civil penalties owed under this Act shall be paid to the Secretary for deposit into the Treasury of the United States and shall accrue to the United States and may be recovered in a civil action in the name of the United States brought in the United States district court for the district where the violation is alleged to have occurred or where the employer has its principal office.

84 STAT. 1608

STATE JURISDICTION AND STATE PLANS

SEC. 18. (a) Nothing in this Act shall prevent any State agency or court from asserting jurisdiction under State law over any occupational safety or health issue with respect to which no standard is in effect under section 6.

(b) Any State which, at any time, desires to assume responsibility for development and enforcement therein of occupational safety and health standards relating to any occupational safety or health issue with respect to which a Federal standard has been promulgated under section 6 shall submit a State plan for the development of such standards and their enforcement.

(c) The Secretary shall approve the plan submitted by a State under subsection (b), or any modification thereof, if such plan in his judgment—

(1) designates a State agency or agencies as the agency or agencies responsible for administering the plan throughout the State,

(2) provides for the development and enforcement of safety and health standards relating to one or more safety or health issues, which standards (and the enforcement of which standards) are or will be at least as effective in providing safe and healthful employment and places of employment as the standards promulgated under section 6 which relate to the same issues, and which standards, when applicable to products which are distributed or used in interstate commerce, are required by compelling local conditions and do not unduly burden interstate commerce,

(3) provides for a right of entry and inspection of all workplaces subject to the Act which is at least as effective as that provided in section 8, and includes a prohibition on advance notice of inspections,

(4) contains satisfactory assurances that such agency or agencies have or will have the legal authority and qualified personnel necessary for the enforcement of such standards,

(5) gives satisfactory assurances that such State will devote adequate funds to the administration and enforcement of such standards,

(6) contains satisfactory assurances that such State will, to the extent permitted by its law, establish and maintain an effective and comprehensive occupational safety and health program applicable to all employees of public agencies of the State and its political subdivisions, which program is as effective as the standards contained in an approved plan,

(7) requires employers in the State to make reports to the Secretary in the same manner and to the same extent as if the plan were not in effect, and

(8) provides that the State agency will make such reports to the Secretary in such form and containing such information, as the Secretary shall from time to time require.

(d) If the Secretary rejects a plan submitted under subsection (b), he shall afford the State submitting the plan due notice and opportunity for a hearing before so doing.   Notice of hearing.

(e) After the Secretary approves a State plan submitted under subsection (b), he may, but shall not be required to, exercise his authority under sections 8, 9, 10, 13, and 17 with respect to comparable standards promulgated under section 6, for the period specified in the next sentence. The Secretary may exercise the authority referred to above until he determines, on the basis of actual operations under the

84 STAT. 1609

State plan, that the criteria set forth in subsection (c) are being applied, but he shall not make such determination for at least three years after the plan's approval under subsection (c). Upon making the determination referred to in the preceding sentence, the provisions of sections 5(a)(2), 8 (except for the purpose of carrying out subsection (f) of this section), 9, 10, 13, and 17, and standards promulgated under section 6 of this Act, shall not apply with respect to any occupational safety or health issues covered under the plan, but the Secretary may retain jurisdiction under the above provisions in any proceeding commenced under section 9 or 10 before the date of determination.

Continuing evaluation.

(f) The Secretary shall, on the basis of reports submitted by the State agency and his own inspections make a continuing evaluation of the manner in which each State having a plan approved under this section is carrying out such plan. Whenever the Secretary finds, after affording due notice and opportunity for a hearing, that in the administration of the State plan there is a failure to comply substantially with any provision of the State plan (or any assurance contained therein), he shall notify the State agency of his withdrawal of approval of such plan and upon receipt of such notice such plan shall cease to be in effect, but the State may retain jurisdiction in any case commenced before the withdrawal of the plan in order to enforce standards under the plan whenever the issues involved do not relate to the reasons for the withdrawal of the plan.

Plan rejection, review.

(g) The State may obtain a review of a decision of the Secretary withdrawing approval of or rejecting its plan by the United States court of appeals for the circuit in which the State is located by filing in such court within thirty days following receipt of notice of such decision a petition to modify or set aside in whole or in part the action of the Secretary. A copy of such petition shall forthwith be served upon the Secretary, and thereupon the Secretary shall certify and file in the court the record upon which the decision complained of was

72 Stat. 941;
80 Stat. 1323.

issued as provided in section 2112 of title 28, United States Code. Unless the court finds that the Secretary's decision in rejecting a proposed State plan or withdrawing his approval of such a plan is not supported by substantial evidence the court shall affirm the Secretary's decision. The judgment of the court shall be subject to review by the Supreme Court of the United States upon certiorari or certification

62 Stat. 928.

as provided in section 1254 of title 28, United States Code.

(h) The Secretary may enter into an agreement with a State under which the State will be permitted to continue to enforce one or more occupational health and safety standards in effect in such State until final action is taken by the Secretary with respect to a plan submitted by a State under subsection (b) of this section, or two years from the date of enactment of this Act, whichever is earlier.

FEDERAL AGENCY SAFETY PROGRAMS AND RESPONSIBILITIES

SEC. 19. (a) It shall be the responsibility of the head of each Federal agency to establish and maintain an effective and comprehensive occupational safety and health program which is consistent with the standards promulgated under section 6. The head of each agency shall (after consultation with representatives of the employees thereof)—

(1) provide safe and healthful places and conditions of employment, consistent with the standards set under section 6;

(2) acquire, maintain, and require the use of safety equipment, personal protective equipment, and devices reasonably necessary to protect employees;

(3) keep adequate records of all occupational accidents and illnesses for proper evaluation and necessary corrective action;

Recordkeeping.

(4) consult with the Secretary with regard to the adequacy as to form and content of records kept pursuant to subsection (a)(3) of this section; and

(5) make an annual report to the Secretary with respect to occupational accidents and injuries and the agency's program under this section. Such report shall include any report submitted under section 7902(e)(2) of title 5, United States Code.

Annual report.

80 Stat. 530.

(b) The Secretary shall report to the President a summary or digest of reports submitted to him under subsection (a)(5) of this section, together with his evaluations of and recommendations derived from such reports. The President shall transmit annually to the Senate and the House of Representatives a report of the activities of Federal agencies under this section.

Report to President.

Report to Congress.

(c) Section 7902(c)(1) of title 5, United States Code, is amended by inserting after "agencies" the following: "and of labor organizations representing employees".

(d) The Secretary shall have access to records and reports kept and filed by Federal agencies pursuant to subsections (a)(3) and (5) of this section unless those records and reports are specifically required by Executive order to be kept secret in the interest of the national defense or foreign policy, in which case the Secretary shall have access to such information as will not jeopardize national defense or foreign policy.

Records, etc.; availability.

RESEARCH AND RELATED ACTIVITIES

SEC. 20. (a)(1) The Secretary of Health, Education, and Welfare, after consultation with the Secretary and with other appropriate Federal departments or agencies, shall conduct (directly or by grants or contracts) research, experiments, and demonstrations relating to occupational safety and health, including studies of psychological factors involved, and relating to innovative methods, techniques, and approaches for dealing with occupational safety and health problems.

(2) The Secretary of Health, Education, and Welfare shall from time to time consult with the Secretary in order to develop specific plans for such research, demonstrations, and experiments as are necessary to produce criteria, including criteria identifying toxic substances, enabling the Secretary to meet his responsibility for the formulation of safety and health standards under this Act; and the Secretary of Health, Education, and Welfare, on the basis of such research, demonstrations, and experiments and any other information available to him, shall develop and publish at least annually such criteria as will effectuate the purposes of this Act.

(3) The Secretary of Health, Education, and Welfare, on the basis of such research, demonstrations, and experiments, and any other information available to him, shall develop criteria dealing with toxic materials and harmful physical agents and substances which will describe exposure levels that are safe for various periods of employment, including but not limited to the exposure levels at which no employee will suffer impaired health or functional capacities or diminished life expectancy as a result of his work experience.

(4) The Secretary of Health, Education, and Welfare shall also conduct special research, experiments, and demonstrations relating to occupational safety and health as are necessary to explore new problems, including those created by new technology in occupational safety and health, which may require ameliorative action beyond that

which is otherwise provided for in the operating provisions of this Act. The Secretary of Health, Education, and Welfare shall also conduct research into the motivational and behavioral factors relating to the field of occupational safety and health.

Toxic sub-
stances,
records.

(5) The Secretary of Health, Education, and Welfare, in order to comply with his responsibilities under paragraph (2), and in order to develop needed information regarding potentially toxic substances or harmful physical agents, may prescribe regulations requiring employers to measure, record, and make reports on the exposure of employees to substances or physical agents which the Secretary of Health, Education, and Welfare reasonably believes may endanger the health or safety of employees. The Secretary of Health, Education, and Welfare also is authorized to establish such programs of medical examinations and tests as may be necessary for determining the incidence of occupational illnesses and the susceptibility of employees to such illnesses. Nothing in this or any other provision of this Act shall be deemed to authorize or require medical examination, immunization, or treatment for those who object thereto on religious grounds, except where such is necessary for the protection of the health or safety of others. Upon the request of any employer who is required to measure and record exposure of employees to substances or physical agents as provided under this subsection, the Secretary of Health, Education, and Welfare shall furnish full financial or other assistance to such employer for the purpose of defraying any additional expense incurred by him in carrying out the measuring and recording as provided in this subsection.

Medical
examinations.

Toxic sub-
stances,
publication.

(6) The Secretary of Health, Education, and Welfare shall publish within six months of enactment of this Act and thereafter as needed but at least annually a list of all known toxic substances by generic family or other useful grouping, and the concentrations at which such toxicity is known to occur. He shall determine following a written request by any employer or authorized representative of employees, specifying with reasonable particularity the grounds on which the request is made, whether any substance normally found in the place of employment has potentially toxic effects in such concentrations as used or found; and shall submit such determination both to employers and affected employees as soon as possible. If the Secretary of Health, Education, and Welfare determines that any substance is potentially toxic at the concentrations in which it is used or found in a place of employment, and such substance is not covered by an occupational safety or health standard promulgated under section 6, the Secretary of Health, Education, and Welfare shall immediately submit such determination to the Secretary, together with all pertinent criteria.

Annual
studies.

(7) Within two years of enactment of this Act, and annually thereafter the Secretary of Health, Education, and Welfare shall conduct and publish industrywide studies of the effect of chronic or low-level exposure to industrial materials, processes, and stresses on the potential for illness, disease, or loss of functional capacity in aging adults.

Inspections.

(b) The Secretary of Health, Education, and Welfare is authorized to make inspections and question employers and employees as provided in section 8 of this Act in order to carry out his functions and responsibilities under this section.

Contract
authority.

(c) The Secretary is authorized to enter into contracts, agreements, or other arrangements with appropriate public agencies or private organizations for the purpose of conducting studies relating to his responsibilities under this Act. In carrying out his responsibilities

84 STAT. 1612

under this subsection, the Secretary shall cooperate with the Secretary of Health, Education, and Welfare in order to avoid any duplication of efforts under this section.

(d) Information obtained by the Secretary and the Secretary of Health, Education, and Welfare under this section shall be disseminated by the Secretary to employers and employees and organizations thereof.

(e) The functions of the Secretary of Health, Education, and Welfare under this Act shall, to the extent feasible, be delegated to the Director of the National Institute for Occupational Safety and Health established by section 22 of this Act.

Delegation of functions.

TRAINING AND EMPLOYEE EDUCATION

SEC. 21. (a) The Secretary of Health, Education, and Welfare, after consultation with the Secretary and with other appropriate Federal departments and agencies, shall conduct, directly or by grants or contracts (1) education programs to provide an adequate supply of qualified personnel to carry out the purposes of this Act, and (2) informational programs on the importance of and proper use of adequate safety and health equipment.

(b) The Secretary is also authorized to conduct, directly or by grants or contracts, short-term training of personnel engaged in work related to his responsibilities under this Act.

(c) The Secretary, in consultation with the Secretary of Health, Education, and Welfare, shall (1) provide for the establishment and supervision of programs for the education and training of employers and employees in the recognition, avoidance, and prevention of unsafe or unhealthful working conditions in employments covered by this Act, and (2) consult with and advise employers and employees, and organizations representing employers and employees as to effective means of preventing occupational injuries and illnesses.

NATIONAL INSTITUTE FOR OCCUPATIONAL SAFETY AND HEALTH

SEC. 22. (a) It is the purpose of this section to establish a National Institute for Occupational Safety and Health in the Department of Health, Education, and Welfare in order to carry out the policy set forth in section 2 of this Act and to perform the functions of the Secretary of Health, Education, and Welfare under sections 20 and 21 of this Act.

Establishment.

(b) There is hereby established in the Department of Health, Education, and Welfare a National Institute for Occupational Safety and Health. The Institute shall be headed by a Director who shall be appointed by the Secretary of Health, Education, and Welfare, and who shall serve for a term of six years unless previously removed by the Secretary of Health, Education, and Welfare.

Director, appointment, term.

(c) The Institute is authorized to—
(1) develop and establish recommended occupational safety and health standards; and
(2) perform all functions of the Secretary of Health, Education, and Welfare under sections 20 and 21 of this Act.

(d) Upon his own initiative, or upon the request of the Secretary or the Secretary of Health, Education, and Welfare, the Director is authorized (1) to conduct such research and experimental programs as he determines are necessary for the development of criteria for new and improved occupational safety and health standards, and (2) after consideration of the results of such research and experimental programs make recommendations concerning new or improved occupational safety and health standards. Any occupational safety and health standard recommended pursuant to this section shall immediately be forwarded to the Secretary of Labor, and to the Secretary of Health, Education, and Welfare.

(e) In addition to any authority vested in the Institute by other provisions of this section, the Director, in carrying out the functions of the Institute, is authorized to—

(1) prescribe such regulations as he deems necessary governing the manner in which its functions shall be carried out;

(2) receive money and other property donated, bequeathed, or devised, without condition or restriction other than that it be used for the purposes of the Institute and to use, sell, or otherwise dispose of such property for the purpose of carrying out its functions;

(3) receive (and use, sell, or otherwise dispose of, in accordance with paragraph (2)), money and other property donated, bequeathed, or devised to the Institute with a condition or restriction, including a condition that the Institute use other funds of the Institute for the purposes of the gift;

(4) in accordance with the civil service laws, appoint and fix the compensation of such personnel as may be necessary to carry out the provisions of this section;

(5) obtain the services of experts and consultants in accordance with the provisions of section 3109 of title 5, United States Code;

80 Stat. 416.

(6) accept and utilize the services of voluntary and noncompensated personnel and reimburse them for travel expenses, including per diem, as authorized by section 5703 of title 5, United States Code;

83 Stat. 190.

(7) enter into contracts, grants or other arrangements, or modifications thereof to carry out the provisions of this section, and such contracts or modifications thereof may be entered into without performance or other bonds, and without regard to section 3709 of the Revised Statutes, as amended (41 U.S.C. 5), or any other provision of law relating to competitive bidding;

(8) make advance, progress, and other payments which the Director deems necessary under this title without regard to the provisions of section 3648 of the Revised Statutes, as amended (31 U.S.C. 529); and

(9) make other necessary expenditures.

Annual report to HEW, President, and Congress.

(f) The Director shall submit to the Secretary of Health, Education, and Welfare, to the President, and to the Congress an annual report of the operations of the Institute under this Act, which shall include a detailed statement of all private and public funds received and expended by it, and such recommendations as he deems appropriate.

GRANTS TO THE STATES

SEC. 23. (a) The Secretary is authorized, during the fiscal year ending June 30, 1971, and the two succeeding fiscal years, to make grants to the States which have designated a State agency under section 18 to assist them—

(1) in identifying their needs and responsibilities in the area of occupational safety and health,

(2) in developing State plans under section 18, or

(3) in developing plans for—
    (A) establishing systems for the collection of information concerning the nature and frequency of occupational injuries and diseases;
    (B) increasing the expertise and enforcement capabilities of their personnel engaged in occupational safety and health programs; or
    (C) otherwise improving the administration and enforcement of State occupational safety and health laws, including standards thereunder, consistent with the objectives of this Act.

(b) The Secretary is authorized, during the fiscal year ending June 30, 1971, and the two succeeding fiscal years, to make grants to the States for experimental and demonstration projects consistent with the objectives set forth in subsection (a) of this section.

(c) The Governor of the State shall designate the appropriate State agency for receipt of any grant made by the Secretary under this section.

(d) Any State agency designated by the Governor of the State desiring a grant under this section shall submit an application therefor to the Secretary.

(e) The Secretary shall review the application, and shall, after consultation with the Secretary of Health, Education, and Welfare, approve or reject such application.

(f) The Federal share for each State grant under subsection (a) or (b) of this section may not exceed 90 per centum of the total cost of the application. In the event the Federal share for all States under either such subsection is not the same, the differences among the States shall be established on the basis of objective criteria.

(g) The Secretary is authorized to make grants to the States to assist them in administering and enforcing programs for occupational safety and health contained in State plans approved by the Secretary pursuant to section 18 of this Act. The Federal share for each State grant under this subsection may not exceed 50 per centum of the total cost to the State of such a program. The last sentence of subsection (f) shall be applicable in determining the Federal share under this subsection.

(h) Prior to June 30, 1973, the Secretary shall, after consultation with the Secretary of Health, Education, and Welfare, transmit a report to the President and to the Congress, describing the experience under the grant programs authorized by this section and making any recommendations he may deem appropriate.

Report to President and Congress.

STATISTICS

SEC. 24. (a) In order to further the purposes of this Act, the Secretary, in consultation with the Secretary of Health, Education, and Welfare, shall develop and maintain an effective program of collection, compilation, and analysis of occupational safety and health statistics. Such program may cover all employments whether or not subject to any other provisions of this Act but shall not cover employments excluded by section 4 of the Act. The Secretary shall compile accurate statistics on work injuries and illnesses which shall include all disabling, serious, or significant injuries and illnesses, whether or not involving loss of time from work, other than minor injuries requiring only first aid treatment and which do not involve medical treatment, loss of consciousness, restriction of work or motion, or transfer to another job.

(b) To carry out his duties under subsection (a) of this section, the Secretary may—

(1) promote, encourage, or directly engage in programs of studies, information and communication concerning occupational safety and health statistics;

(2) make grants to States or political subdivisions thereof in order to assist them in developing and administering programs dealing with occupational safety and health statistics; and

(3) arrange, through grants or contracts, for the conduct of such research and investigations as give promise of furthering the objectives of this section.

(c) The Federal share for each grant under subsection (b) of this section may be up to 50 per centum of the State's total cost.

(d) The Secretary may, with the consent of any State or political subdivision thereof, accept and use the services, facilities, and employees of the agencies of such State or political subdivision, with or without reimbursement, in order to assist him in carrying out his functions under this section.

Reports.

(e) On the basis of the records made and kept pursuant to section 8(c) of this Act, employers shall file such reports with the Secretary as he shall prescribe by regulation, as necessary to carry out his functions under this Act.

(f) Agreements between the Department of Labor and States pertaining to the collection of occupational safety and health statistics already in effect on the effective date of this Act shall remain in effect until superseded by grants or contracts made under this Act.

AUDITS

SEC. 25. (a) Each recipient of a grant under this Act shall keep such records as the Secretary or the Secretary of Health, Education, and Welfare shall prescribe, including records which fully disclose the amount and disposition by such recipient of the proceeds of such grant, the total cost of the project or undertaking in connection with which such grant is made or used, and the amount of that portion of the cost of the project or undertaking supplied by other sources, and such other records as will facilitate an effective audit.

(b) The Secretary or the Secretary of Health, Education, and Welfare, and the Comptroller General of the United States, or any of their duly authorized representatives, shall have access for the purpose of audit and examination to any books, documents, papers, and records of the recipients of any grant under this Act that are pertinent to any such grant.

ANNUAL REPORT

SEC. 26. Within one hundred and twenty days following the convening of each regular session of each Congress, the Secretary and the Secretary of Health, Education, and Welfare shall each prepare and submit to the President for transmittal to the Congress a report upon the subject matter of this Act, the progress toward achievement of the purpose of this Act, the needs and requirements in the field of occupational safety and health, and any other relevant information. Such reports shall include information regarding occupational safety and health standards, and criteria for such standards, developed during the preceding year; evaluation of standards and criteria previously developed under this Act, defining areas of emphasis for new criteria and standards; an evaluation of the degree of observance of applicable occupational safety and health standards, and a summary

84 STAT. 1616

of inspection and enforcement activity undertaken; analysis and evaluation of research activities for which results have been obtained under governmental and nongovernmental sponsorship; an analysis of major occupational diseases; evaluation of available control and measurement technology for hazards for which standards or criteria have been developed during the preceding year; description of cooperative efforts undertaken between Government agencies and other interested parties in the implementation of this Act during the preceding year; a progress report on the development of an adequate supply of trained manpower in the field of occupational safety and health, including estimates of future needs and the efforts being made by Government and others to meet those needs; listing of all toxic substances in industrial usage for which labeling requirements, criteria, or standards have not yet been established; and such recommendations for additional legislation as are deemed necessary to protect the safety and health of the worker and improve the administration of this Act.

NATIONAL COMMISSION ON STATE WORKMEN'S COMPENSATION LAWS

SEC. 27. (a) (1) The Congress hereby finds and declares that—

(A) the vast majority of American workers, and their families, are dependent on workmen's compensation for their basic economic security in the event such workers suffer disabling injury or death in the course of their employment; and that the full protection of American workers from job-related injury or death requires an adequate, prompt, and equitable system of workmen's compensation as well as an effective program of occupational health and safety regulation; and

(B) in recent years serious questions have been raised concerning the fairness and adequacy of present workmen's compensation laws in the light of the growth of the economy, the changing nature of the labor force, increases in medical knowledge, changes in the hazards associated with various types of employment, new technology creating new risks to health and safety, and increases in the general level of wages and the cost of living.

(2) The purpose of this section is to authorize an effective study and objective evaluation of State workmen's compensation laws in order to determine if such laws provide an adequate, prompt, and equitable system of compensation for injury or death arising out of or in the course of employment.

(b) There is hereby established a National Commission on State Workmen's Compensation Laws.

Establishment.

(c) (1) The Workmen's Compensation Commission shall be composed of fifteen members to be appointed by the President from among members of State workmen's compensation boards, representatives of insurance carriers, business, labor, members of the medical profession having experience in industrial medicine or in workmen's compensation cases, educators having special expertise in the field of workmen's compensation, and representatives of the general public. The Secretary, the Secretary of Commerce, and the Secretary of Health, Education, and Welfare shall be ex officio members of the Workmen's Compensation Commission:

Membership.

(2) Any vacancy in the Workmen's Compensation Commission shall not affect its powers.

(3) The President shall designate one of the members to serve as Chairman and one to serve as Vice Chairman of the Workmen's Compensation Commission.

84 STAT. 1617

Quorum.

(4) Eight members of the Workmen's Compensation Commission shall constitute a quorum.

Study.

(d) (1) The Workmen's Compensation Commission shall undertake a comprehensive study and evaluation of State workmen's compensation laws in order to determine if such laws provide an adequate, prompt, and equitable system of compensation. Such study and evaluation shall include, without being limited to, the following subjects: (A) the amount and duration of permanent and temporary disability benefits and the criteria for determining the maximum limitations thereon, (B) the amount and duration of medical benefits and provisions insuring adequate medical care and free choice of physician, (C) the extent of coverage of workers, including exemptions based on numbers or type of employment, (D) standards for determining which injuries or diseases should be deemed compensable, (E) rehabilitation, (F) coverage under second or subsequent injury funds, (G) time limits on filing claims, (H) waiting periods, (I) compulsory or elective coverage, (J) administration, (K) legal expenses, (L) the feasibility and desirability of a uniform system of reporting information concerning job-related injuries and diseases and the operation of workmen's compensation laws, (M) the resolution of conflict of laws, extraterritoriality and similar problems arising from claims with multistate aspects, (N) the extent to which private insurance carriers are excluded from supplying workmen's compensation coverage and the desirability of such exclusionary practices, to the extent they are found to exist, (O) the relationship between workmen's compensation on the one hand, and old-age, disability, and survivors insurance and other types of insurance, public or private, on the other hand, (P) methods of implementing the recommendations of the Commission.

Report to President and Congress.

(2) The Workmen's Compensation Commission shall transmit to the President and to the Congress not later than July 31, 1972, a final report containing a detailed statement of the findings and conclusions of the Commission, together with such recommendations as it deems advisable.

Hearings.

(e) (1) The Workmen's Compensation Commission or, on the authorization of the Workmen's Compensation Commission, any subcommittee or members thereof, may, for the purpose of carrying out the provisions of this title, hold such hearings, take such testimony, and sit and act at such times and places as the Workmen's Compensation Commission deems advisable. Any member authorized by the Workmen's Compensation Commission may administer oaths or affirmations to witnesses appearing before the Workmen's Compensation Commission or any subcommittee or members thereof.

(2) Each department, agency, and instrumentality of the executive branch of the Government, including independent agencies, is authorized and directed to furnish to the Workmen's Compensation Commission, upon request made by the Chairman or Vice Chairman, such information as the Workmen's Compensation Commission deems necessary to carry out its functions under this section.

(f) Subject to such rules and regulations as may be adopted by the Workmen's Compensation Commission, the Chairman shall have the power to—

(1) appoint and fix the compensation of an executive director, and such additional staff personnel as he deems necessary, without regard to the provisions of title 5, United States Code, governing appointments in the competitive service, and without regard to the provisions of chapter 51 and subchapter III of chapter 53 of such title relating to classification and General Schedule

80 Stat. 378.
5 USC 101.

5 USC 5101,
5331.

84 STAT. 1618
Ante, p. 198-1.

pay rates, but at rates not in excess of the maximum rate for GS–18 of the General Schedule under section 5332 of such title, and

(2) procure temporary and intermittent services to the same extent as is authorized by section 3109 of title 5, United States Code.

80 Stat. 416.
Contract authorization.

(g) The Workmen's Compensation Commission is authorized to enter into contracts with Federal or State agencies, private firms, institutions, and individuals for the conduct of research or surveys, the preparation of reports, and other activities necessary to the discharge of its duties.

Compensation; travel expenses.

(h) Members of the Workmen's Compensation Commission shall receive compensation for each day they are engaged in the performance of their duties as members of the Workmen's Compensation Commission at the daily rate prescribed for GS–18 under section 5332 of title 5, United States Code, and shall be entitled to reimbursement for travel, subsistence, and other necessary expenses incurred by them in the performance of their duties as members of the Workmen's Compensation Commission.

Appropriation.

(i) There are hereby authorized to be appropriated such sums as may be necessary to carry out the provisions of this section.

Termination.

(j) On the ninetieth day after the date of submission of its final report to the President, the Workmen's Compensation Commission shall cease to exist.

ECONOMIC ASSISTANCE TO SMALL BUSINESSES

72 Stat. 387;
83 Stat. 802.
15 USC 636.

SEC. 28. (a) Section 7(b) of the Small Business Act, as amended, is amended—

(1) by striking out the period at the end of "paragraph (5)" and inserting in lieu thereof "; and"; and

(2) by adding after paragraph (5) a new paragraph as follows:

"(6) to make such loans (either directly or in cooperation with banks or other lending institutions through agreements to participate on an immediate or deferred basis) as the Administration may determine to be necessary or appropriate to assist any small business concern in effecting additions to or alterations in the equipment, facilities, or methods of operation of such business in order to comply with the applicable standards promulgated pursuant to section 6 of the Occupational Safety and Health Act of 1970 or standards adopted by a State pursuant to a plan approved under section 18 of the Occupational Safety and Health Act of 1970, if the Administration determines that such concern is likely to suffer substantial economic injury without assistance under this paragraph."

(b) The third sentence of section 7(b) of he Small Business Act, as amended, is amended by striking out "or (5)" after "paragraph (3)" and inserting a comma followed by "(5) or (6)".

80 Stat. 132.
15 USC 633.

(c) Section 4(c)(1) of the Small Business Act, as amended, is amended by inserting "7(b)(6)," after "7(b)(5),".

(d) Loans may also be made or guaranteed for the purposes set forth in section 7(b)(6) of the Small Business Act, as amended, pursuant to the provisions of section 202 of the Public Works and Economic Development Act of 1965, as amended.

79 Stat. 556.
42 USC 3142.

ADDITIONAL ASSISTANT SECRETARY OF LABOR

SEC. 29. (a) Section 2 of the Act of April 17, 1946 (60 Stat. 91) as amended (29 U.S.C. 553) is amended by—

75 Stat. 338.

(1) striking out "four" in the first sentence of such section and inserting in lieu thereof "five"; and

(2) adding at the end thereof the following new sentence, "One of such Assistant Secretaries shall be an Assistant Secretary of Labor for Occupational Safety and Health.".

80 Stat. 462.   (b) Paragraph (20) of section 5315 of title 5, United States Code, is amended by striking out "(4)" and inserting in lieu thereof "(5)".

ADDITIONAL POSITIONS

SEC. 30. Section 5108(c) of title 5, United States Code, is amended by—

(1) striking out the word "and" at the end of paragraph (8);

(2) striking out the period at the end of paragraph (9) and inserting in lieu thereof a semicolon and the word "and"; and

(3) by adding immediately after paragraph (9) the following new paragraph:

"(10) (A) the Secretary of Labor, subject to the standards and procedures prescribed by this chapter, may place an additional twenty-five positions in the Department of Labor in GS–16, 17, and 18 for the purposes of carrying out his responsibilities under the Occupational Safety and Health Act of 1970;

"(B) the Occupational Safety and Health Review Commission, subject to the standards and procedures prescribed by this chapter, may place ten positions in GS–16, 17, and 18 in carrying out its functions under the Occupational Safety and Health Act of 1970."

EMERGENCY LOCATOR BEACONS

72 Stat. 775.   SEC. 31. Section 601 of the Federal Aviation Act of 1958 is amended
49 USC 1421.   by inserting at the end thereof a new subsection as follows:

"EMERGENCY LOCATOR BEACONS

"(d) (1) Except with respect to aircraft described in paragraph (2) of this subsection, minimum standards pursuant to this section shall include a requirement that emergency locator beacons shall be installed—

"(A) on any fixed-wing, powered aircraft for use in air commerce the manufacture of which is completed, or which is imported into the United States, after one year following the date of enactment of this subsection; and

"(B) on any fixed-wing, powered aircraft used in air commerce after three years following such date.

"(2) The provisions of this subsection shall not apply to jet-powered aircraft; aircraft used in air transportation (other than air taxis and charter aircraft); military aircraft; aircraft used solely for training purposes not involving flights more than twenty miles from its base; and aircraft used for the aerial application of chemicals."

SEPARABILITY

SEC. 32. If any provision of this Act, or the application of such provision to any person or circumstance, shall be held invalid, the remainder of this Act, or the application of such provision to persons or circumstances other than those as to which it is held invalid, shall not be affected thereby.

APPROPRIATIONS

SEC. 33. There are authorized to be appropriated to carry out this Act for each fiscal year such sums as the Congress shall deem necessary.

EFFECTIVE DATE

SEC. 34. This Act shall take effect one hundred and twenty days after the date of its enactment.

Approved December 29, 1970.

LEGISLATIVE HISTORY:

HOUSE REPORTS: No. 91-1291 accompanying H.R. 16785 (Comm. on
               Education and Labor) and No. 91-1765 (Comm. of
               Conference).
SENATE REPORT   No. 91-1282 (Comm. on Labor and Public Welfare).
CONGRESSIONAL RECORD, Vol. 116 (1970):
     Oct. 13, Nov. 16, 17, considered and passed Senate.
     Nov. 23, 24, considered and passed House, amended, in lieu
        of H.R. 16785.
     Dec. 16, Senate agreed to conference report.
     Dec. 17, House agreed to conference report.

Index